SECRET SERVICE

SECRET SERVICE

Untold Stories of Lesbians in the Military

ZSA ZSA GERSHICK

alyson books
los angeles
Celebrating Twenty-Five Years

Manufactured in the United States of America.

This trade paperback original is published by Alyson Books,
P.O. Box 4371, Los Angeles, California 90078-4371.
Distribution in the United Kingdom by Turnaround Publisher Services Ltd.,
Unit 3, Olympia Trading Estate, Coburg Road, Wood Green,
London N22 6TZ England.

ISBN 0-7394-5423-4

Credits
•Cover photography by John Sann/Stone Collection/Getty Images (cadet) and
  Davies & Starr/Image Bank/Getty Images (dog tags).
•Cover design by Matt Sams.

Contents

Acknowledgments vii

Foreword • Col. Margarethe Cammermeyer ix

Introduction xiii

Twenty-two Years of Undetected Crime: *Shirley Geiling* 1

About Face: *Wendi Goodman* 25

Once They Tag You, You're Always on the Edge: *Diana Kerry* 26

About Face: *Belle A. Pellegrino* 44

I Am a Marine 100 Percent: *Lance Cpl. "Rhonnie"* 45

About Face: *Judi Carey* 56

My Life Ends When I Walk Out the Door: *"Major Maureen"* 57

About Face: *Barbara Owens* 75

They Consider Us Less Than Human: *Angel "Mousey" Ramirez* 77

About Face: *Jamie P. Roberson* 91

We're Soldiers First: *Brenda Hammer* 92

About Face: *A.G. Flynn* 108

That's Just My Demographic: *Rebecca D.* 110

About Face: *Sandra A.* 126

Made in Japan: *Caroline Riso* 127

About Face: *Melissa S. Embser-Herbert* 147

We Were Number 1: *Kelly Mohondro* 149

About Face: *Barbara Owens* 163

We'll Have to Issue Soap-on-a-Rope: *Lara Ballard* 164

About Face: *A.G. Flynn* 187

Dinah Shore Made Me Do It: *Shalanda Baker* 188

About Face: *Belle A. Pellegrino* 204

Sergeant Mom: *Ziva Mataric* 205

About Face: *Wendi Goodman* 218

Smile and Look Pretty: *Major Jane Wilson* 219

About Face: Jane 239

Okay, I Won't Wear Shorts: *Donna S.* 240

About Face: *Jamie P. Roberson* 255

Pick It Up, Put It Down: *Vicki Wagner* 257

About Face: *A.G. Flynn* 279

Able v. United States of America: *Brenda Vosbein* 280

Glossary of Military Terms 303

About the Author 307

Acknowledgments

I owe an enormous thank-you to all the servicewomen—named and unnamed—who responded to my Web postings and overtures and graciously and bravely took time to answer my frank queries. To Aaron Belkin, director of the University of California, Santa Barbara's Center for the Study of Sexual Minorities in the Military, whose networking skills and generous support were invaluable; to the men and women of Lambda Legal Defense and Education Fund, Servicemembers Legal Defense Network, and American Veterans for Equal Rights who continue to fight the good fight for fair and equal treatment; and particularly AVER's regional vice president (Region II) Lara Ballard for her unfailing good humor, initiative, and direction. To Noel Riley Fitch for her ongoing mentorship and unflagging confidence; to the Foxy Ladies, who reminded me of my primary purpose; to Alyson editor-in-chief Angela Brown, a woman of great patience and skill, who kept me in the saddle; and to my extraordinary spouse, Elissa Barrett, can-do attorney by day, crack transcriptionist by night, who cheerfully sacrificed a year of weekends—100 words a minute—that I might have a precise and faithful rendering of every conversation.

Foreword

Col. Margarethe Cammermeyer,
U.S. Army (Ret.)

Secret Service: Untold Stories of Lesbians in the Military is an extraordinary compilation of interviews with lesbians who have served, or are serving, in the American military. The stories you will read are the real, everyday experiences of women as they traverse the pitfalls set by the law prohibiting lesbians from serving openly.

As you read these stories, imagine yourself in their shoes, away from any support system, having to survive, living a lie in silence. Such is the plight of gays and lesbians in the military.

I can only speculate what it was like being a light-skinned person of color trying to pass in white society. I can only intellectually, and superficially, imagine what it was like for a Jew to try to pass as a Protestant to survive under Nazi rule. But I don't need to imagine or speculate what it was like to serve in the American military as a lesbian because I did: I am a retired military officer who served for thirty-one years, who just happens to be a lesbian.

When I read these interviews with lesbian service members, I had flashbacks of the emotional stress, the feeling of alienation, the rejection I experienced as I faced discharge because of who I am as a person.

As you read their stories try to imagine the experience of giving up personal freedom to serve in the military. Imagine love of country, pride in service, working to "Be All That You Can Be." Imagine that pride of wearing the uniform, and then imagine that despite your best effort, being an extraordinary soldier, you can summarily be separated.

Women in the military live in constant fear of becoming a target as a lesbian. And even if a service member is not a lesbian, how does she prove it? Lesbians live in fear of discovery, intimidation, and threat. And then there is living with the interrogations, the alienation, and the confinement until you either are discharged or transferred.

Even if you are transferred, it may happen all over again.

In 1993, Congress enacted the "don't ask, don't tell" law that permitted homosexuals to serve as long as they did not acknowledge their nonconforming sexual orientation. Under the law, disclosure would result in separation from the military. This meant that serving in silence, always serving with fear of unintentional disclosure, of being blackmailed, serving in fear of sexual or physical harassment, became a way of life for lesbians in the military.

Since the law was enacted, three to four service members are discharged daily because of being perceived as homosexual. These individuals are not discharged because of misconduct, but purely because they have been targeted. The Servicemembers Legal Defense Network in Washington, D.C., is the one organization in the country that keeps track, reports, and assists service members under investigation. Their statistics clearly demonstrate how women are disproportionately pursued, since they make up only fifteen percent of the military but are more than thirty percent of those discharged for homosexuality.

The red herring used against permitting gays and lesbians to serve in the military is that they would "undermine morale and discipline." But gays have served in the American military dating back to General Von Steuben working for General Washington during the Revolutionary War. Regardless of which regulation is in effect, during wartime there are fewer troops discharged for homosexuality than during peacetime. This means, of course, that homosexuals do not undermine morale and discipline: If that were true, they would not be able to do their jobs during wartime.

The law as it stands does not make sense. Why? Because it is based on the ignorance of many and the discomfort of a few, resulting in the indescribable loss to the military of dedicated servicewomen and the unbearable emotional burden borne by those serving in silence.

It is very hard to mask your life, to withdraw so that you keep a personal and social distance from your peers and comrades, and still be part of a unit and contribute to unit cohesion while living a lie. Yet that is the mandate imposed upon gay and lesbian service members in the U.S. military. That is their obnoxious burden, superimposed upon their sacrifice of serving and being willing to die, fighting for the freedom of others while being denied their own.

Why should you care about the life experiences, the sacrifices of lesbians in the military? Why should you care about women persecuted for being perceived as lesbians because of their demeanor, their rejection of male sexual advances, or just for being more competent in a competitive military milieu? Would you be offended and demand change if this behavior was targeted toward your mother, your daughter, your sister, or your spouse?

You should care because the law permits the federal government to discriminate against a group of people, different from the majority, but whose personal characteristics have absolutely no bearing on their ability to perform their role in the military, no bearing on their love of country, their dedication, nor their willingness to give their lives for America.

You should care because these women cared enough about America to serve in the military, were willing to die for just causes, and were denied their own humanity. You should care because only you can help overturn the "don't ask, don't tell" law by challenging your congressional representatives and senators. These women and thousands like them deserve to serve with dignity while living their personal lives without fear of retribution.

Introduction

This book is dedicated to the legions of lesbians—black, white, Asian, Latino, nurses, pilots, skippers, clerks, cooks, MPs, artillerymen, and all the rest—who've served America's armed forces bravely and well. The stories in *Secret Service* underscore what people in uniform at both the highest and lowest echelons already know: Lesbians (and gay men) serve and have served proudly and well in all branches of the American armed forces (and openly in the militaries of many of our allies). We often are uncommonly dedicated—the sharpest troops found anywhere, wearing the glossiest boots and earning the highest performance evaluations. We neither disrupt good order and discipline nor impair unit cohesion—something African-American and female troops also were accused of when their full integration into the military was nigh in the 1940s and 1970s, respectively.

In fact, the real bar to good order and discipline, the real destroyer of unit cohesion—a fact well-documented but continually denied—is bad behavior on the part of heterosexual men and a military establishment that fosters and excuses it. These bad behaviors include widespread sexual harassment of women and violence toward GLBT people (or those merely perceived to be).

Sexual harassment is something all the women in *Secret Service* report.

I am a veteran and know these facts firsthand.

Frankly, my service in the U.S. Army Reserve from 1978 to 1983 as a broadcast journalist (71R) and medic (91B) was unremarkable. I joined because I thought it was the roughest, toughest, nastiest thing a nice Jewish girl could possibly do. Once there, I met many young men and women—some gay and lesbian—for whom the service was the best among limited options.

I did my basic training at Fort Jackson, South Carolina, in the fall of 1978, part of an experimental cycle that threw a handful of females into training with men. The Women's Army Corps had only recently been dissolved, and the Army was trying on coed training. I was promptly made squad leader and put in charge of the female barracks. When I made the women cry, I was placed in charge of the men. There I took delight in barking orders and "dropping for twenty" 18-year-olds the size of refrigerators.

It seemed a kind of golden era for lesbians (although the Department of Defense had actually strengthened its anti-gay policy during the Carter Administration): The Army—fresh from the PR crisis of Vietnam and the disposal of the draft—needed bodies. I had checked "no" to question number 37f: "Have you ever engaged in homosexual activity (sexual relations with another person of the same sex)?" on my enlistment form, but I looked like one thing: a "baby butch," as my friends teased. I didn't "tell," but everything about me was telling.

God, it is said, protects fools and children.

Two incidents stand out for me still.

During our basic training a male drill sergeant from another company raped one of our trainees, a petite girl from somewhere in Michigan. The girl was discharged; the drill sergeant transferred. (A common story, well-documented most recently in an award-winning series in *The Denver Post*, "Betrayal in the

Ranks.") At the command level there were no consequences.

(Sometimes there are even rewards. Maj. Gen. Robert T. Clark was post commander of Fort Campbell, Kentucky, when PFC Barry Winchell—suspected of being gay by fellow soldiers—was bludgeoned to death in 1999. Clark, at the urging of the Bush administration, recently has been promoted to lieutenant general. Never mind that a spree of anti-gay harassment during Clark's watch was documented by the Department of the Army's Inspector General.)

I graduated from basic with a commander's letter and moved on to AIT—advanced individual training—at Fort Benjamin Harrison, Indiana, then home of the Defense Information School, DINFOS, trainers of all military public affairs people, scribes, and broadcasters.

At DINFOS, the cadre told us plainly that women may be fine as print journalists, but none on the broadcast track—newly opened to females—would survive the course. Twelve weeks later all the women had indeed been washed out—except for me.

As the women were cashiered one by one, I loudly protested to anyone who would listen. On the eve of graduation, in a closed-door meeting with the school commandant, a senior Air Force officer, I was told that though my performance had been only "average," I would be "allowed" to graduate.

They were happy to get rid of me, he said.

I served with a psychological operations unit until joining an evac hospital—the 352nd, Col. Margarethe Cammermeyer's unit, though I did not know her personally—and cross-trained as a medic at Fort Sam Houston, Texas. Everywhere I went I met gay and lesbian active and reserve soldiers, sailors, airmen, and Marines who were outstanding, who loved the service, and who were working hard.

And then it was over. I went on to college and work as a reporter and editor.

Later, in my early 30s, a new seriousness upon me, I

thought about reenlisting. *What could I make of such an opportunity now?* I asked myself. I knew I could do better, really "be all that I could be," as the recruiting slogan had urged me a decade before.

A couple of things stopped me: First, I was very out, and there was plenty of evidence of it. My byline had appeared on GLBT reportage; I'd been on a speaker circuit. It wouldn't be as simple as checking "no" to question number 37f. And did I really want to lie about something so essential—something about which I had no shame—and could I feel good about myself in doing so?

Thirty is not 18.

Secondly, Bill Clinton was running for president and promising to overturn the military ban on gay men and lesbians serving openly, and I had begun to interview GLBT service members for a series of profiles. What I learned moved me: Though I had skipped unmolested—in a variety of ways—through my service, many, many gay men and lesbians with "201 files" full of commendations had been harassed, interrogated, stripped of benefits, and thanklessly discharged for nothing more than their sexual orientation—a part of themselves they'd kept utterly private and off-post.

(Even the women who had evaded others' gaydar still reported having been harassed as women. And the most circumspect servicemembers feared the "lesbian card." Any competent female can lose her post if a male—especially one who wants her job or fears she'll get his—plays it.)

The 1992 election came and went. President Clinton, knee deep in kimchi, struck his compromise with a recalcitrant Congress and Joint Chiefs of Staff: "Don't ask, don't tell," later, "don't ask, don't tell, don't harass, don't pursue," a de facto ban, arguably left us worse off, not better. The short form was this: Under the old Department of Defense policy, the military had to prove the accused was gay; under "don't ask, don't tell," now federal law, the service member had to prove she wasn't.

Moreover, commanders no longer had any discretion in whether to retain or discharge a troop.

Ten years after its passage, nearly 10,000 highly motivated, keenly trained GLBT service members—including much-needed Arabic and Farsi-speaking linguists—have been discharged under the policy, one-third of the 30,000 new recruits the Army now says it needs to combat terrorism. And though, at this wartime writing, GLBT discharges have dropped to an historic low, what happens to those troops at war's end is what bears watching. An Army nurse who served in the first Persian Gulf War told me that her hospital unit had an enormous GLBT presence, including the ward masters and many of the nurses and medics. They served with distinction, she said, and when, at conflict's end, they returned stateside for promotions and benefits, all summarily were discharged for being gay.

Translation: If you're gay, you're good enough to die but not good enough to honor or retain when the shooting stops.

This book is for all GLBT service members who've experienced—or who may yet experience—such ingratitude for a job well done—an injustice that is costly, counterproductive, and contrary to our nation's ideals.

—Zsa Zsa Gershick

Twenty-two Years of Undetected Crime

Shirley Geiling

This chapter takes its title from the book Shirley Geiling says she could write about her two-plus decades in the Navy. The crime, of course, is the love that dare not speak its name.

Geiling was raised in Indiana and Illinois, an "artsy" child who loved to read. Her dislike of the color green combined with the grim, mannish appearance of the Army females she met at the local recruiting office, she says, made her turn toward the Navy.

She had slept with women but hadn't heard of the L word. She was 18.

"I read once a long time ago that the definition of a lesbian is a woman who says she is. And at that particular time, I hadn't decided I was," says Geiling, who served from 1964 to 1987, with a year break spent in the reserve, and retired a Hospital Corpsman Chief Petty Officer (E7).

"It was one of those things in the era, in the 1960s, in Indiana. The word queer *didn't even come up for women because* queer *was limp-wristed men on the street corner. I knew this was something that was not for the public, you know, in the back of my head. I shouldn't flaunt it that I was sleeping with women. But* queer *was all men and had nothing to do with women."*

She completed boot camp at Bainbridge, Maryland, and hospital corps-man training at Great Lakes. Her one civilian job had been in high school, serving as a curb hop at the local Steak 'n' Shake. The Navy suited her fine.

"Initially, the recruits, the first-year people, are the ones that end up with the most scut work, and have the most difficulty, and have every-body telling 'em what to do," says Geiling.

"But the longer you're in, there are fewer people who tell you what to do. Then you get to tell some other people what to do. You just ease your way into it. If you follow the rules, you don't have a problem."

* * *

You were in the first wave of women to serve aboard ships in the early '70s. How did the men react to that?

SG: Of course there was the, "Oh, women can't do as much as men," "Women aren't as strong as men," "Women shouldn't be aboard ships." But we had more problems with the men's wives than we did with the actual guys on the ship. The wives were just having a fit. They thought there was going to be all this hanky-panky going on. And our contention was, "Well, they're gonna go to the Philippines and do it anyway, so what difference does it make?" [*Laughs*]

Did that hanky-panky happen?

SG: Of course it did! There were some liaisons. There always are. I don't care if you're at a shore station, you're on an airplane, where you're at. Somebody's gonna do it.

Were most of those hook-ups heterosexual in nature?

SG: Oh, yeah! Definitely. I don't recall any of them being gay or lesbian.

When you went to the recruiting office, wasn't there a question on the form?

SG: The only one I remember is on the medical form, and that was: "Have you ever had homosexual *tendencies?*" And I could rationalize that one out because how can you have "tendencies" when you are one? So, you can truthfully say, "No, I don't have homosexual *tendencies*," and not lie about it.

Because you're a full-blown *homosexual?*

SG: Exactly! [*Laughs*] There it is!

Once you were in boot camp, did you see other women whom you recognized as lesbian?

SG: I didn't recognize lesbians at the time. I didn't even recognize myself by that name. There were some women who were more masculine, who had shorter hair, carried themselves differently. At that time, my head said, *tomboy.* I'd never met anyone who said they were a "lesbian."

I remember in boot camp hearing that if a woman comes up to you and says she doesn't have any friends and wouldn't you like to be her best friend, beware! [*Laughs*] When I look back on this stuff, it cracks me up. [*Laughs*] And you can't sit on someone else's rack because that might be construed as a "homosexual act." Oh, please!

I thought, *What's the problem?* I don't understand why they can't be in the Navy just like everybody else. I didn't understand why it was such a big deal. Of course, that was before I understood homosexuality in the military was a "detriment to morale and good judgment" and because homosexuals could be blackmailed for top secret information. It's a catch-22: If you didn't have to hide, then you couldn't be blackmailed. I don't get that either, but that's what we were told.

At age 21, you'd discovered something about yourself; the light came on. How did that happen? And how did that affect your being in the military?

SG: I found this woman that I was attracted to, and I said, "No, I'm not gonna do this because the Navy doesn't approve of it."

Of course, that went out the window in about two seconds. And so I was sleeping with this woman who said *she* wasn't a lesbian. [*Laughs*] The whole thing was kind of a comedy of errors. And I finally admitted to myself that if I'm sleeping with women and enjoying it, then I must be a lesbian. You think? [*Laughs*]

It was difficult to accept it for a while. I had a little problem with that. It wasn't a societal norm. It wasn't a military norm. I didn't know anyone I could talk to about it that had some authority, that had some experience, that had some background, that had some knowledge, anything. You wouldn't dare talk to anybody for fear that you'd get caught and canned. It was hard to come out to yourself without someone to talk to.

And yet you did it.

SG: Logic prevailed. If you figure you like sleeping with women, and you are identifying with women, and you're going everywhere and doing everything with women, and you could really care less if you go with guys, then that must tell you something.

And how did you meet her?

SG: We met in the same barracks.

How do you get from A to Z in that environment?

SG: You walk on very soft shoes around the block a lot before anything happens. [*Laughs*]

And from there, you got to know other gay men and lesbians.

SG: It's the gaydar that you develop when you're in the military so that you learn to recognize somebody. I don't know how to explain it. It's just a feeling. You say, "Well here's somebody." You look at 'em and you go, "Well, gee. I wonder if this woman's a lesbian?" It's some sixth, seventh sense that you pick up from hiding all those years.

And I imagine you especially need that gaydar if the woman is very femme in appearance.

SG: Those are the hard ones! If a woman is very feminine in appearance, it's very difficult. The gaydar doesn't work most of the time on that. And some women are fairly borderline.

I think lesbians carry themselves differently from straight women. They're more assured in the way they walk. I'm not talking about swagger. It's just that they put one foot in front of the other, and they go from place to place. They don't pussyfoot and mince. Really. They have a purpose. That doesn't necessarily mean that every woman who strides is a lesbian, but lesbians just seem to have more purpose. [*Laughs*]

Well, they certainly do look you square in the face.

SG: You get eye contact. You get truth. You get that stuff. And there's other things that get you a gaydar twiggle. I don't know how to explain it. A lot of it is intuitiveness from hiding all those years.

And when you're in the service, if you think another woman is a lesbian, then there's the feeling-out period. Making friends and talking with them to start off with before you actually drop the bomb on their head and scare them off.

Sometimes it's like, "Well, where are you from?" "Where have you been stationed?" "If you've been stationed at such and such a place, do you know this bar?" "Do you know so-and-so?" Maybe you can make the connection with a place or a person because sometimes that makes the difference.

Did you go to gay bars?

SG: First time I went to the gay bars was when I was stationed in San Diego. And the first time I came out here was 1967. I had never seen a gay bar. I had never been around women who were lesbians and actually saw women in an embrace or a kiss. I had never seen that until I came out here and went to a bar. I mean, I only had myself and the other person I was involved with. Before that, when I was at Bethesda.

How did you react to seeing that?

SG: I thought, *Wow! This is really cool! I'm not alone. There are other people here. These women do this, too!* [*Laughs*]

Were you afraid to go to that place?

SG: I was that concerned the military would have spies, and I would get caught and kicked out of the Navy. The one thing that I recall—to digress just a moment—is a woman I knew when I was stationed at Bethesda, somewhere in like '65, '66, who was being kicked out because she was a lesbian.

They sent an administrative letter to her parents, telling them why she had been discharged from the Navy, which I thought was pretty damn tacky. That's what the policy was at the time.

So when I was here in San Diego, and going to these bars, that was my concern, that I would be caught and discharged. And not necessarily for myself, because I figure, *Hey, you know, I'm 21, 22, I could always go find a job, so what's the big deal?* But for them to write a letter and tell my parents that I'm a homosexual, that was the fear.

You wrote to me that since you came out after you were in the Navy, hiding was second nature.

SG: Yeah. It's like you don't talk to a woman on the phone and talk about your love interests. You don't write notes. You don't do anything on the base. You don't hold hands. You don't give certain looks. You don't do any of that stuff. You don't trust anybody either. It takes a lot before you trust someone to share this information with.

How long would you have to know someone and what hoops would he or she have to jump through to earn your trust?

SG: That's really a tough one because the military did plant people. They really did. They'd get somebody in a pickle. They'd get somebody and say, "Hey, you know, you've done something against the Uniform Code of Military Justice, and we'll let you off the hook if you'll turn in all of these lesbians."

How do you know that happened?

SG: Because I managed a barracks when I was an E5 here in San Diego. And I worked as base police for my duty. You know because the Navy likes you well enough, once every four to six days they let you work an extra twelve hours, right? It's called "duty." So I had to drive around in a cop car and all that kind of stuff. Security, in effect.

When the criminal investigators would question someone

that they thought was a lesbian, they had to have a female present. And because I got to drive around in the little cop car at night, they chose me to sit in on and listen to the conversations and the questions that the NIS would ask these women about being lesbians.

What did they ask them?

SG: Point-blank questions. "Are you lesbian? We know you are. So-and-so told us this, or somebody told us that, so you might as well fess up," and that kind of stuff, which was all crap.

How did you feel when a girl would be sweated in front of you?

SG: Glad it wasn't me. What else could I do? Gee. I'd feel sorry for her. I'm sorry it came to this. But hey, it's either you or me. And it sure as hell ain't gonna be me. So I'm just gonna sit here and shut up.

Did you know any of those women?

SG: I knew one. Didn't know her well. I didn't associate with her.

When you were sitting in the same room, was it likely she knew who you were?

SG: Yeah. I think she did.

But she didn't give you up?

SG: No. She wouldn't give anybody up. She was a doctor. She said, "Okay now, if you guys want to know things. Here, you talk into my recorder, and you tell me who my accusers

8

are. I want to face them now, or I'm getting up and leaving." And she turned off the tape recorder, and they're all standing there going, "Uh, uh, uh." So she says, "I guess this conversation has ended." She got up and left, which is what she should have done in the first place. They had no grounds. There's no way to prove it. Unless somebody says, "Yes, I am," they can't prove it.

Was that just a run-of-the-mill sort of harassment?

SG: Absolutely.

And she got up and left.

SG: Yup.

And nothing happened.

SG: Nope, not a thing. Of course, they watched her like a hawk. They tried to get someone to rat on her. And that's the way that they worked. Finally, they'd harass you so much, you'd say, "Oh, yes I am," just to get out and get away from it.

How is that justified, do you think?

SG: I don't know. The only thing I can come up with is the top-secret clearance stuff. We're gonna go blab to whoever we're fighting this week and tell up all the secrets because we can be blackmailed because we're in the Navy and living this double life.

How much information is a hospital corpsman going to know?

SG: Not a hell of a lot! [*Laughs*]

Does Osama bin Laden really want to know how many Q-tips you have on hand?

SG: Let me see. Uh-huh. Absolutely. It was a scare tactic, and it was effective.

Was there any time that you sat in on those interrogations that you were afraid for yourself?

SG: There was one time. I didn't sit in on an interrogation, but there was a birthday party. I went to a birthday party with another woman, a birthday party of someone I did not know. There were probably about twenty-five or thirty women at this party. Then come to find out that there was a plant from NIS, and this person was giving names and so forth to NIS. There was this whole list of names. And for the people she didn't know, she just said "and others." And I was one of the "others." So I was fortunate. I didn't know hardly anybody there. That was a little scary.

How did the fact of the plant come to your attention?

SG: Because the woman I went to the party with knew the other women, and the other women had been called by NIS and asked these questions. And the rumor mill is really good. [*Laughs*]

As soon as you had enough stripes, you lived in apartments out in town. Were you ever afraid that the NIS was hiding out and watching your house?

SG: Well, we never did anything with curtains open. [*Laughs*] And how are they gonna prove it? Photographs are inadmissible evidence, and you're not gonna let three people watch? I don't think so. [*Laughs*] So how are you gonna get caught, unless you go, "Yes, I am"? They could have someone say, "I saw her at a party." "I saw her at a bar." But just because you're in a public place with a bunch of people doesn't mean you are what they are. I mean, I could go to the Marine Corps Ball. Does that mean I'm a Marine? I don't think so. It's all scare tactics. And I was what you call a "sea lawyer," one of those people who knows enough about the regulations to get around them.

Unless it's an NIS person that you went to bed with.

SG: Well, that's a drawback. Absolutely. But then you got them! There's two of us. We did this together. And if you think you're turning me in, I'm sure as hell turning your ass in. Because if it's my ass or yours, it's yours, baby! [*Laughs*]

You mentioned to me that men in your duty stations seemed to be threatened by the fact that women didn't need them for sex or anything else.

SG: That's just a general observation. There are a lot of men who do not deal well with aggressive women. They don't know what to do with us. First of all, there's only two kinds of women in the military. There's whores and queers. Pick one! [*Laughs*]

Yes, that's what I heard in the '70s as well. Was that the rule of thumb in the Navy?

SG: I'd say at least for the first ten years that I was in, yeah. It got a little bit better during the '70s because of "love and peace" and trying to get through Vietnam. I think men changed a little bit, and some of the people in authority were a little easier, had a little more brains, had a little more exposure to things other than themselves so that they could understand a different lifestyle or a different way or whatever.

The military is really hard-pressed to change, but it does change a little bit when society changes. Not much, but a little. [*Laughs*]

Well, what's true is that societal change happens incrementally. We have bursts. Then we have a backlash. Then we inch along again.

SG: And I think that men getting in touch with their feelings didn't hurt anything either. That's still going on. When men are allowed to hug each other and men are allowed to cry in front of their peers, that helps the rest of us. They don't have to deal so much from within. They have a little more resource outside themselves.

It's not that I hate men. I dislike what peers do to them, to their heads, you know? That macho bullshit just drives me crazy. And the Navy? I don't think they float on oceans; they float on testosterone.

When you think machismo, you think of the Marines and you think of the Army. But the Navy swaggers, too?

SG: Oh, God! Are you kidding? Oh, yeah. Absolutely! Not as bad as the Marine Corps. I think the Marine Corps has got the worst case.

I've heard from others that the leading fear among non-gay servicemembers is that if gay men and lesbians are allowed to serve openly, we'll devour them in shared foxholes, tents, and showers. It's the old "don't drop the soap."

SG: Oh, for heaven's sake, yeah! Oh, they're all gonna get attacked in the shower. Every damn one of them. [*Laughs*]

Female servicemembers comprise a disproportionate number of people who are separated under the ban on homosexuals serving openly in the military, but I understand there are more gay men actually serving. Why do you think women bear that burden?

SG: Because we won't sleep with the men! We don't need

them. What do we need them for? And it's threatening. That's the problem.

You're saying it's not necessarily the lesbianism, it's the independence.

SG: It's the independence, therefore it's the lesbianism. They'd let us stay if they could watch. Don't you think? [*Laughs*]

No one would get any work done.

SG: Do they now? [*Laughs*]

Well, I don't know. They're fretting and obsessing quite a lot.

SG: That's a full-time job, isn't it? [*Laughs*]

And an expensive one, borne by you and me and other taxpayers.

SG: Really!

It seems when there's war on, when "good order" and "discipline" and "maximum readiness" are needed, we're fine to have in the ranks and discharges decrease. But then, when our bodies are no longer needed, suddenly we're a problem. Can you explain that contradiction to me?

SG: Sure. We're back to square one! Look what they did to Rosie the Riveter. Look what they did to her. They gave her a refrigerator and made her wear an apron and said she was happy. [*Laughs*] That's amazing. And Rosie bought it. That's the worst part of it. Oh, my God. Oh, yeah. Let's go home and have babies now. We're done. [*Laughs*]

I wonder if they authentically bought it? Certainly there was a lot of Miltown[1] being consumed in the '50s.

13

SG: Jeez. [*Laughs*] I haven't heard of that in years. *Valley of the Dolls*, eh?

That's right. Maybe women didn't really. They thought they should buy it, so they bought it. Then they had a hard time living with it.

SG: That was the whole purpose of the WAVES. So we could do the jobs on shore while the men were all out to sea fighting. Hello? Wasn't that what happened with the Army, too?

That's right. "Free a man for the front."

SG: Yup. They needed us then because all these macho dudes were gonna go to war, and they had to have somebody to flip papers. As soon as we're done with the war, the guys can go back to their jobs, and we can go get a refrigerator! [*Laughs*]

When you were in the service, did you think about that? "I'm good enough to be here, as long as they don't know."

SG: Not in those terms. Being in the Navy was a game. I was playing a game. I'd drive by the naval hospital down here in San Diego and see a wheat field when I wasn't working here. It was a game.

It was a means to an end. You played by the rules. You get around it the best way you can. You make friends. You do whatever. You get on with your life. And when you're there, you're working, you're Navy. And when you're not there, you're somebody else, somewhere else, and the Navy doesn't exist.

You got out before "don't ask, don't tell." Is it your sense that the policy has made any difference?

SG: No. I have a friend, a gay man, who retired a few years after I did, and he was in for "don't ask, don't tell." This man is an intellectual and he's a wonderful person. He's a physician assistant now, working up in San Francisco. He thought it seemed to be as bad, if not worse, initially because people were misusing and misinterpreting it. And you still can't come out! You can't say anything! How does it change anything? Because they can't ask you?

But they can and do. And if they still suspect you, for whatever reason, they can still investigate.

SG: Yeah.

One might ask, what constitutes fair suspicion? Is it just that you have short hair or that someone saw you fornicating in the day room?

SG: I think in some cases it's, "You didn't fuck this guy, so that makes you a lesbian. So we're gonna investigate you." I'm sure that there are women who are investigated because they are good at their jobs and actually better than their male counterparts. So they are investigated and gotten rid of.

A man is competing with you for a promotion and it looks like he might lose. He can always play the lesbian card?

SG: Oh, hell yeah!

When you were in the ranks, did you ever see gay men terrorizing straight men or lesbians terrorizing straight women in the barracks?

SG: Not ever.

That's the big fear.

SG: The women that I hung out with, the other lesbians I knew when I was in the Navy, we all thought, *Why would I want* *to go put the make on some straight chick? What fun is there in that? Why bother? [Laughs]*

It's a trifle arrogant. I'm straight, and all the lesbians are going to come after me because I'm so fabulous and irresistible.

SG: [*Laughs*] Then there's the other side of the coin. If someone finds out you're a lesbian, then the men are saying, "Well, I know what you need! You just need one good fuck and you'll be cured! Ah-ha-ha-ha." Oh, please. [*Laughs*]

Did it occur to you to do that in order to put up a heterosexual front?

SG: No. But it happened in a couple bars here in San Diego. Guys would come in and try to pick up lesbians, because they thought they could "cure" 'em. We all laughed them out of the bar. [*Laughs*]

These are guys who like rejection.

SG: Evidently!

Is there a shift in understanding coming? Does the military have to lag so far behind society?

SG: Does it have to? God. I think it depends on the type of people who go into the military. That's what makes up the military mentality. If you have a lot of people who are not well educated, not worldly, very young, very protected, then I think it's gonna be very difficult to change the mentality, because it'll be a mob mentality, so to speak. And they feed off of each other. It's very difficult to change that, an attitude.

And if someone writes a regulation and says "you will," then it's only going to make it worse because these people with their narrow minds and narrow mentalities will pick out those for whom "you will" applies and make life miserable for them. That's the way it works.

The '70s was a good time to start that. I was the senior enlisted woman on the USS *Sanctuary*, a hospital ship, for a period of time as an E5, and the captain of the ship called me up to his cabin one day. And he said, "We're putting this book in the library. What do you think of it?" And it was *Our Bodies, Our Selves*, by the Boston Women's Collective. I stood there and I said, "I think it's a good book, sir." And he said, "I would like everyone to read it at their leisure and take heart with what it says."

Everyone? Meaning every woman and every man?

SG: Yeah. He wanted everybody to read it. Not to say that this is an order, but he would like everyone to. He said, "What people do on the beach—in other words, off the ship—is their own business." He said, "Here. Take the book and put it in the library."

And that was the end of it. I about fell over dead. Because this was an admission on the part of someone who was in prime authority, who knew what was going on, and as long as it did not happen where he had to act on it, he was not going to. And he let that be known in the best way that he could, because of his position. I thought that was pretty good.

He knew there were lesbians on his ship. Not anyone having acted out, not anyone having told him, not seeing anything—but ten percent of the population is, so why not? It's gotta be.

That goes to the idea that it really begins at the top.

SG: Yes, uh-huh.

If the commanders don't set the tone, especially in the military, which is very hierarchical, where is it going to start?

SG: That's right.

I'm thinking of Harry Truman who desegregated the military in the 1940s, mandating that blacks and whites would serve together.

SG: Yup. I bet that went over real big, didn't it? [*Laughs*]

But it did happen.

SG: Yep. I don't know which methodology would be better. Do we one day say, "Okay, this is the way it is," or do we work into it? It's really difficult. If you just throw an ideal at a mass of people who are so anti-lots-of-things, they're going to do everything in their power to go against it and still follow the rules.

Aren't they doing that now?

SG: Yes. In effect. But it'll just make it worse. The more open everything becomes, the worse it becomes for the rank-and-file people. When we had racial sensitivity training in the '70s so that we could understand about blacks in the military and how blacks felt about whites, everybody had to go to these classes. And what it boiled down to was that the white people called it "Watermelon U," and it just pissed them all off. And it made it worse for the black people.

But it was an effort.

SB: It definitely was an effort. The only thing you can do is start. And just say, "Okay. This is the way it is. And if you don't like it, get out!"

But you make a good point because that effort was begun in the 1940s, and you're talking about troops having a reaction to racial sensitivity and calling it "Watermelon U" thirty years later.

SG: Well, I remember the USS *Kittyhawk* here in San Diego in the '70s. There was so much racial hatred and violence they had to lock down the crew and separate them all.

So it seems to be that you have to make a start, a bold start, and then deal with the fallout. There's going to be foot-dragging either way.

SG: Absolutely. The problem also is that the people who are in charge don't run the show. It's the middle management that runs the show. And the middle management are the ones who are the most prejudiced.

Education has a lot to do with it. Fear of the unknown: It's the fear of unknown stuff.

You know, my father was a bigot. My father hated anybody that was different from him. I don't care what it was. And I know a lot of that is because he was not well-educated, he was not well-traveled, and his fear of the unknown. He hated Mexicans. He hated blacks. He hated lesbians. He hated gays. He hated everybody equally. I'll give him that. He was a well-rounded bigot! [*Laughs*]

If you're not around a person, or this person is not allowed to be himself when you're around him, then how are you ever gonna learn that we're all just people? We have things about each of us that we like. We have things about each of that we dislike. We have things about each of us that are different from everyone else. Little things. But we're all people. How are you going to learn that if you never sit down and talk to somebody about it? Or read about it? Or face your own fears? How's it ever going to change?

What you are presenting is an argument in favor of making everything aboveboard. Opening the doors.

SG: Open the doors. Absolutely. And then carry a sidearm! [*Laughs*]

Are the stresses of hiding as a gay man or a gay woman in the military harder on enlisted people or on the officer class?

SG: It's probably harder on the enlisted class because they're the ones who have to put up with the uneducated middle-management people.

The officers at least have a four-year degree. They're a little older when they start out being in the Navy than the rest of us. They're like 22, 23, and a lot of enlisted people go in at 18. They have a few more years there, a few more books, a little more exposure to the world. And I think that makes a difference.

What would you tell a young lesbian or gay man who was thinking about the military? Would you say, "Oh, yeah, go," or "Think about it"?

SG: I would do both. I would recommend anybody go into the Navy for four years. If you don't like it, don't do it again. It's like being a lesbian. If you don't know, you want to try it, you like it, do it again. If you don't like it, don't do it again. Do something else. [*Laughs*] And I'd tell 'em that if you're self-proclaimed and you're out, you're gonna have to hide. And if you don't want to do that, don't go in, 'cause it ain't gonna work.

But if you start out hidden, you don't know any better, it doesn't matter until it's all over. If you're used to hiding and you started out that way, it's just everyday stuff. But if you've never done it, I would think it would be extremely difficult.

Have you suffered ill effects related to such hiding?

SG: No. You know, it was a learning experience. It was a means to an end. It ended. I met a lot of good people. I met some bad people. I went some good places. I went some bad places. Whatever. You know? I wouldn't trade it because I learned, I grew, I was able to do things I would never have done, go places I would never have gone, meet people I would never have known, all over the world.

How do you do that when you're 18 or 19? It was a valuable, learning, growing experience for me, and that's why I would recommend it to anyone. Like I said, if you don't like it, don't do it again. What's four years out of a ninety-year life span? It's nothing.

I found the Army medical corps very queer indeed. Did you find the Navy hospital element very gay, or did you think you were the only one most times?

SG: Oh, God, no. Honey, there were dental techs that I thought were flaming faggots everywhere! [*Laughs*]

I imagine that helped you not to feel alone.

SG: Absolutely. And every duty station that I went to, I made it a point to find one person, if I could, that I felt comfortable enough to connect with so I would at least have someone that I could talk to. So that I could say "lesbian," you know? When I was up in Iceland, the first six months there was nobody. And it was the pits. [*Laughs*]

Then I was working, and this woman came in and stomped across the entranceway and stomped back to the records office, and I went, *There's one!* [*Laughs*] So I sought her out to make friends, and it turns out I was right! And it was nice to have somebody to talk to.

I remember at times being in training situations with almost all men and feeling like I just had to get out of that supermasculine environment. I just wanted a woman to talk to.

SG: Yeah. You get tired of playing "mine's bigger than yours" after a while.

Exactly. Because mine isn't very big!

SG: And that's all they do. You know, "When I was in, and I did this, and we went there, and we did that, and I did this and that." Oh, Jesus! Give me a break.

I just wanted to be around someone who smelled sweet and seemed soft and had a nice, pleasant voice.

SG: [*Laughs*] And sat down when they went to the bathroom!

That's always nice.

SG: You know, there's two kinds of guys that come to sick call. There's one that'll come to sick call and say, "Um, is there a guy here?" And there's the other one that'll say, "I came to get my *crank* checked." You know? There's nothing in the middle. There never was.

"I came to get my 'crank' checked"?

SG: Thought he had the clap. And I'd say, "Well, that's nice. Why don't you take your crank over there and undress it!" That'd shut 'em up. [*Laughs*]

Didn't want to stay for twenty-five?

SG: Well, you know. I probably would've stayed until

thirty, but I just got tired of dealing with assholes and idiots. [*Laughs*] Oh, God!

Are there more than in corporate America?

SG: Oh, I doubt it. I think it's pretty well spread out. We just have a different kind of asshole and idiot in the Navy. [*Laughs*]

And you were tired of that variety?

SG: Oh, yeah. You know? I'm tired of working for men who don't know what the hell they're talking about and try and foist everything off onto you. I was just up to the top of my nose with it. You could hardly see over it! [*Laughs*] Jeez! You know? We're gonna bluster our way through everything because we're a Man. Oh, please! I'm tired of this shit, and I'm gonna go home. [*Laughs*]

And the thing, too, that I noticed, since I enlisted in the Navy until I retired—there wasn't this great revelation, but change was happening, slowly, little by little, in a lot of ways. Women were put into better jobs, different jobs, into male-dominated jobs, because we could actually do that stuff, contrary to popular belief. Instead of the secretarial shit. Because when I went in, the only thing that I could do was be a radioman, a corpsman, a yeoman. Medical, dental, and secretarial stuff was about it.

A friend who went in, that I met later on in life, wanted to be in the Navy band. Well, women couldn't even be in the Navy band in that era.

Is that a supermasculine thing?

SG: Oh, God, gee. Must be! You know, walk up and down and play an instrument. Damn! That must be pretty masculine. [*Laughs*]

But I did see change, and it happened a little at a time. There was progress being made. So in the next fifty years maybe we'll get this done and over with.

Note
1. Meprobamates, a variety of tranquilizer, include Miltown and Equanil. The first of the minor tranquilizers when marketed in 1955, they were considered mild, safe, nonaddictive anxiety relievers. Users discovered their euphoric barbiturate-like effects and "Miltown" became a household word. The high-addiction and overdose potential of the drug was not realized until later.

About Face

This eighteen-year Army veteran served two years as a recruiter isolated in a "redneck dive."

I had seen Army recruiters in high school. My father had been in the Army, and my best friend's father was also in the Army. I just thought it was a good way to go. I knew I didn't want to flip burgers. I knew I didn't want to go to college. And here was somebody offering me training and jobs and money and a way to get out of Chicago, so I took it.

I spent two years as a recruiter in Peoria, Illinois. Holy moly! Have you ever been to Peoria? It's the armpit of Illinois, a redneck dive.

I don't think I ever really ran across anybody who was gay in Peoria. That's the truth. There was one gay bar in Peoria at the time, and I didn't go because I was afraid of being outed. I was in the public eye: I was in the high schools. I was in the malls. Everybody in town knew who all the recruiters were. I hid so far in the closet it was unbelievable. It was just me, and I really, really felt isolated.

If I needed an escort to a company function, I had a good friend who lived forty-five miles away. He's straight, a guy I've known since I was about 10. And he would drive in and take me. And people would assume what they would assume.

The other recruiters were a bunch of big macho men. I was the only woman. I went to work everyday in my Class A's, with my makeup and my hair done. I don't think anybody ever really suspected.

—Wendi Goodman, Staff Sgt.
U.S. Army, Ret.

Once They Tag You,
You're Always on the Edge

Diana Kerry

Capt. Diana Kerry, not her real name, recently retired from the Navy after twenty-five years. Well regarded, she served in command capacities around the world.

Though she led a quiet, deeply closeted life, she was investigated for homosexuality by the Naval Criminal Investigation Service three distinct times, in 1981, 1983, and 1989. The first occurred when someone stole a bus. Each time the results were inconclusive.

Kerry attributes this attention, in part, to the fact that she often served on remote duty stations—"locations most people never heard of"—where the spotlight was always on and it was difficult to blend.

Other lesbian officers she knew were far more "blatant," she says, indulging in all the simple pleasures she denied herself: get-togethers, friendships, affection.

She chose the Navy for two reasons, the second sartorial.

"I actually had wanted to go Coast Guard because they were letting women do shipboard duty," says Kerry, whose father, a Navy veteran, insisted she go to college first.

"But the Coast Guard was full. They were letting only X number of women in. The Air Force made women wear skirts. The Army didn't attract me, so a really stupid second reason for the Navy was that it was one of the first services to allow women to wear pants."

Out now and free to be herself, the reserved 40-something says it's hard to break the hiding habit.

"People ask me, 'Well, gee, you don't have anything keeping you from a relationship now,'" Kerry says. "But I've not gone out looking for it in so long that it's just not part of my lifestyle."

* * *

You were an exemplary officer who'd had high-level posts around the world. You played by the rules and led a circumspect life. Yet in 1981 you were investigated, and an administrative discharge board was convened. Why?

DK: The short answer is that I was with somebody, and our names were brought up by a couple of other people as their way to avoid getting in trouble. It was kind of like, "Let's get the limelight off of us. Let's shoot it over to somebody else."

The old "naming names."

DK: Yeah. They were being investigated for stealing a bus.

A bus?

DK: A bus. Having knowledge of that. And in general questioning, the NCIS, said, "Are you aware of any other things going on that are against regulations?" And they said they knew of some lesbians, and it went from there. The fingers got pointed toward me and my partner.

What did the authorities do with that information?

DK: They immediately removed us from our jobs. Both of us were in a classified environment, and they reassigned us. It was a remote installation. It was probably the closest you can ever imagine to being ostracized because immediately everybody knows something has happened, and it doesn't take long to find out why. The command we had been assigned to also told all of the officers they were not to talk to us, even in a social environment.

And did they tell them why?

DK: Yes. They all knew. And the lines were drawn. With the exception of one individual, I would say the other fifteen or twenty did ignore us.

How were you made aware of the charges against you?

DK: We were brought in separately, and they said they had information that we were homosexuals, and that they could kick us out of the Navy. Back in the old days, it was kind of a good cop–bad cop thing: "If you work with us, things will be a lot easier on you than if you don't work with us."

What goes through your mind when you're presented with something like this?

DK: At the time for me, it was kind of funny because I was like, "What are you talking about?" And then I was kind of like, *How did they get this information?*
I basically went into the clam-up, to see what they're gonna go with. My partner took a different route, and hers was to defend everything: If they say one thing, you say why it can't be true, which, to this day, I would still say is probably not a good tack to take.

Why do you say that?

DK: Because I think you'll slip, and she hit a couple of slips. I think if you defend things too long, you just give them more information to run with. If you just sit silent, they have nowhere to go, other than to develop their own information.

Was this the first time you had been investigated?

DK Yes. That investigation resulted in an administrative discharge board. We both requested that it not be held on the installation because everyone on the base had already made a determination one way or the other.

So we had it convened in another city. My lawyer went with me. And we were found not guilty of the charges. My lawyer was a military lawyer.

Did your colleagues present evidence or character testimony? How was it that you won?

DK: Well, there was a specific incident in which the guys said they had walked in on two women in a particular room. They stated a time frame that it happened and everything.

The fact of the matter was my partner had not even been on the installation during the period of time they said it had happened. And it was a one-time incident.

And the fact was we actually *knew* the two people that they did walk in on. They *did* walk in on two women. But they didn't walk in on us.

When we presented all that information before the boards, we presented it separately. We presented that she was out of the area. We had the ticket to prove it. And the government basically knew they weren't going to win, so they wouldn't even bring the accusers.

Part of my lawyer's tack was, if we can't even interview the guys accusing them of doing it, how can they defend themselves? The board basically concurred.

How long did the proceeding take from start to finish?

DK: The actual board took about four hours. From the time of being accused until we got to go to an administrative board, it was six months.

Did you and she live together?

DK: No, we lived separately in the BOQ, bachelor officers quarters.

What impact did that have on your relationship?

DK: It destined it to fail. We went another three years together, another investigation together, and then that was the end.

You were investigated again together?

DK: Yes. We were investigated at another installation the second time.

How did that happen?

DK: I'm not sure what started it in particular, but they began interviewing neighbors and people with the command and everything. And they called us in again because the other investigation had remained open in the NCIS files, although it was expunged from our personnel files.

They said it had to do with our security clearances, and we went through it all again. And this time they didn't gather enough information to send it to a board.

And how long did that investigation take?

DK: Well, we didn't lose our clearances, so it kind of all died down in three months.

Were you aware of that same sort of thing happening to other people at the same time?

DK: For the first one, when we got accused, the CO, the commanding officer, immediately wanted to go out and do a witch hunt. I credit one male, a chief petty officer, for stopping the whole thing. He just walked in to this commanding officer, and he said, "Stop right there. You don't have any information. You leave the women alone. There's nothing to be gained by doing any of this." If he had not intervened, I really think that at least eight people—women I knew— would have gone down.

What is the justification for doing a witch hunt like that?

DK: There isn't. There isn't justification, but I think they feel they're cleansing the military of deviants.

It seems to me that the services don't have a lot of trouble from lesbians. Most of the instances of harassment and other bad behavior involve heterosexual males. So it's curious that there's always this attention on lesbians.

DK: I think other people have hit the nail on the head. It's certainly not my own insight or would say it is. The military attracts the short-male syndrome. You know, the guys who are smaller in stature than the average population, very much in need of being in control. And as a general population, lesbians are very self-confident, very much willing to take charge, good workers. We typically don't have the family to have to come home to, the kids, the whatever, so you can spend more time at work. So you're a general threat to their looking good.

I understand that recruitment figures for women in a number of the different services are down. It doesn't seem like much of a mystery. You want really good women, but you don't want lesbians. Who's left?

DK: Who is left are the women they really don't want—women with issues. By issues, I'd say women who have trouble keeping jobs, who have some medical problems, or whatever. They don't want that.

The other side of it, I think, is this: I went in twenty-five years ago. I was attracted to the military because it was equal pay for equal jobs. I knew that, as a whole, the guys and I were all going to get promoted at the same time. We were all going to get the same pay. There was nothing they could do to get ahead of me. And that was attractive.

In today's world, women can do a much greater variety of jobs. They may not get the same pay, but I think it's so much closer now if you are aggressive. If you really want to go out and do things, you'll do it in the civilian sector because it's greater pay. That's an opinion, strictly an opinion.

When you joined, did you know you were gay?

DK: No. I had been to parties. Well, let me put in this way: I had not executed any feelings. I knew people who were. I hadn't engaged with anybody.

What was your initial reaction to the Navy? Was it everything you had hoped it would be?

DK: No. My initial reaction was shock. The first thing I was exposed to when I got to my duty station was drugs. I just couldn't believe it when one of my superiors was doing drugs.

The second thing that happened was that my command failed major inspection. You know, that's not a good thing.

The next thing that happened—I just couldn't believe it. You know, everybody tells you, "It's the real Navy." This executive officer, the number 2 in command, entered my BOQ room at night and basically sexually assaulted me.

This was my introduction to the Navy. All within a period of, say, three months.

Did you file a report on that?

DK: Yeah, right! No. I think I held the upper hand: I just did the big threat with—excuse the language—"Get the fuck out of here, or your wife will become aware of this."

And I didn't have any trouble after that.

It was not what I expected. You have this vision of discipline and everyone being very by-the-book, not as freewheeling as everything seemed to be.

How far into your service were you before you realized you were gay?

DK: That would have been 2½ years. I certainly had all the friends (even in the military) who were gay. And then I was on a softball team. We went out of town. And one of the other officers and I were roommates, and she basically made moves on me, and I just accepted them. As they say, "The rest is history."

Were other people aware of the presence of gay servicemembers, or was it an underground sort of community?

DK: I would say it was underground, and the reason I think I was accepted is that everybody just always assumed I was. I hate to say it, but back then it was a lot easier to figure out who was who.

How so?

DK: Personality. Behaviors. Softball used to be the going thing. You know, jeez, there goes the softball players. So be it. Either we're not attracting as many now, I'm too old to recognize them, or they're just a lot different. I certainly can't pick them out.

Some women I've talked to completely avoided softball because they figured that's where the CID, the NCIS, Air Force security, and all the rest of them would immediately go first.

DK: Probably so, and they would have been right going there! [*Laughs*] I mean, that would probably be the easiest place to go hunting.

So you felt fairly comfortable. You and your fellows. Did you worry about witch hunts?

DK: I had to complicate the issue by being an officer. You are always on guard and can't hang around the enlisted that much. I was always on guard. I was always paying attention to how often I did something with anybody. To every bit of what I did, I paid attention.

What kinds of things would you not do?

DK: I never went to the parties with the enlisted, unless we were in a big group, lots and lots of officers. I just didn't do it. I didn't go to the bars. If I did sports, I did softball just a little bit, but not that much. I'd play sports with guys, too. Like I said, I kept in touch but didn't get really involved.

Do you think it's harder as an enlisted person or as an officer to navigate that very tricky trail?

DK: Officer. One, there's fewer of us. And two, if they want to make somebody fall big, they'll make an officer fall.

Because you are held to a different standard, a different code of conduct?

DK: No, we're all held to the same code of conduct. We're all held to a pretty high standard. It's just that we happen to be higher up the food chain.

So for the NCIS, CID, whatever branch we're talking about, an officer is a bigger fish?

DK: Oh, yeah. You figure you're more visible. The fear factor will run faster.

There's more to lose.

DK: There's definitely more to lose.

What were the stresses, if any, associated with hiding such an essential part of yourself?

DK: You don't let your guard down, so you limit your social life severely. And when you have to go to social stuff with work, you just do that on your own. You can't take your partner. Like I said, you're always paying attention.

Did you ever take a beard, a male escort, with you to functions?

DK: No. Being an officer, once again, you're in a more limited environment, you know, as to males you can date. And I certainly didn't meet any out in town that I would use as a cover.

When people would say to you, "Diana, how come you're single?" How would you respond to that?

DK: I had a pretty canned answer, and I don't think it's a wrong one. I basically said, "Any guy that I would be attracted to, that I would like to be with, would not accept my lifestyle. And anyone who would accept my lifestyle wouldn't attract me. I don't want a guy that just follows me around." So, I said, it makes it pretty tough.

And that was accepted?

DK: Most people understood that. And they understood that I transferred every two years. They understood I was in locations where there's just not a lot of breaking in to get a social interaction going. And I was an officer. So it just wasn't like other people in the command. Most of my career, I was within the top three positions of the command. I was the commanding officer, the executive officer, or the operations officer, so there's not anybody at those levels that you can date.

Pickings are slim. It's kind of like being in the upper strata of a corporation. If you're a CEO, you need a CEO or better.

DK: Right, and you put me off places where there's no civilian population, so there's nobody.

Critics of gays and lesbians serving openly in the military say our presence in the ranks disturbs "good order and discipline" and negatively affects "unit cohesion." How do you respond to that?

DK: Personally, I do think it would affect unit cohesion because I don't think that people attracted to the military are that accepting. On the male side, it attracts a very gung ho, macho, enforcer type of personality, and that doesn't jibe with being accepting of people with an alternate lifestyle.

Is that a matter of education?

DK: It might be a matter of their environment. Diana Kerry's opinion. Enlisted, as a general group, don't even come from Middle America. Most of them come from a less-than-Middle American background. And given that, they don't have exposure.

They come from a world that is smaller and not as open. If you get into the officer ranks, most of them, they've been to college, so they've been exposed to things. But it's the same as ethnicity. It is a bigger issue for the enlisted than the officer ranks because they haven't been exposed. So I do think it's an issue. I don't know that we're ready for military people to bring their partners to family functions.

I'm thinking back to the 1940s when a number of the same arguments we hear opposing gay men and lesbians in the military were used for African-Americans.

DK: Yes.

Harry Truman was a very brave fellow. He didn't really wait for the Joint Chiefs and the rank and file to be okay with integrating, he demanded it. I'm wondering if that's so very different from the situation we have now.

DK: The military as a group is probably the easiest to manipulate because they take time out for training and things like that. They demand diversity. They demand safety. They demand a lot of things. My guess would be—if they did all of a sudden say "gays can be in the military"—you're gonna have a reduction in recruitment of straights for a period of time because "I'm not gonna serve with those people."

Although the joke is, they already are.

DK: Yeah, but, you know, it's kind of like, my parents may know that I am but choose not to talk about it. "Let's not bring it up." And I let 'em go with that.

You're saying it's one thing to know plainly and another to have a vague idea.

DK: Confirmation is one thing, but suspicion is another.

I think about what you endured during these various proceedings: You're a dedicated officer, educated, committed, and yet for something that really doesn't matter, you were put on the hot seat.

DK: Other people have said I was successful despite myself. Three different times in my career, they went after me. And I still made captain. Finally, on the third one, I said, "Look, either come up with something solid, or leave me alone."
But the last one cost me a relationship with a civilian. She didn't want to play a part in that anymore, got tired of it.

How did the third investigation go down?

DK: On this one, my partner was a Navy reservist and was going for a security clearance. And in part of the paperwork you have to say who's your roommate, and she wrote down my name. So they started an investigation. They called her in and said, "We're not after you. We're after Diana."
My file was still open. We suspected they had been tapping our phone because on our answering machine you could hear the click when somebody connected. We knew they were watching our house. We saw them.

What did you see?

DK: We actually saw guys out, sitting in cars, watching us come and go. During that period of time, my security clearance was actually pulled again. But I was a security officer, so I read the message. It said, "Effective immediately. Suspend Diana Kerry's security clearance until further notice."

So I'm the only one that gets the message. I call 'em up and say, "Why are we doing this?" (I just said I was the security officer, I didn't tell 'em who I was.)

They said, "Well, there's some investigation going on again." So I just buried the paperwork for a while and kept checking in every once in a while to see where the investigation was.

How do you feel when you have people sitting out in front of your house? I would be very on edge, if not down right paranoid.

DK: It goes back to you're always paying attention. You're always paying attention. The investigation in '89 ended up costing me that relationship because it was just too much work. You couldn't even live a normal life.

You had to pay attention that nobody could see in any window—period, ever. You never did an inadvertent touch anywhere outside. You had to pay attention that two sets of bedroom lights went on and off at different times. You had to walk in front of windows so that shadows would indicate that you were in different rooms. Stuff like that. It's almost like you have to have a schedule. It's very, very taxing.

There's so much effort going into pretending that you can't really live.

DK: I couldn't. Like I said, part of that is because of the locations I was at. I was always pretty remote. Remote being more than 2½ hours or sixty miles from a major base.

The other part is—and everybody does—you quit using pronouns. You just say "my friend" or "they." You never do a "he" or a "she." People start to figure it out after a while. Or, every once in a while, you change the pronoun to fit. It was a lot of work.

Then I turn around and look: I've got two very good friends right now, officers, who both retired at the same time I did, who were with somebody their entire career and didn't suffer any of the same consequences, didn't have any of the same problems.

What did they do differently?

DK: They lived in big cities. They did Washington, D.C., the big areas, where it's a little easier to blend in.

That alone accounts for that disparity?

DK: That was a big factor. The second one is that once they tag you, you're always kind of on the edge.

And your friends were never tagged?

DK: No. And I actually think they were much more blatant than I was, but everybody can say what they want.

What kinds of things do you think are "blatant"?

DK: Going to the bars is pretty blatant. Dangerous. Having parties. At the end, I had a farewell, my retirement party. I had the general one, and I had a friends one.

If anyone had been watching me like they had during the third investigation, where they were sitting outside the door, they could've taken license plate numbers and a whole bunch of people would've gone down. I never had group parties or any of that stuff.

Do you feel freer today to say, "Hey, I'm gay!" Or are you still quite circumspect about that?

DK: It depends on the arena I'm in. I would never outright do it, for my parents. Out of respect for them I wouldn't. Around my sister and her husband I'm very much out. They even laugh. They've been very funny about it. They'll call me and say, "Hey, do you realize this is Gay Day at Disney?" Or "Do you realize this is National Coming Out Day?" It just depends on the environment.

If a young gay man or lesbian came to you today and said, "I'm thinking of joining the military, and I know you retired. What should I do?" What would you tell them?

DK: I wouldn't tell them *not* to join the military. I'd probably ask them why they picked the military. And then I'd just be very honest, saying there's a different set of rules that goes on there. You don't have the luxury of saying, "Hey, here's my two-week notice. I quit."

If you have this need to be around gay people and you can't contain it, you might get kicked out. Can you live with that? If you're willing to play, you gotta be willing to pay.

I'm thinking about the idea of "containing" one's self. If I'm hetero-sexual, I don't really have to contain myself. But if I'm gay, I can't even have my wife's photograph on my desk because that is "telling."

DK: I agree. To me, it's just a whole different lifestyle. The rules of the game. I didn't have a problem with that part of it. I understood those rules, but I don't think I would do it even out in the civilian world. I wouldn't put my partner's picture on the desk.

Knowing what you know and having gone through three investigations, would you do it all again?

DK: You know, I like the fact that I'm retired. I love that I had great respect for the people that I worked with. I'm not sure I would do it again just because I have become a loner as a result of it.

Being in the military, you don't gain equity in things, in relationships, in your family, your parents, whatever. You're not there to put those investments in. Still, I certainly like the fact that I know what my retirement check is every month.

I think you earned that.

DK: Well. Other people have earned the same check, and I'm not sure we put in the same difficulties.

Every other tour I had I would run into a male who just could not stand a female in the position I was in. Let me give you an example: I was up in the northeast. I was the second in command, the XO, doing really well. And I got a brand new boss.

The first thing he did when he called me in was say, "I want your replacement to be a male." This guy had been in thirty-one years, had been in submarines, had never worked with a military female in his entire career, and then he runs into me.

I said, "Okay." So I made the phone call, and I said, "When you replace me, they want it to be a guy." And I got the old laugh, and they said, "It's not gonna be a guy, so he can just get over it."

So I went back to him and said, "Sir, there's not any guys in the pool to replace me." And he says, "Well, then I want somebody who is married." Now you start taking it personal. Okay, he wants a guy, and now he wants somebody married.

So I called back, "When you replace me, can it at least be somebody who is married?" They said, "Well, we can do that."

He and I ended up working together for another year. And in the midst of it, he completely changed his opinion. He really liked me. He started helping me learn things and teaching me stuff. And when I left, his wife actually came in and told me, "He respects you more than any other officer he has ever worked with. You'd be amazed how much he talks about you." I said, "Well, that's kind of good considering where we started from." She goes, "Yeah. And he knows that."

He had high hopes for the female who came in behind me, but he picked the wrong criteria. Her number 1 criteria was her family. She didn't want to learn what I learned. She didn't want to do the job that I had done.

He and I are in touch to this day. And he apologizes on a routine basis. So you run into those. Then I turn around and run into the guy I just left, who, from day one, was gonna make sure I didn't look good. But he couldn't do it. I was good at what I did, and you couldn't deny that.

About Face

This Marine realized she was gay during advanced training. Another awakening: When going to a gay bar, leave your low-quarters in your locker.

First time I went to a gay bar alone, I spent four hours in the parking lot terrified to go in. The next night I went back and spent three hours in the parking lot before finally saying, *Get up off your duff and do this! Don't be an idiot!*

I walked in with as much bravado as I could muster: I didn't have a clue what to expect. Out of the corner of my eye, I noticed this very tall, very muscular-looking older woman wearing motorcycle boots. I thought, *Oh, jeez! What have I gotten myself into here?* I decided I would just play it cool. I stood there for a few minutes. Then I heard this deep, gravely voice say, "If you don't want anybody to know you're in the service, then you shouldn't be wearing boondocks." I just rolled my eyes, groaned and looked down at my feet. *Oh, yeah. Dumb ass!* I was wearing my boondockers, which is what we called our military work shoes.

There I stood. I was like, *Oh, God!* She started chuckling, a deep kind of chuckle. She had been a woman Marine in her day, and she said, "Damn, I get you guys every time. I've never seen anything like it. Only Marines come wandering in wearing boondockers." She kind of took me under her wing, and we got to be friends.

—Belle A. Pellegrino, PFC
USMC, 1968–1969

I Am a Marine 100 Percent

Lance Cpl. "Rhonnie"

*Rhonnie, not her real name, is a lance corporal on active duty some-
where in the United States. At 19, she joined the Marine Corps because
she wanted to be the best—and to escape a dead-end world of drug
addiction in the small Southern town where she was raised. She is just
past the halfway mark in a four-year hitch.*

*At the Military Entrance and Processing Station (MEPS) where
she was inducted, the recruiters didn't ask about her sexuality. There
were posters on the walls, though, she recalls, explaining homosexuality and warning of the penalties for being gay. The recruits were
told to read the posters carefully, and each signed a paper saying she
understood.*

*"I felt like I was totally just walking right back in the closet again,
and I hated the way it made me feel," says Rhonnie, who answers questions with a crisp, "Yes, ma'am."*

*"But it was something I had to do in order to get the hell out of that
crack-head country I was living in. At home, I couldn't ride my truck
down the street without some crack-head hollering my name to sell me
something. So when I stood there and thought about not living the rest
of my life like that, I knew I had to do it. And I believe I did the right
thing. You gotta do what you gotta do in life."*

She's dismissive of the military's "don't ask, don't tell" policy and says that while people usually won't ask her face-to-face, some will go to others, trying to sniff out her sexuality in a roundabout way.

"It's not avoiding detection as much as not giving any evidence," Rhonnie says. "There are a lot of Marines that people assume are gay, but what can they do about it if they give them no proof? I have known some people that have been asked outright if they were gay. So far it's working out okay for me, but I hope it just stays that way."

Completely clean now and totally can-do, Rhonnie says she's a Marine through and through. "I am a Marine in my heart, and I just wish I could be myself to my Marines. My sexuality has nothing to do with my ability to be a Marine, so I just wish they would chill out."

* * *

You wrote, "I just wish I could be myself to my Marines." If you were yourself, how would that look and what would you do differently?

R: A lot of times on the weekend people ask, "Where you going? Whatcha doing?" People ask me to come over to their house, and it would be cool if I could bring my friends, but they all look like dykes. Or my girlfriend. It's kind of hard when everybody has their families around, and we have barbecues at work and stuff like that. It's like, you can't really be yourself.

I wish I could bring my significant other to gatherings like the Marine Corps Ball because I just don't think that it is fair. And also, it takes away from how much my girlfriend understands me as a person because I am a Marine 100 percent.

She doesn't understand how strict the rules are and how tripped out I get when I take her on base. It's not that I don't want to take her. I just don't want anyone to question me. And she doesn't understand why I can't say "I love you, too" on the phone at work. There's a lot of things she doesn't understand.

You always have to put up a front. Have a fake boyfriend or something. You know? It's hard.

When men ask you out, if they do, do you have a fake boyfriend?

R: Oh, yeah. His name's Michael. [*Laughs*] My imaginary boyfriend. I say, "Oh, I can't do that. I have a boyfriend. He'll be mad. I can't go out with you tonight."

And do they believe that?

R: Oh, yeah! A lot of them do because, I don't know—I think that I'm a pretty girl, and there's maybe only five females that live in the barracks, and the rest is males. So you get harassed constantly. It's really no good at all. You have to, like, say something. Otherwise, they'll be like, "Oh, you dyke!" You know?
Some of them do know, and they're cool with it. There are certain people you wouldn't want to know that.

How do you know that they know?

R: Well, cool friends, like my neighbor. He knows. And he's cool about it. But, at the same time, everybody wants to be like, "Oh, it's just because y'all haven't found the right guy yet," and all this crap.

That's the same thing people have been saying for decades and decades.

R: It's ridiculous.

Is that a large barracks that you live in, and are the women on a separate floor?

R: No, the women are scattered around, and like my

neighbor, he's a guy. I'm the only girl that lives in my section. Right now, it's probably only fifty percent filled in the barracks. But it's a pretty big size. I estimate maybe about 100, 200 people at the most.

Is that bachelor-enlisted quarters?

R: Yes, ma'am.

You mentioned that, most of the time, Marines are not accepting—unless they become close friends with you and they begin to love you as a person. What do you think it is about knowing someone and getting to know someone that helps people overcome their prejudice?

R: Well, a lot of my friends I made because I was on guard duty for like eight months, hanging out there fifteen hours a day with people. You start talking to them. And after a while, you really can't help but like 'em. You know?

Then a lot of times we work nights, so you get off work at 7 o'clock in the morning, and there's nobody to hang out with because everybody's at work, except the people you're on guard duty with. So you're around them twenty-four hours a day, pretty much, except when you're sleeping, and that's maybe four hours. And people will start coming up and telling you things about themselves, like they were molested as a kid, or just crazy stuff. Like their whole life story. After a while, you get close.

I just think you have to watch who you say certain things to, but you can just tell in people. After a while, you know them as a person. You can tell how they'll react to it. I don't know. But you gotta pick it closely.

You have to be really careful.

R: Yes.

Is guard duty something everyone does on a rotating basis?

R: Well, it's supposed to be a three-month thing. We went out because of the war and stuff. But it ended up that I was on it for the whole eight months, and they never pulled me off. In my shop, they like totally forgot about me out there. I was loving it, though. I love guard duty. I like it better than working in my shop.

What do you like about it?

R: I was working with the military police, and I just like the way they handle things a lot better. It's more Marine-like. They seem more professional because it's a more serious job. You're holding a shotgun or a 9-mil or an M16. You have to be careful. It's more Marine Corps.

Did you find that there were a lot of lesbians in your boot camp?

R: Actually, there were probably only five of us all together. But then when we went to MCT—Marine Combat Training— after boot camp, everybody, all of the girls, were turning out to be gay.

MCT is like thirty days up in Camp Lejeune. You take ten days' leave after boot camp, then you come back and they teach you how to be a Marine and not a recruit anymore.

You shoot weapons and go out on patrol. It's more like wartime. And almost every single girl in the platoon was gay, and like everybody was hooking up in MCT. They let you do more things. You can smoke and stuff like that. So, everybody! I don't know what the deal was.

And now some of them I talk to on e-mail and stuff, and like, they have code words. Some of them still are gay. Like, they *are*. And some of them are just freaking nuts. I guess they just hadn't had a guy for so long they were like, "Well, a cute little dyke would be all right." Or something. I don't know.

Your roommate in MOS school was a lesbian who married another girl.

R: Yeah. She got kicked out of the Marine Corps. She hooked up with the girl in MOS school, and they were just really loud about it. My roommate was really obnoxious and like just a really butch girl. I think she even invited the CO to the wedding. That didn't go over too well. [*Laughs*]

That would be a mistake.

R: Uh, yeah. A big one.

One of the issues straight people often raise is that of privacy. They're worried about being objectified in the showers. They're thinking gay people are going to attack them.

R: Ha-ha. That's crazy!

What's your view of that, and have you ever seen such a thing?

R: Naw! I've never seen such a thing. When you're in boot camp is the only time that you shower with other Marines anyway. And you're so disgusting and so dirty, and they only give you five-second showers. Like, you don't even get wet in the shower! And then on Sundays, you might get like an hour of free time, so you take a long shower. But you're so disgusting in boot camp, and you see everybody that way.

Personally, when I got back from boot camp, I was like, "I'm not even gay anymore!" I was so disgusted with women. They aggravated the hell out of me. I didn't want to look at any of them. I thought they were disgusting. They stunk. We all stunk. I don't think any of us were looking at any straight females like that in boot camp.

Some people who have those ideas have never been through it. As you point out, you're much too exhausted. You don't care. You smell. And you just want to go to bed.

R: That's right. You just want to not get yelled at. You know? Anything to bring attention to myself, I really didn't want to do.

I think people need to grow up and treat people with respect. If nobody ever told you, then you would never know who is gay or straight. It's not about that. We have all been trained in the same training, and all of us, as Marines, know how important it is to react quickly in a wartime situation. There is no way that a Marine, just because they were gay, would let themselves get caught up in looking at another Marine in a sexual way when rounds are being slung. No Marine wants to get killed.

Exactly right. Did you find boot camp a challenge?

R: Yeah, I found it challenging. It really, really was like the suckiest thing I ever had to do. But it was physically challenging. I'm not a very physical person. It was really the fact that they make it seem like you're never gonna get to go home again. It's just so terrible. But I kind of thought it was a game. I thought the drill instructors were all acting. It was almost like comedy at times because I don't take things very seriously. I got in a lot of trouble because I'd think it was really funny, and I'd laugh.

What does it mean to be "100 percent Marine," and how is that distinct from being any other way?

R: You have to be a Marine in and out of uniform and hold yourself with pride, tuck in your shirt, wear a belt, have respect for other people, and take care of each other. Make sure everybody's okay. If you go out there, make sure everybody gets home safe. Stuff like that. Look out for people. That's about it.

So Marines are really looking out for each other?

R: Yeah.

Do you worry that if it becomes known that you're lesbian, your fellow Marines won't look out for you?

R: No, not my fellow Marines. Not the ones I work with. In my shop, my staff sergeant, she's gay. And I go out with her all the time. And then my master sergeant, he's always preaching "don't ask, don't tell" and puts up a big ol' stink and acts like a macho man, but he's gay also.

So I've got a lot people who will cover my ass. Like my master sergeant. I've seen him every single day just get angrier and angrier. I think he's been in the Marine Corps too long and hiding himself. He just needs to get out. I think he would probably lose his mind if somebody would try to mess with me about it.

People make a big stink about how when Marines are inspecting our rooms, they can't dig through any of our stuff. Because a lot of people will do that. They'll dig through your things and try to, you know, see if you've folded your clothes or whatever. But he's like, "No. I don't want y'all looking, trying to find anything incriminating on your Marines. It's not right. It's 'don't ask, don't tell.' So leave each other alone."

He's really setting the tone.

R: Yeah, he is. He's kind of like almost out to the whole shop, but he thinks he's not

You mentioned that he's getting angrier and angrier, and it's taking a toll on him. What kind of a toll does hiding take on a troop, do you think?

R: Like me, personally. I love the Marine Corps. If I could stay in, I would, probably. I just can't take it. I go home on leave and have such a good time! And it's like I don't have to worry about anything, anybody messing with me. I can be myself. I can make out with anybody that I want. Just kidding! [*Laughs*] I can do whatever I want to and have a good time partying with everybody. You know? I don't care. Damn!

Then I go back to work and feel this weight on my shoulders, like it's just everything I have to push back in the closet again. And I think of him, and he's been in the Marine Corps for twenty years and it's like—to have to hide yourself for twenty years! I'm on two years, and I want to shoot somebody. I just don't think I could do it. After a while you'd lose your mind.

Would you ever go to a gay club or join a softball team, or are those places that you would naturally steer clear of?

R: Oh, I go to gay clubs all the time. Sometimes we go on Friday night. A bunch of Marines. Like, girls. You know? We all go out there and have a good time. Like this staff sergeant I'm friends with: She trips not to show your military ID, and all this, and make sure you keep your butt clean and whatever. But I don't think anybody's really tripping about it.

So you don't think that's a dangerous thing to do.

R: No. I don't really care. If you're in a gay club, you ain't got no business talking about me. If you see me there, then you're there, too.

You mentioned you were addicted to crack cocaine. Did you kick that all by yourself?

R: Yes. That's why I joined the Marine Corps—I figured it would be better than a rehab on my résumé. It's three months long. That's how long rehab is. That's how long it takes for cocaine to be pretty much out of your system. I thought I might as well be the best while I'm at it, so I joined the Marine Corps. Maybe two weeks before I joined I was still smoking crack. I figured I just needed to get the hell out of there. It made boot camp really challenging. Most people were like, you know, trippin' 'cause they were tired from the day. Trying to, you know, fall asleep real fast. I was up sweating. Up in my rack feelin', *My God, I'm gonna die.* Like I'm gonna have a heart attack. But you know, I was fine.

It was God, though. It wasn't really me. There was nothing I could do with it. I had to get away from it. God helped me out. So that's what I did. I just chose the Marine Corps 'cause I figured it would be the best thing for me at that time.

Has it been everything that you wanted and expected, pretty much?

R: Not really. It's a lot easier than I thought it would be. I see a lot of Marines that are so lazy. They get in the Marine Corps, and they don't have any goals for anything. They just sit around. It's like the boringest thing ever to me. I thought it would be more exotic than it is. Plus, the pay sucks, dude.

Can you make ends meet?

R: Yeah, I'm doing okay. I'm paying my bills. And I got a bunch of retarded stuff. I got AOL. What more do you need?

Would you advise a young gay or lesbian person to go into the military?

R: I would ask them why they want to join. If it was for college or something like that, I'd be like, just join the National Guard. But if that's what they really want to do, then do it. It's really good for you as a person. If you're immature, it helps you get away from your family and have to do things on your own. But I would just tell 'em to think about it. You know? Make sure that's what you want to do because it's a commitment. Once you sign that paper, you're gone! [*Laughs*] You gotta stay until it's done.

About Face

This Coast Guard boatswains mate served both shipboard and shoreside for more than twenty-one years.

I was one of the original twenty-four women sent to sea in 1976–'77 as part of an experiment. Twelve were on the Coast Guard Cutter *Morganthau,* out of the San Francisco area, and twelve were on the Cutter *Gallatin,* out of New York City. I was on the *Gallatin.* Through the power of association, I found myself in Greenwich Village, seeing lots of new things and feeling quite at home. This was the late 1970s, and the fear of being caught for any reason by Coast Guard Intelligence was a big deterrent.

[To avoid detection], the party line was, "Lie and don't ever change your story or give any names." Nancy Reagan would call it the "just say no" defense. It worked. I always claimed ignorance. After a few years, when I noticed the climate had changed and I had gained some rank and notoriety, I usually told people either to mind their own business, or I let them take me out.

I did also see a lot of gay members marrying each other to keep the investigators away. The message sent from the investigators must have been that married couples can "swing and experiment" without fear of being labeled.

I don't recall anyone ever being thrown out just for being gay. Many gay people I knew were above-average performers whose coworkers either knew or suspected they were gay. Usually it was ignored due to that performance. A Coast Guard unit usually had just enough or not enough people to be fully manned. Every person is needed at operational units, and the person they might be saving doesn't care who pulls them out of the water—just that they are pulled out.

—Judi Carey
BMC, USCG, Ret.

My Life Ends When I Walk Out the Door

"Major Maureen"

"Major Maureen," not her real name, is an Army combat service support officer on active duty in the military district of Washington, D.C. She is approaching her twenty-year mark and retirement.

Maureen has enjoyed the Army, she says. She appreciates its values and traditions. She likes the people she's met and considers herself fortunate to have traveled the world.

But constantly having to take the temperature of the environment and everyone in it, gauging how real she can be at any given moment, has worn on her, she says.

At one point her ambition was to go the distance, become a general. Deciding not to compete was a watershed moment.

"I just didn't want to be in a position of having my life that exposed to people looking at it," she says. "And I think that's too bad for the Army: There are a lot of good officers choosing not to go into leadership positions because they don't want to put themselves in the position of having their lives examined.

"There are a lot of gay women who decided to stay in and have had really successful commands and are now general officers. And I know that people know they're gay, and they're still successful, so I guess it

works out for them. But they really have to leave part of themselves behind."

When she retires, she hopes to work for the United Nations.

"I don't need to live like this anymore," she says of her round-the-clock closet existence. "I can still serve the country but without having to hide half my life while I'm doing it."

* * *

You didn't realize you were gay until you'd been in the Army for nearly three years. Did you think about leaving at that time?

M: You know, it didn't even cross my mind. I was really scared that someone would find out, but it was much more personal to me at that point, discovering that I was gay and what implications that had on my future and what my family would say. The military was kind of secondary to that. And I've kind of always been a little bit femme, so I could play it off pretty easily. But I think probably more people knew than I thought. And I was probably not as cool as I thought I was being. [*Laughs*]

Do you think they thought, "No big deal. Why bring it up?"

M: Yes. At that point I was just a lieutenant. I don't think anyone was even paying attention to me besides my peers. It didn't seem to be that big of an issue. It startled me later to find out that people had suspected me more than I thought.

Do you remember the first time you heard that?

M: There were a couple of times. Once I was playing basketball, and I got hit in the face and broke my nose. And I had just left an overseas post, and someone back in my unit said, "Oh, what? Did she turn around and run into Janet?" You know, like you're always together. [*Laughs*]

And much later, my executive officer was traveling on a plane and happened to sit next to someone I had worked with. She wasn't even in the Army anymore, and she kind of outed me to him, and he came back and told somebody else, who told me. He said, "I couldn't believe she did that. It was totally inappropriate. And I didn't talk to her the rest of the trip." I guess if she had talked to the right person maybe it would have made more of a difference.

That could have been very dangerous indeed.

M: Yes. But in this case, my executive officer was very supportive of me, and I think he had lesbian friends in the military, too. He was always hinting to me. Like, "I know these two women," trying to get me to be more open with him.

You didn't take the bait?

M: No, no. I try to stay away from that. Even with people I trust. They can think anything they want, and I generally know if they know and are supportive and will open my life a little bit more to them. But I will never say affirmatively that I am gay.

How do you know, from what they say and what they do, when people are in your corner?

M: You get a sense of who they are by just working with them. Generally, people in the Army are pretty conservative. Some of them are very religious and will say things about being gay not being right. And sometimes they will just generally talk about what's on TV, or if something comes up in the news, they will comment on whether they think that's okay or not. And sometimes they even comment, I think, to let me know that it's okay. It's kind of a little game, of feeling each other out.

People at work now know I have a roommate, and they know that we're looking at buying a house together, but I think they just want to assume what they want. People will believe what they want to believe. And they really will go out of their way to convince themselves of something that they want to believe. And they *still* believe I'm straight. [*Laughs*]

You know, I try to be careful, but I'm kind of getting tired of hiding my life. So I am less and less. I'm just pretty apathetic about it now. I'm like, "Whatever. Believe whatever you want." I used to really care. Now I don't care that much.

You once had more of an "I am straight" approach?

M: Right. I would really go out of my way to make people believe I was straight. And now I just tell people the truth, without telling them everything. Like the fact that I have a roommate. [*Laughs*]

You say, "She's my roommate." You don't say, "She's my wife."

M: Right.

What is an example of the lengths to which you would go, in that day, before you became more "apathetic"?

M: We would go out in a group, and I would flirt with guys. I would really purposefully—and I kind of still do—dress a certain way when I am out with people. You know? Like if it comes down to whether I should wear a dress or pants, sometimes I'll wear a dress on purpose. It confuses them. They're really kind of easy to confuse because they so want to believe you're straight. Interesting, isn't it?

Well, I think it's shorthand: dress + mascara = heterosexual.

M: Yeah! [*Laughs*] Exactly. And back in the '80s and early '90s that was way more the case. Because you didn't see lesbians on TV. You certainly didn't see the ones who looked good, like on *The L Word*. Now I guess that doesn't convince people as much. The people who are aware aren't convinced by how you look.

I think people are still pretty convinced. Though she doesn't mean to, my own spouse flies beneath the radar even of gay girls. They think she's a soccer mom.

M: Oh, really? [*Laughs*] That's great! You know, one of my Army friends who looks a little less "straight"—I'm going to use that terminology as shorthand, but that's a very prejudiced way of talking—said I had "straight privilege."

How do you feel about that?

M: I have spent seventeen years acting, and it's almost second nature now. It's a little bit scary to automatically do things. Sometimes I catch myself doing them and am aware I'm trying to present a certain image. It's kind of soul-destroying to have to pretend all the time. And that wears more and more on you as the years go by.

What kind of damage does that do, and how are you aware of it?

M: Well, one, I was raised Catholic. Then I joined an institution that didn't accept me. So my whole life I've had something telling me that what I was doing was wrong. And I think I've probably taken that on and am apologetic for being gay, a little bit.

Instead of just being open and living my life and being comfortable about that, I feel like to live my life openly is putting it in someone's face and making them uncomfortable, and they shouldn't have to deal with that. And that's the message that I've gotten and had to live. And I think it really means that I don't value my relationships and really myself as much as other people do.

If you were going to do some of those little things that your brain tells you are "flaunting it," what would those little things be?

M: Really just being honest. And I think bringing my partner to events. And I would think less about what I was wearing. You know, sometimes I'll take a purse to something, just to make the extra point. It's all that extra thinking, how other people are going to view you.

Would you have your partner's picture on your desk?

M: Yes, yes. I have other friends' pictures up and not hers. It's like really going out of your way to make sure nobody has any sense. Maybe I would invite colleagues over to my house, which I don't do now. But I think it would just be that I would be more honest in how I project myself to them. Or, really, less concerned about what they were thinking.

How does your wife deal with being invisible?

M: I'm not allowed to get married.

Even so, I insist upon using the term.

M: Well, thank you! I appreciate that. She hates it! She hates everything about it. She is not in the military.

And what do your coworkers know about her, that she's your "roommate"?

M: Some know that she's my partner, and they're very supportive about it.

Where's the disconnect, then, from the top brass who make pronouncements about gay men and lesbians "disturbing good order and discipline," and these people with whom you work, whom you meet in the hallways, and who say, "Oh, how's Mary?"

M: Well, one defense is that the people I work with are smarter than other people. [*Laughs*] They get it a little bit more. But I think sometimes people are saying things because they believe that's what other people believe. There are truly some senior people who are very religious and very conservative, and I really think they believe that good order and discipline will be harmed.

But in my experience, for the most part, senior leaders know that gay people work for them. They know they're gay, and they know they're good. And, in my experience, very few people will really go out of their way to kick someone out.

I can't then reconcile that with the number of people who are getting kicked out. I don't know where that disparity comes in. The senior officers I work with very closely are really kind of accepting of many different types of people, and I think really just wouldn't go after someone. It's kind of live and let live.

Again, a part of that is gay people "playing the game" and keeping a low profile and maybe doing subtle things. I have a friend who works in another office, and she wears a wedding ring, and she talks about her "roommate," and nobody asks her any questions. That's the way it is.

And I guess as long as you're doing your job and you're not really saying, "Hey, I'm gay," and putting up HRC stickers in your office, I don't think people care, at least in my experience. Now, I'm not in a combat arms unit. I'm not out on the line. I do get the sense that guys are much more sensitive about having gay guys in their units than gay women.

Do you think women largely don't care?

M: I think guys are a little more threatened, and so will be less comfortable and will take more positive action against someone, against another guy whom they think is gay in their unit. They will either try to bully him into getting out or convince someone to chapter him out.

I wonder how much of that is projection? There seems to be a lot of sexual harassment and general bad behavior among straight men in the military. Perhaps they think that gay men will do to them what they themselves do to females.

M: Yes! There's all sorts of psychology that can go into it. Maybe they have gay tendencies and are afraid of facing them. Honestly, my partner gives me a little bit of a hard time for seeming to defend the policy, which I don't at all. But in my experience, the gay people who have had trouble kind of get caught up in dramatic events that bring it to the attention of others.

What might some of those be, for example?

M: One is coming on to someone who is not gay. One is getting in a fight with your girlfriend in the hallway of the barracks. Or, often, getting caught in bed with your same-sex partner in the barracks. While a straight couple would just get into trouble, a gay couple would get kicked out.

It's especially hard on junior enlisted who must live in the barracks. People listen to your phone conversations; people know who you're hanging out with; when you're gone and when you come home; and also who you're sleeping with. The barracks are also open to inspections and that kind of stuff. It's a hard place to carry on a straight or gay relationship. Unfortunately, you can get kicked out for one.

Did the recent coming-out of retired brigadier generals Kerr and Richards and rear admiral Steinman make an impression on you?

M: I thought people were going to be able to write it off. That was my general impression when I heard about it, that people would say two things: (1) Okay, but they "played the game"; and (2), as long as nobody knew, nobody knew, and that was cool.

That's really the thing: People know there are gay people in the Army. They just want to hide their heads in the sand. They don't want to have to face it. And as long as you don't make them face it, like these generals and the admiral didn't, then they're okay with it. It's not logical at all, but that's the way it is.

What was the buzz in your hallway? Or was there any?

M: Nothing! No response at all.

What do you make of that?

M: I don't think that people pay attention to gay news. It was in *The New York Times*, but I think people will just read right over those stories. They just dismiss it out of hand. It doesn't mean anything to them.

Why wasn't there a woman among the generals, do you think?

M: Well, for a few reasons. One, because there are a lot fewer women who achieve that rank. Right now, I know at least two or three general officers who are lesbians. Besides the Nurse Corps, combat service support is where you would find most women achieving that rank. That's not to say there are no retired general officers who are lesbians; I just don't know them. I'm assuming there'd just be a lot fewer. I also believe that there are a lot more lesbians in the Army than gay men, even given the disparity of men and women in the service.

Why do you say that?

M: Because I know a lot! [*Laughs*] My soldiers, the soldiers that I had [charge of], the vast majority of them were women [lesbians], and finally, just kind of intuitively, you would think that lesbians would come into the military because it's a job they would like, and gay men would kind of avoid that.

Unless they were butch guys.

M: And, again, that is stereotyping, but I think it holds true in this case.

Many women I've interviewed have told me that being closeted made it almost impossible to sustain a lasting relationship. How have you done that?

M: Well... [*Laughs*] It's been hard. I've had three long-term relationships. My current relationship, I've been in for eight years. And I have two answers to this. One, yes it is very diffi-cult in the military. And I don't know if being closeted makes it hard—it adds an extra strain to long-distance relationships because you can't get stationed together. And then you don't have the support you need to maintain the relationship over a distance. Also, maybe they're giving too much credence to being closeted: I don't know many non-military lesbian relationships that last a really long time. You know what I mean? I don't want to write that off altogether, and I don't mean to dismiss it as problematic.

A portion of this might be part and parcel of the career field and its demands.

M: Yes, definitely. The career field because you move apart from one another. Two of my relationships were with people in the military, so it was kind of an understanding that you would be closeted, and we both were comfortable with that. But for anyone trying to have a relationship with someone outside of the military, that would break up a relationship pretty quickly.

Although your spouse is not in the military.

M: That's right. But I'm an exception to the rule. [*Laughs*] You know, I'm a little older now and just a little more ready to settle down. And it hasn't been easy. It hasn't been easy at all. We just both kind of decided to make it work.

It's very frustrating for my partner for a variety of reasons. One, she doesn't know what's going to happen next. She doesn't know when I'm moving next, and that's very unsettling. We lived together for a few years, and then I was gone for two years, and that's not the kind of relationship that she wanted. She didn't have the support of anyone, except people outside the military, during that time. And I was overseas, too, so I really didn't have a chance to come back.

And then she has a career, and she's really put her career in jeopardy at points. *Jeopardy* is a pretty harsh word for that, but she hasn't been in a job for more than five years before she's had to move. Besides the retirement that she doesn't get, she has to just start all over, and on the résumé it looks like she's not really settling into any one job.

But also she can't enjoy the kind of financial safety net that the spouse of a male officer would.

M: Exactly. In particular, health care. That's a big one, especially as we talk about having a family and the potential, at this point, of me staying in a few more years and her staying home. That's just an extra financial burden that wouldn't be comfortable. But the other part is retirement benefits, and I've got to think through this one. I know that if I retire and then something happens to me, usually the spouse would receive retirement benefits up to a certain point. We don't have that option.

Given that, how have you bound yourselves legally to each other without revealing your relationship?

M: We have a lesbian lawyer who works with second-parent adoptions and also has had military clients—not tons, but she has. And so we have wills, and we do have powers of attorney. And having a lawyer is an additional cost. I don't want to complain too much, but I could go to a military lawyer and get my will done, but I can't if I want Mary to be my partner in it. It's just crazy. And stupid.

There'll be an added layer of paperwork—and a greater possibility of being discovered—if you have a child as a couple.

M: Yes. I'm to the point of not really caring as much what people think. And they'll just think I'm a single woman having a child. If people get it, they'll get it. But I'm not concerned so much that people will think I'm having a child with my partner. There might be questions, but I really want to have a child, so that's part of the reason we're doing it.

We're getting inseminated through a private gynecologist, and if I do get pregnant I will go to a military hospital and have the baby in the military hospital, which, again, is quite frustrating because I can't be open about my partner. But the expense of having a baby outside without health insurance is kind of prohibitive.

Do you feel as though you're living dangerously?

M: No. At this point I feel like I have a lot of people taking care of me. I'm really pretty smart at work about what I say and what I do. I don't want to sound too cocky, but I have a good reputation at work. There are a lot of people who would support me and keep me from getting kicked out—unless I did something really, really stupid. If someone just kind of thought that I was gay, I would have a lot of people coming to my rescue, I think.

Would there be any "getting over" the policy? It seems that good conduct and a personnel folder full of commendations and good works cited isn't much of a defense.

M: Right. I guess what I'm saying is that it would never get to the point. I think it would get quashed very early on. I hope I'm not sounding too hopeful or Pollyanna-ish. I just know that people have my back. I just don't see it happening in my current workplace either. I work for a three-star general, and I don't think he would really want me to get kicked out. I had a friend, a woman, who had an affair with her battalion commander's wife.

That's chutzpah.

M: Yes, it is. And she admitted to it. Because she didn't want to lie, in the initial interview she admitted to it. And people kind of bent over backwards to try to find a way for her to stay in because she was good. And eventually it came to her getting an honorable discharge. Now she had eighteen years in the military, and she couldn't get retirement, which would just suck at this point. So I'm very cognizant that it could happen.

Why couldn't the powers that be have stopped that?

M: Because the battalion commander was really pissed off. [*Laughs*] And he had really specific evidence. So they said, "Look, we've got too much here, and you admitted to it. There's only so far we can go, and this is what we can give you, an honorable discharge." Otherwise it was going to be a court martial. So she decided to get out.

At any time you might run into someone who doesn't accept you, and that person has the power to end your career.

M: And those are the people you have to watch out for. Maybe I've just learned over time how to measure my interaction with individuals. Instead of having just one way of acting, I act very subtly [in] different ways with different people.

Once, when I was overseas for an extended period, I witnessed a commander actively try to enforce the policy against adultery by investigating field-grade officers en masse. I realized at that point that at any time I might run across a commander who would feel so strongly about sexual orientation that he or she might take a small piece of information and conduct a widespread investigation. I felt very vulnerable.

Another part of the reason I'm kind of willing to take a bit of a chance now is that I really haven't been living my life. It hasn't been the best life I could have been living for myself, and there's a balance, you know. And if part of the balance is taking a little more of a chance at work, that's okay.

You have used this phrase a number of times, "playing the game," that you get through by "playing the game." What does a day in the life of playing the game look like?

M: My life, as I want it to be, ends when I walk out the door of my house. And from that point on, I am extremely aware of who is around and who is paying attention to me.

When I'm in another city, I hold hands with my partner in the street because no one's going to be around that I know. But here? Anyone I work with could be anywhere, so I'm very careful.

I try to gauge what the doorman is thinking, like how many times have I been out with my partner versus how many times have I walked out the door alone, so that people can't kind of put it together.

When I go to work and people talk about what's been happening at home—"How was your evening?" or "How was your weekend?"—I measure what I say. I measure every *thing* that I talk about and every *word* that I say. And I am pretty vague in what I say. I'll say, "I went bowling with friends," and let them assume it was a mixture of men and women. And they'll say, "Oh, what friends?" And I'll say, "Oh, they're not in the military." I just answer the question with a vague answer that doesn't really answer the question.

Is that good enough for most people?

M: Interestingly, it is. I think that people find me secretive because of that. But I try to balance that with being open about other things, like I'll talk about my brothers and sisters and my mom and dad. Just something else. I'll talk about watching a show and let them into how I feel about what movie I saw. I'll be very open about those kinds of things and then very vague about others. So I think I confuse people.

71

That sounds like a tremendous amount of energy to do all that.

M: Oh, my God! [*Laughs*] It's a tremendous amount of energy, and it's hard. It's hard to keep up on a daily basis, and that's the kind of thing that messes with your soul. It just hurts your insides to act every day. And to be so aware of people's reactions to you. I measure every reaction. And I pay attention. It's a constant. That's "playing the game": It's a constant understanding of how people are thinking of you. It's something I cultivated over time. I don't like it, but it's how you survive.

You mentioned that the discharge of the Army's gay and lesbian linguists in 2003 highlighted to the world the stupidity of our policy of exclusion. What was the buzz about that among your fellow officers?

M: When that happened, we were tracking the war and everyone knew what shortages there were, and that just kind of came and went without much comment at all. Isn't that odd? Now that I think about it, most things that come up, as they apply to gays in the military, are not discussed. It's just a taboo subject. I don't think people quite know how to handle it.

So it's not that it's a non-issue. It's a taboo issue, too hot to handle.

M: Yeah. I don't think that people quite know what's okay to say. I don't know that people really understand the "don't ask, don't tell" rules very well. And I don't think that anyone in the military who disagrees with the policy—and many probably thought this particular instance was pretty stupid—will come out and say something against the policy 'cause they're afraid of what other people will say about them.

There's a very, very conservative culture about what you're

allowed to talk about and what you're allowed to be for or against, and I think there's kind of a silent majority who are quite okay with gays in the military, but they're not going to come out and say it.

If the majority remains silent, how does that change?

M: By someone having the nerve to stand up: Straight, senior officers getting together and saying, "This is silly. Enough." And I think the consensus right now among senior leaders is that there is no reason for the policy. Except they're afraid of the American public, mothers and fathers, and what their reaction will be. But I don't think that individually, personally, the majority of senior leaders in the Army are in favor of the policy. I don't think Colin Powell is for the policy.

Although publicly he says differently.

M: Right. But everyone's afraid of Mom and Dad.

It's interesting about Colin Powell: As an African-American he doesn't seem to connect the dots. The things that are said about gays and lesbians are the same things that were said about African-Americans in the 1940s. They're unfit. They'll be disruptive. We can't maintain order if they're a part of us. And it took Harry Truman.

M: Someone to say, "No, this is the way it's going to be." But when it has anything to do with sex.... I don't know how you feel about this, but the reaction to the breast-bearing of Janet Jackson, I thought, was totally outrageous. I didn't think it was that big of a deal.

We've all seen breasts.

M: Right. There's some of the show that I thought was a bit racy, maybe not prime-time stuff, but *whatever* about the breasts. But that's where our society is about sex. They're totally freaked out. And as long as being gay is associated somehow with sex, then people are going to have trouble with it.

About Face

When a "bevy" of lezzies was discovered at an Army post outside of Washington, D.C., the yeoman next door said, "I do."

I worked at the Naval Security Station, which is way across the other side of town, almost into Maryland. But the women's barracks were in Virginia, right across the street from the Army's Fort Myers. There was nothing there, not even a movie theater, so we had to go across the street, and we got to know the girls over there.

I saw a headline in the paper one day that said something like, "Bevy of Lesbians Found in WACs Barracks." Right across the street from us! Some of them knew me and others as well. I saw the handwriting on the wall. It was only a matter of time. I figured the only thing I could do is get out, if I wanted an honorable discharge, so I asked this nice guy in my office if he would marry me. I wouldn't have thought of marrying him under false reasons. I told him the truth, and he said, "Sure." So we did. And I got out.

Everybody else waited and got kicked out. I don't know whether they thought, *Everything'll be all right* or *They'll never come to me*, or what. A couple of them got married, too, but it was too late in the investigation. I did it so soon that they hadn't started to clamp down on our side of the street. They were still after the WACs.

—Barbara Owens, CT3
U.S. Navy, 1952–1953

They Consider Us Less Than Human

Angel "Mousey" Ramirez

Angel "Mousey" Ramirez's reasons for joining the Army in 1994, at the very opening of the "don't ask, don't tell" era, are the same most people cite: She needed employment, wanted to travel, and thought the service would offer a challenge.

But the 24-year-old Brooklyn native got more than she expected.

Ramirez completed basic training at Fort Jackson, South Carolina, and was sent to Fort Gordon, Georgia, for Advanced Individual Training (AIT) as a wire systems installer (31-Lima). She completed the course, but when her security clearance hit a snag, after a yearlong wait, Ramirez was sent to the Army's Aberdeen Proving Ground for a second AIT to train as a diesel mechanic (63-Whiskey). After graduating, she was assigned to permanent party at Fort Irwin, California.

Ramirez entered the Army a private (E1) and 3½ years later was honorably discharged a specialist (E4). Two surgeries left her unable to pass the Army's physical fitness requirements, and she was released early on a medical.

Such details can be found in her 201 file. What won't be evident is the nearly nonstop anti-gay harassment Ramirez says she endured.

Though she would never "tell," her boyish appearance and assertive manner were nonetheless telling, she says. And though they could not ask, her NCOs made it their mission to remove her from their ranks.

* * *

I didn't know much from the military before I signed up. I just basically saw commercials and heard that you get to travel, see different states and different places. I thought that would be really nice.

I first tried to join the Air Force, and I failed the test. Then they directed me to the Navy, but that didn't work out neither. I was too honest with them when they asked me if I ever tried any drugs. I said, "Yeah, when I was a kid, I did, marijuana." They said, "Aw, we can't accept you." They told me to try the Army or the Marines. I heard that the Marines was really strict, so I thought the Army would be better.

And you took the test and you passed.

AR: Correct.

Did you want to be a diesel engine mechanic?

AR: No, actually my primary MOS was 31-Lima, wire systems installer. I'd finished the course, but I couldn't get my secret security clearance. Somehow—this is what I was told—they got a report that an Angel Ramirez from Brooklyn, New York, had been incarcerated. I've never been incarcerated. So I pleaded with them, "Are you sure you checked the right Social Security number?" 'Cause one person only has one Social Security number. There aren't duplicates. And for some reason they got it twisted, and they just basically gave up. So they forced 63-Whiskey, which is a diesel engine mechanic, on me. They said, "Either you take this MOS, or you leave." Because I was a holdover for about a year.

You said that when you enlisted you answered "no" to the question about homosexuality.

AR: I answered no because "don't ask, don't tell" says they can't ask you and they can't pursue you. So lying wouldn't be no detriment to me. But for a second I hesitated.

And what did you think in that second?

AR: I thought I should leave because I was going to feel uncomfortable, you know, that I have to be in the closet, which I was [in the Army]. But not completely. I was like half in the closet, but still half being me. But I felt almost like a little heat wave come over me. An uncomfortability. And I thought, *Well, if they can't pursue, then it can't hurt.* So I just put "no" and kept moving.

What half of you went into the closet?

AR: Well, I had to be choosy with who kept that confidence. I don't like to hide being a homosexual because I feel I'm just hurting myself by doing that. There were some people that I befriended, and after a while I did let them know. But I basically kept to myself. I didn't socialize much. And you know, although there were women that did confront me in the service, I didn't flamboyantly expose myself. They just knew. That was the part of me that didn't go in the closet. I guess they seen through me. And they said, "Hey, would you like to go to bed with me?" I was like, "Hey! Why not?" [*Laughs*]

Women would approach you just like that?

AR: It wasn't in basic training. It started in the first AIT. Then a lot in my second AIT. And when I went to my second duty station, at Fort Irwin, my roommate hit on me.

You were two enlisted girls in the same room, and she just came on to you?

AR: Yeah. After a couple of weeks of being roommates, I guess she just saw that I was different. That I wasn't heterosexual, and I was more drawn into myself. And she would start, you know, putting on the lingerie, asking me to take provocative pictures of her.

My.

AR: And then eventually, little by little, she said, "We've been friends for a while, why don't you tell me the truth? I won't tell anybody. Do you like females?" And before we knew it, we ended up doing somethin'.

She was a gay girl who was in the closet also?

AR: No. I don't know if this is appropriate to say, but I'll say it anyway: She was a nymphomaniac. With guys. I don't know if that was her way of trying not to show that she was bisexual or somethin'. But she was well known to be a lay. An easy lay.

And did she keep your secret? And hers?

AR: Yes she did. I was never asked up-front if was I a lesbian. I was asked a couple of times why I wasn't dating anybody. Why did I choose to be by myself? And why not hang out with the rest of the people? And I said that it takes me some time to get used to being around new people 'cause I'm a loner. That's the excuse I gave, which was somewhat the truth. And it was also an excuse I gave because when you hang out with them—and you know everybody drinks in the military—they're gonna start trying to pry into your personal life. And that's what I didn't want to happen, because you can't trust everyone.

Even though I didn't let no one know it, I didn't go fully into the closet. I let myself be me. I didn't wear no ties, but I wore my baggy clothes. You know? I have three earrings in my left ear, one earring in my right. I guess you could say that I dressed like a child that's from the village, New York City, Greenwich Village. And all the other females was wearing tight pants and exposing more of their flesh. And a lot of the company, you know, they did wonder why I didn't have a male companion, and why I wasn't like my roommate, a nymphomaniac, having sex with everybody in the company.

And I would get picked on by my peers. They would always tease me whenever I'd fall out the run. I'm small—I call myself petite, not skinny—and they would say, "How in the heck can you be a diesel mechanic? You're so small. You can't lift a wrench!" And when I got promoted to a specialist, the whole company could not believe it. They said, "How the hell could she get promoted to specialist?" And the same time I got promoted to a specialist, I got my good conduct medal. And they could not believe it. They just felt that I was undeserving of it, and I couldn't understand why it was their business to say I was undeserving of it. I did a very good job.

At my second AIT, at the Aberdeen Proving Grounds, they had

an investigation going on, drill sergeants fraternizing with female enlistees.[1] And I was being interviewed by this sergeant first class. And she gave me the highest compliment that I could ever have: She said she could see me as a sergeant major. And I'm thinking, *Wow!* You know, everyone's picking on me, and I'm getting so much trouble. And when I try to do things right I still get in trouble. And she gave me that compliment. I was overwhelmed by it.

Why were you the focus of the company's wrath?

AR: The only reason I can come up with is that, deep down inside, they knew I was a homosexual. But because of the "don't ask, don't tell" policy, they could not pursue me, and that's what aggravated them so much: I was able to continue serving. And, of course, being a female and them being males and being drill sergeants, and they can't get into my pants. I think it irritated them even more.

Did they try?

AR: Yes, they did. One drill sergeant, the senior drill sergeant in my company, he propositioned me. And then I had a drill sergeant that was not even in my company try it. This is when I was in Fort Gordon, Georgia. He was on the other side of the post, and I just happened to be walking around, leisurely walking around, and he decided to approach me. He was very insistent. I managed to get away. My company wouldn't believe me because I always used to get into so much trouble in my company. They would try anything to give me counseling statements and Article 15s.[2] They wouldn't say anything straight out, so to speak. It would be roundabout ways, trying to catch me doing something wrong. Like, "Where was you? Why wasn't you at formation at so-and-so time?" When they knew I was working. They were just trying to get me in trouble.

They didn't want me there. And, you know, I couldn't figure it out. What is it that I'm doing? I make my bed correctly. I keep my area clean. When they tell me to post CQ, I post CQ. I don't go to sleep on CQ. I do my PT. What is it that I am doing wrong? And I could not understand it. They just had it out for me. I can imagine if I was a gay male I would have got it a thousand times worse.

So they said, "This woman is a lesbian. We recognize her, and we're going to make her life hell."

AR: Yes.

Do you think a part of that harassment was the fact that they considered being a diesel engine mechanic a men's gig and, in their way of thinking, you were violating their territory?

AR: In the beginning, yes, that did cross my mind. Almost like an initiation kind of thing. There wasn't that many women at Fort Irwin. And there was maybe six or less that worked as mechanics. Everyone had that hassle in the beginning. You know, "A female can't do a man's job." But eventually they would back off. "Oh, look. She did three engines in one day. She's pretty good!" I did that work as well, but I was still ridiculed. So that led me to thinking that no, it's not just that I'm in a man's job.

You've said that the people you encountered in the Army were very homophobic.

AR: Yes. They'd say, "The 'don't ask, don't tell' policy is a bunch of BS," and that if they knew someone was a homosexual, they would beat them up. They would talk about—I forget what it's called, where they strap a sheet on you and everybody takes turns beating on you?

A GI party.

AR: Yeah. They'd talk about bringing that back. And the drill sergeants would say they wished that things in the olden days would be brought back, where they were able to lay hands on the enlisted. That faggots had no place in the military, and they're less than men. The comments were more towards gay men, but lesbians they said they would basically—what's that terminology again? Gang-rape 'em. That's what they'd say about the lesbians.

If they discovered a lesbian, they'd gang-rape her?

AR: Right. And that had me really, really nervous because I'd been raped prior to the military. I know it's hard for a woman raped in the military to prove it. So that made me really scared. Then someone would change the conversation or something. But me, I wouldn't even get into the conversation. I would act as if I didn't even hear anything. I would act as if I was really stupid. I don't know nothing. I don't see nothing. I don't hear nothing.

Did you have a sense that, if something were to happen, you could go to your supervisors?

AR: No. If something was to happen, I could not depend on my company chain of command to help me out because my company chain of command was the one that was doing it. They basically wanted to boot me out the military, to get me on any infraction. So I knew that if that was to happen, I couldn't depend on my chain of command. And to go outside my chain of command is not really allowed. But I would have to do that, to be heard. I'm not one to just stay quiet. Even though I'm petite, I have a lot of strength inside of me.

You've said that critics of gay men and lesbians serving in the military are "full of shit."

AR: Hell, yes. They are! They consider us less than human because of our sexual preference. But then when manpower is low or we're needed because there's a crisis going on, then it's okay if you're a homosexual. Then you'll be considered a soldier. So yes. The critics are full of shit. I'm talking about the generals and all them big brass people. When there's no conflict going on, we're considered less than. Like we're freaks. We don't bleed the same color. We're not smart. You know, we can't be strong. We're weak-minded. All of this. They create it. And I think a lot of them are in the closet themselves or bisexual.

You can't really have it both ways, can you?

AR: No. That's why I'm in an organization called AVER–New York. American Veterans for Equal Rights. And we're hoping to end the "don't ask, don't tell" policy because that's a crock of shit, too. Excuse my language.

People really do still ask, don't they?

AR: Yes. I was asked by people that I felt were homophobes, what I would call rednecks, who I felt intimidated by because they are the ones you read about gay-bashing someone. And I would just ignore them. Try to change the subject. Or say, "Listen, don't be asking me no personal questions because you are not my friend." They asked me, "Do you have a boyfriend? I've never seen you with any guy. Do you *like* guys?" And I would just tell them, "Off-duty, it's none of your fucking business what I do!"

Would they back off?

AR: Yes, they would back off, and I think that would have them inquire more. "Yes, she must be lesbian because she comes off so nasty with her answer." And basically the reason why I come off nasty is because it really is none of their damn business. They're trying to get into my private life.

How can you answer that question and win, whether you're nasty or nice?

AR: There was one time that I was trying to be nice. I told them that I did have a boyfriend, and he was back in New York, and that we was gonna get married. That I wasn't going to cheat on him, so that's why I'm not with nobody. And then they would ask me, "Well, don't you think he's cheating on you? It should be okay if you cheat, too." I said, "Listen, if he cheats, I'm not thinking about that. I'm just thinking about doing my job here and eventually, you know, we'll get a place together and get married."

I made that up for a while. Then I got tired of even making that up because then they'd ask me more questions about my so-called fiancé in New York. They knew it was a lie. So I just stopped altogether and didn't answer any questions. "Listen, I'm just here to do my job. Just let me do it. And if you have any questions, let's just relate it to the job. No personal stuff."

At the time, I was smoking, and I said, "I don't even want to take cigarette breaks with you." And you know, that was anti-social, but that's how I thought it best to be. Because when you're in the Army, it's a different world. You can be physically abused. You could be raped. And they could mentally abuse you, too. And in that world, you can have no help if it's coming from someone who has a lot of rank and knows a lot of people. You're basically fucked. So I had to be very cautious.

I don't think people understand how isolated that world can be, especially as a junior enlisted. You really have no power.

AR: No, you don't. Unless you get to know people that has rank and power. And one time I did. I knew that she was a lesbian, just like she knew I was. But we didn't voice it. We didn't say those words. She was from a different company. And she told me, any time I wanted to come to her for advice, she's got an open-door policy. And one time, my company put in the paperwork to discharge me, and I asked her for help. Would she write a letter of recommendation for me? And she definitely did. And because of her rank—she was a captain—it helped me out a helluva lot.

Why did your company want to discharge you?

AR: Because the harassment that I was taking—you know, them always wanting to know my every move, being on restriction all the time—it got to the point that I went on a three-day-weekend drinking binge. Actually went AWOL, with two other enlistees. Fortunately, we wasn't missed at formation for the whole weekend. But when we came back, we were very drunk, and I was the only one they picked out. That's when I felt I had a little nervous breakdown. I cursed out my drill sergeant. I cursed out the first sergeant. And then afterwards—I knew I was in a world of shit—I took a bunch of prescription pills. I knew what the outcome would be.

After they pumped my stomach, they wanted to discharge me. And I decided to fight them because even though I cracked, and they were almost winning, I said, "No, I'm not going to let them win. I'm a stronger person than this." And I bounced back. Went to everybody outside my company that had higher rank, like the captain, and I said, "Please give me a letter saying that I'm a good soldier." And I got a whole bunch of letters, and that outruled their favor. And I think that's really ly why they told me either I take the 63-Whiskey or I'd be discharged from the military. After I beat them, you know, they said, "Hey, I know another way to get her: Who wants to be a diesel engine mechanic? Nobody."

Because you had a spotlight on you anyway, didn't you think twice about going AWOL with those girls?

AR: No. I'd had it at that point. I was at my limit. And I was, like, "Fuck all of this." That's why, I guess, when I came back I snapped, 'cause I left with an attitude of *I've had enough. Enough is enough.*

Do you think they were just waiting for that opportunity?

AR: Oh, definitely. Because every day, like I say, I was being harassed, every day. If it wasn't one thing, it was another. There was a Thanksgiving. What they do on the post during holidays like that is that different officers or NCOs take an enlistee into their homes for that holiday dinner. And the captain I was telling you about invited me to hers. And my company just totally denied me, which was another way of basically trying to fuck with me, to see if I was going to lose it. So every day it was something new to try to get to me, and I did break. But I bounced back.

Is it easier, do you think, for femme lesbians to just pass under the radar?

AR: Yes. Because they're so feminine lookin', they can get away with just wanting to be in solitude. A lot of guys in the military hit on you because they're just a bunch of dogs. And she can turn them down easily and, because she's a femme, probably throw the charm onto them where they'll just be happy to be in her presence as a friend—and hope they'll still get into her pants after a while. But for a person as I am, which I guess you'd call a dyke, it's really hard.

88

So they saw that you were a big dyke, and they were going to turn up the heat and see if they could break you?

AR: Right. Well, actually, I'm just a little dyke. [*Laughs*]

Me, too. But I feel like a big dyke inside.

AR: [*Laughs*] Yes, that's how I feel. Unfortunately, there is no solid proof behind it. I went into the detail of everything that happened to me, every incident. And I said. "Take a look at it, at where the road leads, and you'll see that it's pointing all in the same direction: They discriminated against me because I'm a lesbian, but they couldn't verbalize it straight out, so they just harassed me so that I would leave on my own. And that's how it was.

I really was a good soldier. In my whole company, even though we were mechanics, when formation time came, I had my uniform neatly pressed. My boots shined. I have a gold tooth in my mouth, and I would not be satisfied until I seen my gold tooth in my boots. And I was the only one in my company that had a pressed, shiny-boot uniform. For everyone else it was wrinkled and everything. I couldn't understand. Here I am, and I'm looking good as a soldier, and yet I'm still getting picked on.

You were awarded a good conduct medal, though?

AR: Yes. Yes I was.

So someone was noticing.

AR: Yes. Someone. Someone higher was noticing. But for some reason, the NCOs were the ones that were trying to degrade me. The people above didn't see that: They just looked at my performance. I *know* I was a good soldier.

Whatever they asked me to do, I did it. Why did I have to pull CQ back-to-back when there's other bodies laying in the beds and you're asking me to do this? I still did it. No argument. I stood up and did it. I didn't go to sleep. I know that it was discrimination.

Notes

1. The investigations were triggered by numerous allegations of sexual assault against female trainees by their drill sergeants at the Aberdeen Proving Ground in Maryland. The Army-wide investigations took eight months to complete and resulted in more than 35,000 interviews at fifty-nine bases around the world. "We had a leadership failure," said then Army Chief of Staff General Dennis Reimer, who, in a 1997 CNN interview, cited the need for better selection and training of drill sergeants. Investigators found that sexual harassment exists throughout the army, crossing gender, rank, and racial lines; that sex discrimination is even more common than sexual harassment; that the army lacks commitment to the equal opportunity program; that soldiers don't trust the complaint system; that too many leaders are not trusted by soldiers; and that respect is not well taught in basic training.

2. Within the Uniform Code of Military Justice (UCMJ) a commanding officer's nonjudicial punishment (Article 15) can result in confinement to quarters, duty restrictions, or forfeiture of pay for a prescribed time.

About Face

This Naval officer thought hiding her essential self would be "a piece of cake."

There wasn't a question about homosexuality on the form when I entered. A military physician who was administering my physical asked me about drug use. I told him that I had tried marijuana a couple of times but that I was not a user. When I later reviewed my chart, I noticed that he had a stamp with DRUG USE, HOMOSEXUALITY, ALCOHOL ABUSE, and YES or NO following each in a grid. He marked my response as YES to drug use, along with my remarks, but marked NO to the others without asking me. I had dressed sorority-preppy that day, so he made his assumptions.

It's disgusting to have to lie, lie, lie in a culture that emphasizes honor and respect, at least as an ideal, if not a reality. When I was 19, I could never have realized how bad it is. When you internalize the major core values of honor, courage, and commitment, it all looks really great on paper. And then you have to lie to survive. There's a huge disconnect there.

With every lie, I felt less worthy of respect. And if you really are the kind of person who tries constantly to self-improve, constantly tries to do the right thing, it's toxic. So you're thinking, *Well, I'm just a bad person.* All that military slang: "I'm a dirt-bag." "I'm a shit-bag." And your self-esteem goes to hell.

—Jamie P. Roberson, LT.,
U.S. Navy, 1984–1989

We're Soldiers First

Brenda Hammer

Brenda Hammer grew up in Selma, Indiana, the eldest of six children. At Ball State University, in nearby Muncie, she majored in physical education, intending to teach gym when she graduated in 1975.

But then Women's Army Corps recruiters came to campus looking for juniors to participate in an accelerated ROTC program, and Hammer fell in love.

"We were at Fort McClellan, Alabama, home of the WAC, and it was wonderful," says Hammer, now a school counselor in Austin, Texas. "I knew I was gay at the time, but I didn't know there were other gay women in the Army. I just loved the service. It wasn't till much later that I found out that many of the women who were with me in the program

were gay also. But I was deeply closeted, and so was everybody else."

Earning both her BA and her bars, Hammer returned to Fort McClellan for Officer Basic. Slowly, she learned she wasn't alone.

"We didn't talk about it because we were afraid," she says in a straight-ahead, no-nonsense cadence. "We liked the Army so much. We wanted to stay in, and we didn't want to take a chance on anything spoiling it."

From WAC headquarters she went to Fort Benjamin Harrison, Indiana, for Adjutant General training and then on to Fort Hood, Texas, where she served for three years before heading to Germany, a command, softball coaching, and a CID witch hunt that would result in her discharge.

After a humiliating four-month investigation, the captain's spotless eight-year career was over.

"Although I still feel that the Army is a wonderful organization in terms of learning opportunity, career development, seeing the world, starting a career, [lesbians and gay men who enter the service] need to be fully aware of what could happen to them, possibly being put out years down the road, but also being maligned and hurt by their fellow soldiers," says Hammer, who is now fully out in her life and community.

"I certainly would not want to be serving next to someone who hated me so much because of my being gay that in wartime I might become a casualty."

* * *

In the '70s, what you heard was that the only women who went into the Army were either whores or queers. That's what the men said, and they really looked down on us. But with the Women's Army Corps we were together. And it wasn't until we left there in 1978 that I felt different, left all those women and had to go into units where there were men and women. I had the sense, *Maybe I don't fit in here.*

You talk about confiding in each other, but in the barracks there was no sexual activity?

BH: No. Absolutely no. It wasn't your typical barracks where you see all the bunks. I roomed with one other woman. We shared a bathroom with two other women. We wouldn't have thought about it, not even when we camped out in tents and stuff. We were there to do a job, and that's all we cared about. We weren't out there cruising.

How much time does a girl have in basic training anyway!

BH: You don't! You're hitting the books, preparing for inspections. You're doing uniforms and boots. The only social time that I had was during the weekends, if we got a pass. Then I could be with my other gay friends who were in the civilian world. I'd try to talk to them about the military, but it wasn't easy. They had no conception of what it was like.

Then I was sent to Fort Hood, Texas, as the Rec Services officer. I was in charge of the gymnasium and all of their sports programs. It took me a long time to find out that a group of women even existed. I found out through the sports program.

That would seem to be the best place.

BH: Yes. The gym! I got to play on a slow-pitch softball team, and I met a lot of other gay women who were closeted, too. The thing was, you had to be careful because CID investigates every woman who plays softball. You're obviously a lesbian if you're playing softball. They're terrible. Someone told me, "You're going to be investigated now." And I heard that I was a number of times while I was at Fort Hood, but I was never confronted by CID.

Were you on extra alert most of the time?

BH: I was always very cautious. To me, the military was my job. I was very protective about it. I had an incident once where an enlisted person fell in love with me. And I said, "No, this can't happen. One, it's called fraternization. And two, it's a homosexual act, and that's against the rules, too." That scared me. But it didn't scare me enough. We did finally have a relationship. I visited her in her barracks out of uniform. I would never go up there in uniform. We did occasionally go to lunch and things in uniform. I don't know that I was totally always watching my back. I just did my job and enjoyed life.

Did you ever hear of other gay men and women being harassed?

BH: Yes, I did. I later was assigned to the company commander at Fort Hood. One of my troops came to me, in fact, and said, "Lt. Hammer, I want to get out of the Army." And I said, "We don't have any reason to put you out of the Army." "Well, I'm gay." And I said, "Oh, shit. Don't tell me this. I don't want to put somebody out. You don't want to do this." "Yes, I do. I want out. I want to go be with my lover, and this is the only way that I can do this."

It wasn't so much that company commanders were out looking for these things. But it seemed that the only role CID had was to rid the corps of all the gays and lesbians. And I felt the women were hunted more than the men. Men could get by with it a lot easier than the women could. I sometimes felt that it was because they felt we didn't belong. We shouldn't be here. We were invading their territory. I think it was a matter of discrimination. Blacks had a hard time, too. But women had a particularly tough time. If you were here, it was because you were a whore or a lesbian.

What impact did the dissolving of the Women's Army Corps in 1978 have on this state of affairs?

BH: When they did away with that, we didn't have any-thing to hold onto. In 1979 I was sent to Germany, where I served with the Eighth Infantry Division as a personnel officer. I made captain. I was doing very well, and I was pushing for a company. I wanted a command before going stateside. At the same time, I was coaching women's softball, and we were under scrutiny a lot. We felt like CID was always watching us, investigating everyone who was on the team. It was all very secretive. You could never turn your back. You were always afraid that someone was out looking at who you were with and taking notes.

Were the CID in civilian attire? You could spot them pretty much?

BH: Pretty much. It's kind of like you know who the detec-tives are here in Austin by their obscure-looking cars. They'd pass by and we'd say, "There goes CID! I wonder who they're after now?"

Did they hang around the softball field?

BH: The softball fields were right on post, and we suspected that they were following different players. A couple players came under investigation, but nothing ever happened. I got my com-pany, and I was company commander there at the regional per-sonnel center, and I made some women mad.

This led to your outing?

BH: Yes. One of the women who had worked for me was not doing a good job and got an adverse evaluation. And anoth-er woman decided that she wanted out of the Army and she

96

was going to get out. And she was pissed off at me. So they both went to CID and made statements that they were gay and in a relationship together, and they turned me in also. That was in 1982. I heard it. They didn't tell me.

I came back to the States for graduation ceremonies for my Masters degree at Ball State University, took a vacation with my family and my lover at the time. When I came back from my leave, I learned later, CID was at my company headquarters to arrest me, but I didn't go in. I called in and reported that I was back from leave, and I spent the weekend relaxing. But I felt something was going to come down.

Why?

BH: Because I'd heard a rumor before I went on vacation that I was under investigation. I had a friend who was in CID.

A gay person?

BH: She was closeted, too. She wasn't the one investigating me, but she knew there was an investigation, and she alerted me. I went back to work—I'm thinking it was a Monday, but it may not have been—and I had three CID men, burly men, walk into my office and tell me that I was under arrest.

Early in the morning?

BH: It seems like it was. It was a shitty day! And it was like, *Don't do this to me!* They went through my desk. They wanted to handcuff me to take me out to the car. Here are these three men, and they want to handcuff me because I'm a lesbian. I'm going to do something terrible, you know. But this is in front of my troops, people I supervised. I was humiliated. They took me down to the CID headquarters and put me in this room and tried to interrogate me.

What did they do?

BH: Basically, they said, "We have information that you're a lesbian." I said, "Oh, that's interesting." I refused to answer their questions. I would not say a thing.

Was this the classic light-in-the-face interrogation?

BH: Oh, yeah. They had a light in my face. It was the classic, "Let's see how much stress we can put on this woman."

How big was the room?

BH: There was a window in it, and a door, and a chair, and a table, as I recall. There was nothing else. Like an interrogating room that you see in the movies. I refused to say anything. They advised me to get a lawyer. I did, a military lawyer, and I had to drive an hour just to see him. There was no lawyer in our area. Being in Germany, and not knowing what else to do, I felt so damned isolated.

My lawyer advised me that I needed to do whatever I could to have this go easy on me because they were going to court-martial me. It was a federal conviction, and they were going to get me for lewd and lascivious acts, conduct unbecoming an officer, and fraternization because they had seen me with enlisted people. They had three or four charges that they were going to bring against me, and they would have all resulted in jail time.

You could have gone to Leavenworth?

BH: Oh, yeah! I never did admit to the lawyer that I was gay. I told him I had been gay prior to coming into the Army, but I wasn't practicing now. He told me, "Brenda, maybe they'll do a deal with us. Write this big statement and try to convince them that it's okay for you to get out." So I wrote a ten-page statement.

What did you say?

BH: Basically, how I had my first gay relationship. I would not admit to anything after that. They had made accusations about friends of mine, and I tried to clear their names. They wanted me to name names like these other people had done. They had the two NCOs who had made statements against me, but that wasn't enough. Later they got a West Point lieutenant who felt duty and honor bound to go in and make a statement against another lesbian captain, a doctor, that she had had a relationship with. So they arrested the doctor, who happened to be a friend of mine, and they both made statements about me. Based on those four statements, they came after me.

It was just amazing. It was like, *My God. And these are other lesbians!* The credibility of the NCOs wasn't enough to do it, but when you put a West Point lieutenant and a medical captain and all those statements together, you've got a huge case.

Had you any experience of CIDs following you in Germany? Did they show you photographs of your going into a gay bar?

BH: No. I had gone to some gay bars in Germany, but people would alert us if CID was outside and taking pictures of people and of cars with American license plates. I never had that experience.

But I had taken a vacation in that January of '82 with my lover of the time and stayed at a military hotel. Well, they went and got the receipts from that hotel, showed I had paid for that, and that I had flown her to Germany. They were using all that. She was enlisted and stationed in the States. They were using all that against me, too. They had her in for questioning. Her job was on the line. Fortunately, her supervisor supported her through this, and she remained in.

Another friend of mine who was in Germany, they went through her barracks, tore it up, tried to investigate her. The post commander at the time knew about the investigation, knew the both of us, supported the both of us. Fortunately, she got to stay in. I wasn't going to take any of my friends down. There was no way.

I did not know whether they had enough [on me] or not. My lawyer felt that they did, and if they went to court, they would convict me. So, the lesser of the two evils was to do this. They also made me go to a psychiatrist for a psych eval to make sure I wasn't crazy. That was really humiliating. Everything they did to me was humiliating.

I had to go to work every day during this investigation. They relieved me of my company and put me in the Adjutant General's Office of Division Headquarters, so I had to see all these top-level people who were saying, "Brenda, we're so sorry that this is happening to you. You don't deserve this. But on the other hand, this is CID and this is the JAG and this is what they think should happen." The commanding general also went along with it even though we knew each other and he thought I was a good soldier.

He didn't want to put his neck on the line.

BH: Nope. And I had gotten an efficiency report in June, and it was excellent. I mean, top-block everything. They rescinded that OER a month later when all this happened and put me down in the lowest block. I have a copy of the original one and a copy of the one they re-did. I thought, *How could you assholes do this?*

That's a way to justify their actions.

BH: Right.

From the time CID walked into your office to the time you were out, four months elapsed. How did you handle that?

BH: With my head up. The angry part of me wanted to come out and say, "To hell with all of you." But I didn't know what they would do with that information. If I did, I feared I would hurt a lot of other people.

People you associated with?

BH: Yes, because it was guilt by association. If you're running around with her, then you must be gay, too.

Did you have an experience of your friends stepping back from you?

BH: Yes. I had one very special friend, matter of fact. She and I had been in a relationship for a while. She told me to stay the hell away from her, that she never wanted to see me again. That hurt. That hurt a lot.

My roommate at the time, who was not gay, moved out because she could not handle the guilt by association. She worked for Division Headquarters, and she said, "I can't put my career on the line." She had known I was gay. It didn't bother her until the investigation.

The ones who really stayed around me were the ones who came under investigation, too, and had appreciated what I had done. They did stand beside me.

How did you feel about coming back to the States like this?

BH: I felt lower than life. I was very angry at the world, at life, at myself. I was angry the most because I didn't come out. I'd think, *Why didn't I have the guts to stand up and say, "Yes, I am gay, and there's nothing wrong with me!"* I had nightmares for years. I'd wake up and I'd have been dreaming that I was back in the military, back in Germany, living through all that again.

You know, I never came out to the people after I came under investigation, even my supervisors. They said, "Brenda, we don't care whether you are or not. You've done a great job, but this is the way it's gotta be."

In the last few years, I've been able to sleep quite well. There are occasions that I will have a dream that I'm in uniform again. Those usually come up when the military is in the news, and that desire of mine to be able to serve emerges. But they happen very rarely now. I've moved on.

There are a lot of gay troopers out there.

BH: Oh, a lot! Yes. There are just as many men as women, but the women are the ones who get it the most. I had male troops in my company who were gay and they never got harassed. Never. But the women would.

What kinds of things did you observe?

BH: Just the real nelly stuff. They'd get teased occasionally, but they didn't come under investigation like the women did. I mean, if you looked butch, then you were gay, and you were under investigation. It was like the only job that CID had to do was to investigate and purge the military of all the lesbians.

How about your friend? The lesbian in CID? How could she do that job?

BH: There are a lot of lesbians and gays in CID, and it is hard. It's a job, and it's unfortunate.

It would seem that you would have to dissociate.

BH: You do.

I'm investigating you, but I go home to my girlfriend. That's crazy.

BH: Yeah. Exactly. Fortunately, she wasn't the one doing the investigation. CID also handled the drug and alcohol problems that were going on in the military, and espionage stuff. This was just one aspect to keep them employed.

It's nice to be lumped in with drug dealers and spies.

BH: That's what they thought we were. Criminals.

It's curious to me that we still keep going in even though we know how dangerous it is.

BH: I don't know if I realized how dangerous it was when I first went in. I didn't care. I knew that education was not going to be a profitable field and that the military could provide me a good income. Back then, being a female, there wasn't a lot society allowed us to do where we could make a good living. The Army afforded me that opportunity. And yes, I was asked, "Are you homosexual?" And I put "no."

For the longest time when people asked me, "Gee, Brenda, eight years is a long time. Why'd you get out?" I'd lie. I'd say because I got tired of traveling and I wanted to get back into education. To my gay friends, I would not lie. My parents know why I got out, but we don't talk about it. They would not even tell the rest of my family. They were embarrassed. And when most of your friends are military, that makes it even harder.

Did you feel envy?

BH: Oh, yeah. When I came back to Texas, I missed the military. I ended up getting into a relationship with a woman who was in the Army just so I could feel some connection to it.

I can remember when I was in Germany being the assignments officer. Two friends of mine, who were lesbians, called me and said, "Brenda, we've been assigned to Germany, and I'm going to be stationed here, and she's going to be stationed there. Can you do anything to help us?" Well, sure. I pulled strings and got them assigned together. We did those things, and we still do those things. I have friends of mine, they call other friends in Washington and say, "Hey, can you get us assigned together?" It happens. We had to try to take care of each other because nobody else was going to.

I don't regret being in the military. To me it's still a very important organization, and I think everyone should serve. But they make it impossible. So have my views changed? I guess to some degree. Why should we want to serve if they don't want us? If they want to persecute us, belittle us, beat us down. But it's still an organization that's needed.

Would you have a compulsory system such as the Israelis have?

BH: I think so. It was very instrumental in developing me into the type of individual I think I am today.

What is that?

BH: I'm an independent thinker. Self-starter. I'm disciplined. Yeah, I had some of those qualities when I went into the military, but just the aspect of having served, and of having been a part of that organization, helped enrich that. Of course, all those challenges I faced in those few months, dealing with the issue of my being put out helped make me who I was, too. And at the time I was very angry, and I sort of still hold a lot of anger about that.

When I was discharged, the sexual revolution for the gay and lesbian community had not hit really, particularly not in Germany. Now it's evolved to where, yes, we may still be discharged, but at least if you want to fight it, you know where the support services are. I'm not trying to downplay the pain and suffering that people go through today. I'm sure it is quite similar, but it is also quite different. At least now you can talk about it.

And now there have been so many high-profile discharges.

BH: Oh, absolutely. Margarethe Cammermeyer. And just recently there were a couple of retired generals who came out. I though that was so cool. But why should we have to wait until we retire?

Do you think their views hold weight with the establishment?

BH: As far as the military goes? Not a lot. I think people will go, "Oh, my God, really?" But I don't know it's going to do a lot to change things right now. It's still a political sword, unfortunately.

It seems to be that a part of the problem—at least it was for President Clinton—the minute the Joint Chiefs bridle, they back down.

BH: Exactly. And of course, that's all men. I'm sure there's probably a gay person in there someplace. But their careers are at stake, too. And when you put in twenty-eight years, you don't want to risk losing it all, and I can understand that. That's a helluva lot to lose. Eight and a half, to me, was a helluva lot to lose.

It's a hard choice to make.

BH: Well, it is. And it's something they have to live with every day, as did I. You make those choices. Who are you going to associate with? Who can you trust? If I do this, will someone suspect, or will they say something?

What is the solution?

BH: Well, I think the president's going to have to take a stand and be brave enough to say that people are who they are. Take that stand, and have the balls enough to allow us to be who we are. We're soldiers. And that's the number 1 thing: We're soldiers first.

But the minute gay men and lesbians are allowed to serve openly, it's just going to be an orgy in the showers.

BH: [*Laughs*] When you're on the battlefield, those are not things you're thinking about. You're there to do a job. And when I hear people say that, it's like that's all we think about, sex. And that's not what it's about.

The job is number 1, being able to be proficient and professional. I typically found the gays and lesbians to exemplify that to the utmost, as compared to other soldiers.

Why, do you suppose?

BH: Maybe because we had more to fear, we tried to perform better. You felt as though you had to be the best because you didn't want to risk coming under scrutiny for anything. I can think of so many women, evaluating them, and they were the top soldiers—the way they looked, the way they performed. Their conduct was far and above their peers who were heterosexual. Now, I didn't do any great studies on it or anything, but that was their code: to be the best that they could be.

Some of our leading critics charge that our serving openly in the military disrupts good order and discipline and negatively affects...

BH: [*Interrupting*] And it does because of the homophobia of the other military soldiers who persecute and beat up and kill and malign those who would like to serve openly. That's where the problem lies. It's not because of who we are; it's because of how we are treated.

Does the command fear that gay men will report for duty in feathered boas?

BH: [*Laughs*] I don't know if that's what they think. But I liken it to when the military had segregation. It was an all-white Army, and they couldn't have blacks serve. Then women couldn't do certain things. Well now they can. I foresee some-day it will be that everyone will be able to be who they are, but I don't know if I'll see it in my time. I'm very happy that we've made this progress, but we still have a long way to go.

About Face

This medic/x-ray tech joined the Army in 1981 and was a member of a women's boxing team at Fort Gordon, Georgia, and Fort Bliss, Texas.

I am a tomboy, and even though that does not mean that girls who look like I looked are queer, it certainly was not a secret in my case.

At enlistment, the question on homosexuality was paired with one about marijuana use. The two questions were on a rubber stamp, applied to the nearly complete entrance form. The homo question went something like, "Have you ever engaged in homosexual conduct?" I initialed the "yes" box, and I also affirmed my use of Mary Jane. These responses rated a trip to a private interview room.

A sergeant entered the room wearing Class B's. He was carrying a typewriter, and his fly was down. He set down the honking heavy IBM Selectric on the desk. I asked if that was part of the interview. "What?" he asked. "That you start out with your fly down." "No," he said, "and I'll ask the questions."

First he asked about the pot. How often? (Not very.) When did I start? (After high school.) When was the last time? (This morning.) He's taking notes.

Then the homo questions: When did I start? What did I do? I asked what constituted "homosexual conduct." When the sergeant got to "cunnilingus" in the list he was reading, I asked what that was. He did not know. I admitted at least to holding hands with girls and perhaps at most kissing them. When he got to "Who with and when?" I refused to answer.

In light of my answers, he said, I would be refused enlistment. But they wanted to get me: I had great scores and no criminal record. He offered that if I changed the homo answer, the Army could take me. I agreed, and he whited-out my original answer and had me initial the NO HOMO box.

I finished the physicals, raised my hand, and prepared to ship the following morning. After dinner I smoked a doob and scoped for girls headed to Fort Dix.

—A.G. Flynn

That's Just My Demographic

Rebecca D.

When Rebecca D. graduated from high school at 17, she thought immediately of the military. The Southern California native was young and had no specific plans.

Her first stop was the Marines. Their training program for women, they told her, was the same as the men's. She demurred.

"They told me they'd make a man out of me, says Rebecca, 35, who now works as an investment manager. "I said, 'No, that's not for me. I don't want to be a man.' I didn't want to lose my femininity, but I did want to serve in the armed forces."

She joined the Air Force in 1986, an airman recruit, and completed her basic training and advanced security police training at Lackland Air Force Base in San Antonio, Texas. Following graduation she was sent temporarily to England then became permanent party at Ramstein

Air Force Base in Kaiserslautern, Germany, where she served until 1991, attaining the rank of senior airman (E4).

She was raised conservative Baptist, attended services thrice weekly, and was educated in religious schools. Being gay wasn't an option.

"I didn't even know about gay people. I knew very strongly that I did not want to get married, and I knew very strongly that I didn't want to have kids. And I had absolutely no interest in men whatsoever. I would read Cosmo *and think,* Why do I never have those feelings?

She learned why on the basketball court, after she fell in love with one of her teammates. On a temporary duty assignment with the object of her affection, she made her move.

"We kissed, and that was my girlfriend for the rest of the time I was England, until I got placed in Germany," *she says.* "I had to go back and tell my boyfriend that it was over, and that's the last boyfriend I had."

The military can be a "rough ride" for gay troops, Rebecca advises, and new recruits should enter eyes wide open.

"You have to live under the radar," *she says.* "If you're prepared to do that, then go for it."

* * *

When I entered the Air Force, I was very feminine, and I had long blond hair. I looked like a cheerleader, basically. And when I was in, and all the way up until I got out, people made comments to me not knowing I was a lesbian.

Once I was on a tour of a military prison, Mannheim, in Germany, and they told me if I ended up in prison there, I would have all these bull-dykes after me. And I got a little smirk on my face because they had no idea that I was a lesbian, and that would not bother me whatsoever. [*Laughs*]

You were thinking, Well! That's just my demographic!

R: Exactly. [*Laughs*] I was thinking, *That doesn't sound bad!*

But nobody had any idea. I did not look the stereotypical lesbian.

You just passed beneath the radar?

R: Yeah. I blended. But also, I didn't like hiding my sexuality, and my girlfriends happened to be very butch-looking. And when the guys started realizing, "Hey, she's not doing anything with us, she must be a lesbian," that's kind of how it went around.

How long did it take for them to realize it? And were you already in permanent party?

R: When I was first in England I had a girlfriend, and I don't think people really knew about that. I lived off base, so it wasn't really an issue.

Now when I went to Germany, my girlfriend and I had decided we would try to make it through living in two different countries. So when I got to the base, I wasn't really hanging out with any of the women. I was just doing my job and going back to the dorm. Everybody just thought I was off-limits. Whatever.

But I started getting a lot of the guys asking me out. And you know, I would hang out with the guys, but I wouldn't ever date any of them because I had a girlfriend and I had no interest. I had decided for myself that if somebody started getting close to me and they thought there might be some type of future romantically, I would tell them, "Hey, listen. I'm a lesbian. I'm not into men." But I would have to know this person enough to know that they wouldn't turn me in.

And I met somebody out with a bunch of the guys. A girl, another lesbian. And we ended up talking, getting to know each other better. It was a strain having a partner all the way in England, so we ended up breaking up our relationship. And me and this other girl started dating.

And I had to go out in the field for a week. I was kind of down because we had just started dating, and I missed her, and I would come back to the dorm every day and there'd be a note written on my door saying, "Hope everything's going well out in the field. —T."

A very good friend of mine ended up figuring out that I was dating this girl. So I asked him if he would basically play boyfriend for me. I said, "Let's pretend we're dating. Come to the dorm room, sleep on the floor, and leave in the morning when the other girls are getting up so it looks like I've had a man spend the night because I don't want anybody figuring this out."

People had started doing the sideways-take because my girl-friend had started coming over to my room and hanging out, spending the night and that sort of thing. And she was the very stereotypical lesbian. She had the very short, very butch hair-cut, and I think they kind of caught on to that.

So he said, "Okay. I'll take the role of boyfriend." But then he started telling his buddies, "Listen. She's not into men." And it started spreading until one day I had been out at a wine festival, and I came back and somebody had written CARPET MUNCHER on my door. And it was in big letters. Oh, my gosh. And the next day the same thing happened again. I finally took my board off the door, so people couldn't write on it anymore. And when I would walk into the shower in the morning, every showerhead would turn off and everyone would leave. And that's when I said, *Oops! It looks like everybody knows now.*

It's an interesting thing that the women would leave. It's this idea of the vampiric lesbian: She's gonna get you!

R: Exactly.

And so you began sleeping with men who had big mouths so that it would get around that you can't be a lesbian?

R: That's exactly what. Because not only were people in the dorm starting to know, but I started getting very, very concerned. I thought, *Uh-oh, if this gets back to OSI*—the Office of Special Investigations, which investigated homosexuality in the Air Force—*I'm out of a job! I'll get a dishonorable discharge.* My whole thing was, I was going to do my time and get out with an honorable discharge. There were no ifs, ands, or buts.

And some of the guys I worked with started questioning me. And that's when I started saying, "No, no, no. That's not the case." And basically I knew the guys who would talk to the other guys, and I would go back to the dorm room with them and do whatever had to be done. I knew they would go and tell their buddies, "No, man. Don't worry about it. She's not a lesbian. She's straight. She slept with me."

But what people started saying was, "Well, she may not be a lesbian, but she's definitely not straight. She must be bisexual." So I never got to the point of, "Don't worry about it. She's straight." It was always, "Well, she's bisexual."

That's the point that I said, *This obviously isn't working. I only have a short amount of time left on my tour. I'll get out when it's time to get out.*

How common do you think that sort of ruse was among lesbians who were essentially in deep cover?

R: I saw it all the time. I had very good friends who were lesbians, and they'd go out with a guy here and there just for this very same reason—to cover up whatever might be going on or whatever might be said. These women were lesbians. They had no desire for men. No. It wasn't an "I'm confused" type of thing. It was, "No, I love women. That is who I want to be with. That is who I am going to be once I'm out of here."

But the whole thing about OSI investigating: It was a real threat, and people were very afraid. So they were doing anything they could to keep from getting discharged. One woman actually slit her wrists. It was crazy.

The pressure was just too great for her?

R: Yeah. She ended up getting out, and she's still a lesbian. I'm still in contact with her. She's living fine, has a girlfriend, is happy. A lot of people look at it this way: It happened in my past. It wasn't like I was a career military individual. I did my time and got out as soon as I found out whether I could deal with it or not.

You said that this sort of thing really messed with your head and the heads of others who were under cover. How did that look? What were you thinking? How were you feeling?

R: If I'm on the outside, I would never, ever in the world resort to having to sleep with a man to make sure that everybody knew I was straight. I felt very cheapened by having to do that, and I didn't like it. Every time I did it I felt disgusting, but I knew that, okay, this could possibly keep me from having to deal with discharges, embarrassment, the stigma attached to being gay in the military.

That was the biggest thing, having to do the things you would never, ever do just to hold on to your career and to stay under cover so that nobody found out.

You had the people that you hung out with in your free time, when you were off duty. The good times when you were actually you and going out into the gay bars and meeting up with retired military people who had stayed over there and were out now because they didn't have to be in the closet anymore.

It was a very small group of people that we knew. But if we were in our uniforms and on duty, we might not even acknowledge each other. Because if somebody sees that you're acknowledging each other, then they might say, "Hey, wait a second." So you were one person in uniform and a completely different person out of uniform.

Were you afraid that agents of the OSI would be at the gay bars off-post?

R: Oh, yeah. In fact, sometimes straight people would come in and just harass people. Just flat out harass people. GI's would go in there, and that was their fun, harassing people and calling them "dykes" and "faggots." And the owners of the bar would see it, and they would escort them out. The owners of the bar often knew what to look for, so if they saw something funny, they would turn people away at the door.

What would be construed as "funny"?

R: For instance, I had gone downtown with a friend of mine, a sergeant, and we were just walking around and everything was closing up. We ended up walking by this one gay bar that I had been to very often. And he said, "Let's go in here." And I was like, "No, no. Let's *not* go in here." He's like, "It's open. Let's go check it out."

I was scared to death because I was thinking, *Oh, my gosh! I'm gonna go in there, and people are going to know who I am and say, "Hey, Rebecca! How's it going? It's been a long time."* You know? Whatever!

Now this was my reporting officer, my supervisor. So I was terrified that if he found out, that's it. My job's over. But they let us in, and we started walking up the stairs, and I looked at the owners like, *Please don't let us in.* Because they get a cover before they let you all the way up the steps.

And I don't know what they read on my face, but they looked at him and they looked at me and said, "Sorry. We're closed." And I couldn't have thanked them enough. I just said, "Okay. Thanks!" [*Laughs*] And I just grabbed his hand and said, "Let's go."

When you passed by, did he recognize that it was a gay or lesbian bar?

R: No, no. They were very discrete. A lot of the bars would have a camera outside to see who's coming in the bar, and they would have to buzz you. For my friends, that was horrifying because we would have to stand out in front and wait for them to buzz us in. And there's cars of people driving by, a lot of GIs downtown, so you ducked your head and tried to cover before they opened the door because you didn't want anybody who was driving by to happen to see you go in.

How did you recognize the gay men and lesbians around you in the Air Force? Especially those who were in deep cover?

R: One of the very positive things that happened after they wrote CARPET MUNCHER on my door was that new girls, new cops, would come onto the base, and the girls on the floor would warn them, "Stay away from her. She's a dyke." So what happens? Every single lesbian that came to the base was knocking on my door, saying, "Uh, hi. Do you know where the gay bars are?" [*Laughs*] So I became the new connection for every hot new lesbian cop that came to the base.

My!

R: You still had to be careful. It wasn't like they could just come in and say, "Hey!" They'd say, "Do you mind if we talk?" And we'd sit there and talk for a while. And they'd ask me, "Where do you go, if you go out?" And you had to be very careful. So I'd say, "Well, where do *you* go? Have you been anywhere? Have you heard about any place?" And once they mentioned this or that bar, it was like, *Okay, you are, obviously, so okay.*

They had a lesbian bar in Heidelberg that we would go to.

The other bar, in Kaiserslautern, or K-town, was a mixed bar. It was gay and lesbian. But that was basically how I would meet people. You don't know for sure, until you see them there.

But sooner or later, if they were, they'd end up on your doorstep.

R: Oh, yeah. Or you'd meet them through somebody else that knew them from a base before. But you had to be careful because you don't know who's OSI—on base, in the bar, or anywhere.

Were there tip-offs? For instance, number 1, no one has ever seen this person before. And no one knows who he or she is. But were there other things that would make you suspicious?

R: No. One of the first things I got asked every time I met somebody was, "Are you OSI?" I don't know if that's because people thought that if they asked, and you *are* an OSI agent, you have to admit to it. But I know that a lot of people asked *me* that.

Like I said, I looked like a little cheerleader, and people had no idea. So not looking the part might have been one for some people. You just had to be very careful. And if somebody knew somebody, then you knew it was okay. But if they didn't know them, then you kind of kept your distance until somebody found out by sleeping with them or whatever.

Someone told me a story about an OSI person who insinuated herself into a group. This group of girls wasn't as smart as yours because even though no one knew the woman, they confided in her and let her in anyway. And one day she disappeared, and everyone was under investigation.

R: Yes, I had a friend and the same thing happened to her. It was actually in Florida. All of a sudden, a girl showed up and they accepted her into the group and, from my understanding, some people actually slept with her. One of my exes who was stationed down there was part of the group.

What was the climate toward gay people at your duty station? There was, of course, someone who wrote the unbelievably imaginative CARPET MUNCHER *on your door. But was that common?*

R: It was very hostile. It wasn't uncommon to hear very derogatory terms used even over the radio. I had a friend at work. She was on the radio a lot. And one morning she was calling to say, "Okay, relief is in the area. Everybody get ready to be relieved." And somebody said over the radio, "Dyke!" It's kind of like, "Come on, guys! That's not cool." But she was a lesbian, and she was very, very butch. Comments like that were the biggest thing. All the time! All the time.

You'd just hear this in the course of the day?

R: Oh, yeah. It was very common. It was no problem to call somebody a "faggot" or "queer." Queer was a big one. I knew two gay guys at work. One was very effeminate, and everybody knew about him. The other one, I had no idea until he came out to me. I thought he was OSI because when he came out to me, you would never, ever in a million years know he was gay.

He hung out with the guys. He went out to the strip bars with the guys. I mean, he did everything with the guys. Now I understand it's because he wanted to be around the guys! But at the time he was very much Mr. Manly Man. And he never dated women. And I thought it was kind of odd, because before he actually told me about himself, he wouldn't even pay me any mind. I mean, he wouldn't even look at me. And I thought, *What is wrong with him? Why won't he look me in the eyes or have anything to do with me?*

Whether it's conceit or whatever, I was used to men hitting on me in the military. And the fact that he was basically having nothing to do with me, I thought, *Gosh, there's something really strange about him.*

So nobody knew. But he came into the group and ended up being a very good friend of mine. And then he got out. I thought he was career. But he got out and ended up staying over in Germany. The last thing I heard, he was dating one of the guys and working on the base somewhere.

All I know is, I wasn't ever under investigation, even though a boyfriend that I broke up with—my first and last boyfriend there on the base in England when I was 18—told me I was under investigation quite a few times. But I don't know if that was jealousy or what. I think he was trying to scare me more than anything else. He was trying to play on my fears.

No one else ever said anything directly to you?

R: My commanding officer actually pulled me aside once. My girlfriend was picking me up. She was actually stationed at another base, and she had started coming down to pick me up in the morning after I got off work. As a cop you have strange hours. After I turned in my gun, she would be right there. So it was very obvious I was going home with a woman.

So he pulled me aside and said, "You need to watch the company you're keeping. You can get in a lot of trouble." And I just looked at him and said, "I don't know what you're talking about." And he said, "Do you want to share anything with me?" And I said, "I have no idea what you're talking about. You need to tell me what you're talking about." And he said, "You need to be very careful." And I said, "Who do I need to be careful of?" He said, "Like your friend over there that's picking you up. You need to very careful who you're seen with, and who you're around, and who you spend your time with." And I said, "Well, since you're not going to tell me any more than that, thank you for the advice. But I think I'm going to keep the company that I keep."

That was the extent of it. I was thrown off that this man—he was the *big* guy—was pulling me aside in the parking lot in the morning and telling me to be careful who I'm around and who I spend time with.

Was he was being your friend?

R: Oh, no. I don't think it was like that. He may have been hearing things, and I think it was like, "You're a pretty girl. Quit being a dyke" type thing. That's how I really think he meant it. It was like, "You're wasting your life on women. You need to stay on this side."

Because with all those officers and the sergeants, all you had to do was snap your fingers and they'd roll over for you. Every supervisor I had hit on me. So when they'd find out I'm gay, it wasn't, "You need to be careful because it's for your own good." It was, "No, no. Come on. Don't do that. Come on over to this side." I mean, shift commanders. All sorts of them: "Come on. You're not really like that. Come on." And I'm like, "I am, and I'm not interested in you." I mean, one of my commanding officers, he was married, and he was hitting on me. It was odd.

When you would say "no," would they back off?

R: Sometimes. But that had been happening all the way from training, from tech school. I basically had a superior who told me he would take care of me if I promised to sleep with him.

While you were still a student?

R: Yeah! I said, "Really?" And he said, "Yeah." And I said, "Well, I'm not going to sleep with you while I'm here, but I'll sleep with you after we graduate." He said, "Okay. The day that you graduate, the way you tell me we're gonna do something is you come up to me and have me pin on your badge for you." And I said, "Okay."

So at graduation, I went to my dad, you know, and had him pin on my badge first. Then I took it off and took it over to my training instructor and said, "Here you go." And he pinned it on, and he said, "Great! Thanks!"

Apparently, these three instructors did this with every class. They would find three girls and basically say, "We'll take care of you as long as you sleep with us." And they had an agreement with two friends of mine, too. We knew we weren't ever going to sleep with them. We're thinking, *Well, if you guys are stupid enough to believe we're actually going to do this, then you do what you have to do.* We were afraid that if we told them no, we would be kicked out of the training school.

So at graduation they said, "Okay. You girls get the hotel room, and we'll get all the booze." Because we were underage. And we said, "Okay. Great." We were supposed to meet 'em after, at like 5 o'clock or something, at this hotel. And at 5 o'clock we were sitting downtown in some bar somewhere, having a drink, just laughing and saying, "I wonder how long these guys are gonna wait for us to show up!" [*Laughs*] Then we went our separate ways.

A couple of months later we heard the instructors were actually discharged for sexual harassment. Twenty-year careers shot. It wasn't like we got special treatment. We didn't get higher scores or anything like that. We just knew that all we had to do was flirt with these guys every once and a while, and we'd make it to graduation. They were very high pressure, like, "We can make it tough for you if you don't." So we said, "Okay, cool. Just wait until after graduation." Because once we graduated, there was nothing they could have done.

Were you ever afraid?

R: No. You know what? We took a totally different approach. To us, we were now completely, 100 percent in power over these men who were supposed to be our superiors. We wielded all the power. As soon as we said, "Okay, we'll do your little thing," and they said, "Okay, this weekend," and we said, "No, no, no. We'll get together *after* we graduate," we had them. That's how I took it. These guys actually believed that we were going to meet them at a hotel room and have sex with them? That just killed me. How stupid can you people be?

I was always, always, always a very strong woman. So I feel very bad for any women that really, really honestly thought that something could happen to them if they didn't say yes to these guys. We just kind of laughed it off like, *Okay, buds. That's not the way it's gonna go down, but you can believe whatever you want.* They just thought they were so *rico.* Yeah, yeah. "You get to have a piece of this," type of thing. I'm like, *Oh, please.* They're old men. I'm 17, just turned 18 years old. God, I'm barely not even jailbait anymore.

You know how to handle that if you're someone who is hit on all the time. It's just like, Whatever. I'm gonna bat my eyelashes. I'll flip my hair. I'll do this little thing. You'll be enchanted. And then, while you're recovering, I'm gone.

R: Exactly!

Do you think it's easier for a femme lesbian to slip beneath the radar, especially in the military?

R: Absolutely 100 percent. Yeah.

It's not really what men expect.

R: Right.

What is so upsetting to men about a butch lesbian versus a femme lesbian? A butch lesbian is everything they want in a soldier.

R: I constantly had people, my sergeants or whoever, thinking, *One night with her, and we can change her.* Whereas, they may think a butch woman is just too far gone for that. As long as men had the idea that they could change me, I wasn't going to have to deal with all those other things that a butch woman would have to deal with.

Critics of gay men and lesbians serving openly in the military say our presence disturbs good order and discipline.

R: I would say right now I partially agree with that, but not because of the gays and lesbians serving, but because the military breeds a hatred of gays and lesbians. They are outright harassed and demeaned, and it is allowed and even encouraged.

What's the solution?

R: Allow gays and lesbians to serve openly in the military. That's your solution! When somebody calls somebody a faggot or a queer, something needs to happen to 'em. They need to either be discharged or they need to get some type of disciplinary action. Because people need to respect each other.

That is what they have lost in the military. Nobody respects each other. The husbands don't respect the wives. The wives don't respect their husbands. Everybody's out doing whatever they want to do. As long as they show up for work on time and fight for their country, it's fine. But in the meantime, they can be downtown gay-bashing, and nothing's gonna happen to them. They could be out sleeping around on their wife: When I was in, every man was sleeping around on his wife. You know? Nobody respects anybody. I think you can have a fighting machine, but you can still have mutual respect for the people that you're fighting alongside. And they don't. They don't!

If somebody isn't the military ideal, they get harassed. There was even a guy I worked with who wasn't gay; he was underweight, and he was a more timid guy, and they just harassed him left and right. And nobody did anything about it. Whether they thought he was gay or whatever—they breed that. They breed hatred. And I think if they honestly start saying, "Everybody who is here is going to be respected," we might be able to get over some of these hurdles.

About Face

This Army corporal underwent an eighteen-month CID investigation in the 1970s.

You name it, they asked it. "Did you kiss Pvt. So-and-so? Did you sleep with her? Were you close? Were you drinking? Did you have oral sex? Did you put your fingers in her? Did she put her fingers in you?" Oh, yeah. I wouldn't answer most of it, and the charges were eventually dropped.

The stereotype of what a good soldier is, is what lesbians are: assertive, aggressive, confident, commanding. We're everything the Army wants in terms of a leader, yet they don't want you to be that really, because that means you're a lesbian. It's the catch-22 that women are always in. If a heterosexual woman is like that as well, and doesn't have a visible male partner, she also becomes suspect.

—Sandra A.

Made in Japan

Caroline Riso

Caroline Riso grew up in a sheltered Italian-American family but always felt "different," though she never heard the L word until she joined the Air Force Nurse Corps in 1963.

"I went to Catholic elementary school, Catholic high school, and Catholic nursing school, says Riso, now 59. "You could be sure I never heard anything before that. And when I got out of nursing school, I worked in the Catholic hospital."

She was 25 when she followed some classmates into the service. Her parents, she says, thought she was "nuts."

What she discovered at seven different duty stations over thirteen years was an extraordinary community of dedicated nursing professionals whose commitment extended above and beyond. They were smart. They were skilled. They were lesbian.

And the ones who weren't couldn't have cared less about their colleagues' sexual orientation. It was an era, says Riso, in which many women didn't even know about themselves.

"A friend of mine went to Vietnam. She was at Da Nang, and she found out that she was gay. When she came home, she called me up and said, 'Did you know I was gay?' And I said, 'Well, I sort of thought so, but that was before I was gay, too.' We had a big laugh about it."

Riso retired as a major in 1976. She was 38 and medically discharged after fouled back surgery prevented her from pulling long, physically demanding nursing shifts.

Afterwards, she went to college, worked as a physical examiner for insurance firms, and was part of an NIH-funded research team conducting a long-term study of psoriasis.

She is a member of OLE—Older Lesbian Energy—and NOW in Boston and seldom misses an opportunity to march in that city's gay pride parade. Her years of silence in the military, she says, make it even more important for her to speak up now.

"I don't mince any words now," Riso says. Since I'm out of the Air Force, everybody knows."

* * *

When I got to my first base in Missouri, it had been raining. And coming from the coast—and spending all my life practically at the seashore—when I saw the flat land, it was so drab. I thought, *Oh, my God! What have I let myself in for?*

We got to the gate, and there were men standing with rifles and machine guns. It was during the Bay of Pigs. And I said to myself again, *My God! What have I gotten into?* We weren't allowed to leave the base. This was a strategic air command base. In fact, I didn't get off that base for a month.

My father was horror-stricken when I called and said I went

into the Air Force. "The Democrats are in. We're going to war. You're going to get killed," he said. He went on and on and on. But it turned out okay.

Aside from the topography and the men with rifles, you took to military life?

CR: Yes. After that, it was just like second nature. I was doing what I was trained to do, what I loved to do: I was nursing. And actually, the scenery was very pretty after the rains and drabness and stuff.

After I was there almost a year, we got a black nurse in. I loved her! She was so funny. We all got along. I lived next door to black people in Philadelphia, so it meant nothing to me. But we discovered that it was a big deal the first time we went off base.

The town that the base was in was Knob Noster. It was a one-street town. There was a restaurant and a motel up on a hill. And we went in, and nobody came near us. Finally, a man came over and said, "We're not serving you as long as *she* stays here." So we had to leave. We had the same thing happen to us in Kansas City. They asked us to leave because we had a black person with us.

Through friends in Sedalia, which was about thirteen miles from the base, she found a bar. We used to go there after hours, and we would dance and dance and dance for hours. It was for black people. And they had a trio there. And we'd go in periodically and have a good ol' time. Nobody would bother us there. I hated when I went to the Midwest, but it turned out to be a wonderful duty station. The chief nurse was a survivor of the Bataan Death March.[1] She was just motherly. So that made it easier.

To this point, everything was really platonic between you and other female servicemembers.

CR: It certainly was.

When you first applied, you had no problems with the forms asking about homosexuality?

CR: I didn't. Not a bit, because as far as I was concerned, I wasn't a homosexual. That word never even popped up that much in my line of work. I might have known gay people, all the years that I worked in the different hospitals and stuff, but it never dawned on me. I only knew that I had more caring and was more interested in women.

In high school I didn't date much at all. We used to have parties and stuff. I went out with a couple of boys, and it was just boring as hell. So I thought, *This is not for me*. I think that was one of the reasons I decided to leave and have a career, see a lot of places and do a lot of things with Uncle Sam picking up the bill.[2]

But everything changed for you in Japan.

CR: Oh, it certainly did. When I got there, I met some women who, I found out later, were all gay. I think the whole floor that I lived on was gay. I made another good friend—a very, very good friend. We did a lot of things together. We had a wonderful time. I mean, we worked like hell. But we had a wonderful time partying.

People partied a lot. It was during Vietnam. We used to have pilots and people come in for R&R to the base. And you know, people just partied. Period. They didn't know if they'd be back or not.

And then I met this woman. She was new, and we worked on the same floor, the same ward. She didn't look very happy. And she wasn't. She did not want to be there. And we just took to each other. We used to spend a lot of time together. We went to different places around base and movies and stuff like that. And it was really, really nice to have somebody that I liked so well sitting beside me while we were watching a movie.

Anyway, one day we were sitting in my apartment. There

were only nurses in the building, and we each had a living room, a kitchen combined, a bedroom and a bath. They were tiny places, but we had our own space. And we're sitting there talking, and all of a sudden she says to me, "What would you think if I kissed you on the lips?" And I don't think it took me a second to get it out. I said, "I'd like that." And that was it. I knew. I like to say I was "made in Japan."

Now that you were intimate with another woman, were you careful about how you appeared in public?

CR: I must have been. But the thing is, nobody cared. I mean, we spent the night at different apartments. Sometime she'd spend the time with me. And you'd always have to get up, depending on the shifts you had. And I remember sometimes I'd be working night duty, and she'd come over at the end of her shift, at the end of the day, and wake me up, and we'd spend a few hours together.

It seemed like nobody cared about that. It was all women. And if some did, they never said anything. Because when I look back, everyone that I knew was a lesbian. We were like a big group that hung around together, in quarters and at the clubs.

There were two women that I especially liked, and they were both straight. I know they knew about the sexual orientation of the other women. The women weren't very cautious in our quarters. They'd hold hands or kiss, or they'd have their arms around each other. But all this was for nobody else's eyes, except for people who lived right there. Nobody was ever touchy in public.

Well, any public display of affection—"PDA"—is fairly frowned upon in uniform anyway.

CR: Yes, true. I knew two or three chief nurses who were lesbians. And the chief nurse that was there during some of my time in Japan was a lesbian. I did not know that, but somebody told me, and I said, "You've got to be kidding me!" Come to find out later it was true. And I knew indirectly of two more. I mean, these women were generals.

So no one noticed or minded, and the women weren't overt in public. But people seem to have this fear that suddenly, if people come out, there are just going to be orgies in the barracks.

CR: That's right. And they think somebody's gonna hit on them. They say, "Oh, this guy's going to be after me." And that's not true. It's not true. I mean, I've known a lot of gay men, some of them very flamboyant, but most of them stick with their own. They don't go after straight men. Unless straight men want them to. [*Laughs*]

In which case the straight men aren't very straight.

CR: That's true! I think sometimes it's a fear about their own sexuality when they see these gay men.

At the time you were having a relationship with a woman, did male officers ever ask you out? And how did you deal with that?

CR: I went out with male officers before, but after I came out I don't think anybody really asked me out. In Japan, we were mostly on the base. We didn't go that many places, unless you took a few days off or you had leave. And we partied a lot in the club, and I met lots of guys and danced and stuff. I just don't remember dating.

Before I went to Japan, before I came out, one of the men I dated was an enlisted man. And he was pretty serious, and I just wasn't. I got stationed elsewhere. We wrote a few times, but that was it. I wanted to explore both sexes. I did meet some men, and I did sleep with some of them. That's one thing I could have regretted but didn't. Nothing happened.

Then I was rotating back to the States. I had requested California, and I got it. And I always thought my girlfriend was the strong one, because I was weepy a lot. But a couple of months before I was ready to leave, actually she was the one I had to console.

So I left, and we called a couple of times a week—our phone bills! One time my phone bill was $320, and I was reading it as I was walking outside, and I stepped off the curb and wrenched the hell out of my ankle. I was on crutches for three weeks! Luckily, I was able to pay the phone bill.

I came back to the states in June. We had decided in February, which was her birthday, that I would take leave and go back to Japan. And my chief nurse didn't like it at all that I was going to Japan. She said, "Suppose you can't get back?" I said, "I'll take a commercial flight if I can't get back, because I was going on a hop through Travis Air Force Base.[3]

So I went to Travis, and I knew some women there who had been with me in Japan, and I was there for two or three days waiting for a hop. And they introduced me to these other two women who were in the Air Force and lived together. And come to find out when we were talking that my cousin, who was also in the Air Force, was gay. I never knew that. And they said, "Are you talking about such and such?" And I said, "Yeah. She's my cousin." And they laughed like hell. They said, "Didn't you know she was a lesbian?" And I said, "No, I didn't." So that's two of us in our family.

Anyway, on the third or fourth day, I called Japan, and I said, "I'm having an awful time getting a hop. I'm just gonna get a commercial flight." And she says to me, "Don't come." I says, "What do you mean, don't come?" And she says, "I found somebody else." She said, "I'm not very strong, and I can't be by myself." So that was the end of that.

Was your heart broken?

CR: Oh, God yes. My friends were very consoling. One of the nurses had driven me to Travis. I was about eighty miles away from our base in Sacramento. I called up and said, "Do you think you could come and get me? My plans have been changed."

So she came and got me, and I guess I didn't look too happy. And we were driving back, and she said, "Why don't we stop for a drink?" So we stopped, and we're sitting there and not paying attention to much. And we had a drink, and I looked around, and all of the sudden, I said, "Oh, my God! We're in a gay bar." And she said, "Yes. Aren't you gay?" And I says, "My God! Is it that obvious?" But it doesn't have to be obvious. I think we just pick each other out. I found that to be true lots of times. I don't know if there's a sixth sense.

People commonly refer to that as "gaydar."

CR: I never heard that before. Gaydar! [*Laughs*]

It's standard issue.

CR: Well, we had a brief fling for a time, but she turned out to be not a very nice person. And I was better off not associating with her because she had an alcohol problem. I remember one time somebody telling me, "You gotta come!" And I said, "What's the matter?" She was drunk, and she fell down a flight of stairs at a motel. She broke both ankles.

When I was at my first base, there was a woman there who she had gone to school with, and they both came into the service together.

And this one woman was absolutely gorgeous. She had blond hair. It wasn't naturally blond, but it was a beautiful blond. And she was very, very good looking. I mean, the guys used to be all over her! And she just didn't give them the time of day. But she always gravitated toward me, and I never knew. And when she was drunk, she had her arm around me and all this stuff. And I didn't know then, but I would feel uncomfortable. And she always wanted to be with me.

One night I got a call from her. She had been drunk, and she got in her car and she was going too fast to go out of the gate, and the guard got in front of the car, and she didn't stop and she hit him. So they called me from the jail there. The state police picked her up and brought her back.

She was investigated and got a reduction in pay. And when I found out that I was gay and was thinking back, I thought, *Well, maybe that poor soul was gay, too, and she didn't know anybody else.*

It was not as though you could be open about it?

CR: No. And I didn't even have a clue then.

Once you came out, you just relied on your gaydar?

CR: Yes.

And what if you were wrong?

CR: Well, I'll tell you. Even to this day I don't go after women. I really don't! There was a woman here where I live, and we became very good friends. And I came out to her. And we did a lot of things together. Then one day she said to me, "I don't know how to say this, but I feel a little uncomfortable. I have gay friends, and I like you a lot, but I'm not that kind of person." I said, "You don't have to worry. I never go after straight women." And she said, "I don't know whether to be insulted or relieved." [*Laughs*] I said, "You can take it either way."

While in the Air Force, it seems you weren't too terribly afraid of witch hunts. Did that kind of thing ever happen?

CR: No! We just heard. They would go after males more, and enlisted people. But any place I was, there was never a problem. And every single base I went, there were gay women. Even up in Labrador. We had fifteen nurses and one WAC officer. And I had a relationship with her while I was up at Goose Bay. Four of us were gay out of the sixteen women.

It wasn't an issue. When I think about it, I think, *Well, how could people not know,* especially when I lived in quarters on base, especially in Japan. There were hundreds of nurses. We had a huge hospital and two flight squadrons. And we lived in this three-story building, and it was full of nurses. Some had known each other from before, from another base. And when you were going to your next base, people would say, "Look for so-and-so."

You say it was a mistake to go to Italy.

CR: Oh, I had a bad time.

You were sexually harassed by another lesbian.

CR: Well, this woman was a nut. I knew of her. She was in Japan when I was. But she was at another base, Yokota Air Base, which was not too far from the base that I was at.

So I went to Italy. I got off the plane in Venice and took a train to Pordenone. It was raining like hell, and here I am in the middle of nowhere. And a sergeant came to get me and put me up in a hotel in this town. Aviano was a tiny, tiny town full of sheep and goats and everything else. And I thought, *Oh, God!* Anyway, I stayed there not very long, and she said, "Why don't you stay with me until you find a place to live?" I knew she was gay, and she never said anything to me. I don't even know if she really knew me.

Anyway, I stayed with her. She lived about a twenty-minute ride from the base. There were no telephones and no transportation. She had a telephone. She had to have a telephone pole put up outside the house there. That's what you had to do if you wanted a phone. None of us could do that, except she was the chief nurse, the head nurse. And I felt really isolated there. I couldn't go anyplace, and she'd come home and fix these wonderful candlelit dinners. And I started to feel uncomfortable.

She was putting the moves on you.

CR: Yes! And at the dispensary where I was working, there was a young woman who was a receptionist, an Italian. We became good friends. So she told me about a place that had a vacancy. So I moved.

And this nurse would say to me, "You know, the commander's wife said you don't ever come to the officers club." And I said, "You're right. I don't care to come to the officers club every night and drink because I don't drink that much." And she said, "Well, you should just make an effort to come. People are noticing." And I thought, *Well, that's too bad.*

But I used to go to the NCO club because the two men that lived in my apartment complex were sergeants. And I used to go with them and their families sometimes. And when I was at Goose Bay, I knew this guy who was stationed there, and I got a letter from him that he's coming to Aviano, to the base. He was straight. When he came, he lived in an old farmhouse not far from the base. And I used to go over there lots of times, and we used to visit. He and I both loved to go to cemeteries. I think I visited every cemetery in that area—including one dedicated to Italian nurses during the war. They were very interesting, especially in Europe, because they're very, very old.

He might have known that I was gay, but nobody ever talked about things like that. We were friends.

And how did all these new relationships affect your would-be suitor, the chief nurse? Did they piss her off?

CR: Yes! [*Laughs*] We were at the base of the Dolomites [the pre-Alps] near Piancavallo, which is a huge ski resort there, so what's-his-name and myself used to go up there. He used to love to ski. And I'd sit in the lounge and watch the scenery. We also went to Austria a few times to ski. And I'd just go for the scenery and walk around the towns and stuff.

And she'd always make remarks.

I also became very friendly with an Italian family there. They were like my own family, and the youngest daughter worked in the town hall. And we became friends.

And I remember a couple of times this nurse would come up to me and say, "Oh, is that one of your new *girlfriends?* And I just wouldn't bother. This younger woman wouldn't know what a lesbian was if you spelled it out in big letters!

But despite having a wonderful family and having made friends...

CR: I couldn't stay. I was there for about a year. I did a lot of good work, and I felt very good about myself. There were two doctors there, and we had a lot of dependents. It was a small fighter base. Tactical command. And I organized the wives as Red Cross workers because we had two nurses, period, and we couldn't do everything. And they loved it! They had something to do. I was in charge of the whole thing. The sergeant in charge was really a good guy. We did a lot of good things together. And everybody liked me.

That was bad news—that everybody liked me—and that I never went to the officer's club and drank myself into a stupor. So the last efficiency report I had, I couldn't believe it. It was the worst report I had ever had in my life. I had never had a bad one before. And I thought, *Oh, my God! I can't believe she wrote this!*

The chief nurse poured all her unrequited passion and venom into it?

CR: Yes! So I went to the wing commander. And he said, "This sounds like a personality conflict. On one hand here, she tells how wonderful you were to organize the emergency room, organized the workers. The enlisted people were very happy. And on the other side, it says that you couldn't adapt here because it was a small base." He said, "It does not make sense, but I cannot do anything about it."

So I wrote to this woman who had been my chief nurse in Japan, who became the chief nurse of the entire Air Force Nurse Corps (AFNC). I wrote to her that I was having a really hard time with someone there and that if I stayed, it was going to ruin my career or it was going to ruin me—one or both.

In a month or so, I got letters to go to Spain.

And the chief nurse in Japan, your friend, she was gay?

CR: Yes. She was gay when she was the chief nurse in Japan, and she was still gay when she was the chief of the whole nurse corps.

She was looking out for me. She knew who I was, and we had many conversations. So I really appreciate her doing that. I thought, *If this ruins my career, that's okay. I have got to get out of here.*

The real issue for the woman who was harassing you was not that you didn't go the officer's club but that you wouldn't be her girlfriend.

CR: Yes, and she was very jealous because nobody liked her. And I had a lot of friends there. I remember one time: The people who lived across the street from me were an elderly woman and her husband, who was younger than her. They worked for Raytheon as civilians. And we became friends.

We used to see each other in the club and stuff. And she came to me one day, and she said, "You need to go talk to the commander because I saw Maj. So-and-so in the ladies room making out with another woman. You've got to go and report it." And I thought, *Dear God! I can't do that. What am I going to tell this lady? I'll be outing myself.* So I said, "Don't worry about it. I'll take care of it." And she thought I had reported it.

But I got the transfer. And I got to Madrid. I was at a meeting, because I was a supervisor, and the command nurse, the European command nurse, was there. And she turned and said to me, "You got an intercommand transfer. That's really unheard of. What's up there? Were you in trouble or what?" I didn't answer her, but the chief nurse of the hospital in Madrid said, "We know what your report was like, your efficiency report. We also know you're a good worker. So the only thing we go by is how you perform here," which was great because I didn't have a problem. I worked well, and I never had a problem with anybody.

Even though it seemed there was quite a network of women, you mentioned that you had to be careful nonetheless.

CR: Yeah, because of the way the climate was. We were pretty open with each other. But if anybody discovered, like the woman in Italy, demanding that I go and report this woman.... "She's a lesbian! She's on the base. We don't want her here!" And these are people that I knew and loved. And that's the hard part. People that you know. They love you. You love them. And yet they have the lowest opinions of homosexuals. I have that with my own relatives. I used to want to cry. And you still had to be careful because if it were found out, then you would be discharged. No ifs or buts.

When people whom you knew and loved would say things, how did you feel?

CR: I felt like a worm. But when I was in the military, it didn't happen too much.

How do we overcome these ideas that people have?

CR: You know, the thing I can do now—but I didn't then—is I tell people. I was working in a battered women's shelter when I moved to New England. And I knew this woman. We had had lunch together and talked and stuff. She was a volunteer, and I was a student. And she started talking to me about somebody. And she said, "And you know, she says this and she says that. And she's a lesbian, for God's sake!" And I said, "Whoa, whoa. Just a minute. I'm a lesbian." And she looked at me, her mouth wide open. She said, "Damn it, you never know who you're talking to!"

She had to change her view?

CR: She certainly did!

How do we get the military to change its view?

CR: You know, I don't think we can. I have never before felt so much anger and distaste for our government as I do today. And as far as the fighting now, I think that that shouldn't have happened.

You have called "don't ask, don't tell" a "farce."

CR: Oh, God yes. What people don't know about, they're afraid of. And I can't see how, in all logic, they could say, "This guy is gay. He has to be discharged." How about the year or two years he spent in Vietnam? How about the medals that he had?

How about the people who think that he's a brave man and relied on him for their lives?

You know, you hear people: "I wouldn't want to be in a fox-hole with that guy." Well, I've known a lot of gay men who have risked their lives in the military and who have died also because they were fighting for their country. They fought alongside their fellow men. If people would delve into it and think logically, maybe they would understand a little bit more.

But I don't see it in my lifetime. People are too ignorant. They don't want to know. They were the same way with black people. You know? We had a civil war, and what good did it do? It didn't do that much good, especially living in the South of the '60s. Then living up here, I couldn't believe the prejudice in New England against black people. So you know? What are you gonna do? You do the best you can. And sometimes you can change people's minds, and sometimes you can't.

We used to joke a lot about it when I was in service and even after. If all the gay people got up and left, there wouldn't be anybody. They would have half a force, if that.

You had written that one of the ways you all dealt with stress during the Vietnam era was that all the medical people partied.

CR: You had to do something. Three of my good friends were stationed in Da Nang. My cousin flew out of Saigon, a flight nurse. The things that they saw were horrible, and how do you deal with something like that? You party. You try and get it out of your mind. I used to love to watch *China Beach* because it's exactly what it was like.

And I always thanked God that even though I drank so much in those years in the Air Force—not every day, but especially when I was over in Japan—that I never became an alcoholic and I never suffered any ill effects. Because that was what you did.

And I worked, I worked all over. In the Air Force, I worked

everywhere except pediatrics and the operating room. And in Japan, I worked for a while in the casualty staging unit that was separate from our hospital. Our hospital was over 300 beds. But we had about ten Quonset huts that had ninety beds each. This was a couple of miles from the hospital, near the flight line, because planes came in day and night from Vietnam.

My friends that were in Da Nang, at field hospitals, they never talked about it. And I can understand why. I can't imagine the things that they saw.

Is your being so active once you got out of the military a kind of response to how circumspect you had to be while in the military?

CR: Oh, yeah. I just hated that we were discriminated against because I knew the people who were gay. I knew what kind of people they were. They were just like everybody else! They did everything that other people did. They did more. They risked their lives. And I used to get very upset with people who would say, "Oh, you're in the military for twenty years. You're young when you come out. What a good life!" I'd say, "Are you kidding? Twenty-four hours a day they own you! I had a $200 paycheck when I went in. And unless you're a colonel or a general or somebody, you don't get a good pension. So I used to get angry at people who thought that military people had it made. We earned it.

Having gone through everything that you've gone through—tussling with benefits, having to hide while you were in uniform—if a younger person came to you and said, "I'm thinking about joining the Air Force, Navy, Army, Marine Corps. Should I do it?" What would you say?

CR: You know, I wouldn't do it again in this climate. I wouldn't do it again. Because I think it's a different military than I knew. But I would have to tell them that there are great opportunities to be had in the military, especially if you want to have a trade or a profession. You can go to school. Several of the nurses went to school. They went on to get their Masters degrees while they were on active duty, and they paid back the Air Force, two years for every year.

But I don't know. I've seen a lot. I don't think there's the discipline and respect in the military that there used to be. And I know several of my friends would say the same thing. But it is an opportunity to go and make something for yourself, especially today when jobs are so hard to get and education is so expensive. But I have mixed feelings today because all these guys are going over to Iraq, getting killed. I mean, after Vietnam. You know, it's the same thing all over again.

Are there parallels for you?

CR: Yes. I mean, we didn't win in Vietnam, and there were thousands and thousands of people who got killed. I think they just said the count in Iraq was 500, which is a lot.4 Five hundred lives is a lot for the time we've been in Iraq—especially since they've declared that the war is over.

That's something to think about before you go into the military because I just don't think it's the same. It's like I said: I just don't have the respect. They play with people's lives.

One of the saddest things I saw was a young black man. They wheeled him off the plane. He was on a stretcher. And he must have heard me talking. And he said, "Excuse me. Excuse me. Could you come here?" So I went over, and I said, "What can I do for you?" He was blind. And he must have been about 18 or 19 years old. And he said, "Who are you?" And I said, "I'm a nurse. An Air Force nurse." He said, "Oh! Please hold my hand." He said, "I haven't seen or heard an American woman in a long time, and I feel so safe that I'm here now." And I thought, *Jesus! Here's this kid. He's 18 years old, and he's blind for the rest of his life. God.* I cried a few times. You just turn your head. You go away, and then you come back.

When I came out, I volunteered at an Air Force base in Florida. I worked in the clinic, and I did volunteer work. And they asked me would I work in the emergency room because they were really short of help. So I went to the emergency room, but I couldn't stay there. I could not tolerate people coming in, in pain. I wasn't able to do it. And I thought, *Jeez! This is horrible. How can I help anybody?* That was the end of my nursing career.

Do many nurses reach that point of critical mass?

CR: I think a lot of them were burned out, especially military. And like I said, the women that I knew that were over in Vietnam didn't talk about it. One of my friends used to write me all the time. They'd go to bed with a flak jacket and a helmet on. And when they heard shooting, they just fell out of their beds and went under their cots. They saw so much, and they worked and worked hours and hours and hours. One of my friends got Agent Orange. She has a disability from the VA.

Which wasn't supposed to exist, really.

CR: That's right. It wasn't supposed to exist, and they finally admitted it and are treating people. People lie a lot. I lied a lot.

Truth is, I really loved being in the Air Force. I loved doing what I was doing. I was representing my country. I got a lot of experience nursing, and I traveled tremendously, as much as I could, being that it was during Vietnam.

And it was great getting a hop. The guys were all wonderful. Especially if they knew you were a nurse, they couldn't do enough for you. Even over here. I've been out of service a long time now, but I was over at the American Legion, and one of the guys said, "What did you do?" And I told him that I had been a nurse. And he said, "Let me shake your hand." I thought that was really nice of him. I have a lot of good memories.

Notes

1. No military nurses are recorded as having been a part of the actual eighty-plus-mile forced march of starving and wounded American and Filipino soldiers by Japanese from Mariveles to San Fernando after the fall of Bataan during World War II. The nurses—also known as the "Angels of Bataan and Corregidor"—were a part of the "Battling Bastards of Bataan" who suffered intense shelling by the Japanese but were evacuated primarily to Corregidor, where they were captured by the Japanese and sent to POW camps in 1942. They were repatriated to the U.S. in 1945.

2. More than 265,000 women volunteered in the U.S. Armed Forces during the Vietnam era, and more than 7,500 women saw duty in Vietnam between 1962 and 1973. Almost 6,000 of them were nurses and medical specialists. Seven Army nurses and one Air Force nurse were killed.

3. Members of the uniformed services and their reserve components are permitted to travel for free on aircraft under the control of the U.S. Department of Defense when space is available. This benefit is often referred to as "space A" or "military hop."

4. As of January 2004. As of January 2005, that number, at roughly 1,350, has more than doubled. More than 10,200 are reported wounded, though VA sources report that the actual figure could be three times that number.

About Face

This Army MP served during what some consider a more permissive period, ending with the introduction of tighter regulations in the early 1980s. But sometimes the enemy came from within.

We probably had about eight drill sergeants. One of them was a woman, and she happened to be a lesbian. She was actually somewhat harassing, although I hesitate to use that word because it has a broader meaning these days. Teasing is almost a better word. Of those of us that recognized as lesbians, I was a couple years older than most recruits. And I'd be like, *She's one of us.*

I ended up seeing someone I was in basic with, and we were in AIT at this point because we would go away on the weekends. And we got back, and one of our male drill sergeants called us in and said, "Look. I know what's going on here. And you just got to realize that this is the Army. You got to be a little more discrete." Then he proceeded to reference this woman, this drill sergeant. And he said, "But you really want to steer clear of Drill Sgt. So-and-so. She really doesn't like the fact that there are lesbians in her Army." And I sat there thinking, *You have got to be kidding me!*

The one thing I can remember is being on the pistol range, facing the target, and having her come up to me and just lean over, to the side of my head, and say something like, "Got any letters from Germany lately?" A woman that I had been involved with was sending me cards and things from Germany constantly, and they hand out your mail in formation. So she knew I was getting mail, and she knew that this woman had come to see me graduate basic. It was little things like that. Nothing that was ever, in its language, inappropriate. But it was, "I know that you know. And you know that I know. And neither of us is going to do anything about it."

—Melissa S. Embser-Herbert
U.S. Army, 1978–1981
U.S. Army Reserve, 1981–2000

We Were Number 1

Kelly Mohondro

Though anti-gay crusader Anita Bryant's national "Save Our Children Campaign" [1] *was well under way in 1979, Kelly Mohondro grew up in small towns in Washington state and never heard the L word before joining the Navy that same year.*

She was 19 and wanted to "see the world, do something for others, and get an education by joining the military."

"My father had been a Marine, so I didn't want to go into the Marines," says Mohondro, 44, now a doctoral student in psychology. "The Coast Guard was aboard ship, and I was afraid of that. And I'm afraid of flying, so I did not go in the Air Force."

The Navy was her last, best choice, and as it turned out, a perfect fit.

She was the lead recruit in her boot camp and later was part of a helicopter training squadron before becoming a company commander— the Navy's term for a drill instructor.

But her celebrated six-year hitch came to a crashing halt when an NIS informer infiltrated her group of gung ho gay and lesbian sailors at the Recruit Training Center in Orlando, Florida.

Though the E6 escaped the Navy dragnet, the experience, she says, soured her on the service.

"I'd decided I was going to be a lifer. I was going to stay in twenty or thirty years. I had advanced really quickly. I loved what I did, and I was really good at it," says Mohondro, who was honorably discharged RE1 in 1985 and hopes one day to use her experience to help the military overcome its prejudice.

"Because of that investigation, I didn't stay in. It kind of stopped me in my tracks, and I had to go in a completely different direction. It did a positive thing and a negative thing: It pissed me off, but in pissing me off it probably made me a better person."

* * *

You mention you were shocked when your recruiter asked you a question about your sexuality. What did he ask?

KM: The question was something like, "Are you now, or have you ever been, a homosexual?"

That's very McCarthy.

KM: It was very weird for my 19-year-old ear, mainly because I was already questioning who I was. I'd always wondered about being lesbian, but I didn't really have a name for it. I hadn't seen or heard or read anything. I just knew I frequently double-dated with my good friends, and rather than being in the front seat with the boy I was with,

I always wished I could be in the backseat with my best friend.

But when you got to boot camp, it seemed that a huge portion of your company was lesbian. How did you know that, if you really didn't have the language?

KM: Because people were pretty open about it. I was selected in my second week as the RCPO, the lead recruit. That's the recruit who kind of stands off to the side and runs the drills, and is in charge of the company. I was responsible for all of the recruits, and I'd come across girls in bed with each other, girls kissing, girls showering together.

No!

KM: Yeah! And it was kind of accepted. I don't remember anyone in my company saying that this was wrong, this was bad. And in fact, starting right before work week, which was the fifth week when we'd go out and do work for the other recruits, like run the mess hall and stuff like that, the gays or lesbians in my company started integrating me into their group, and we all started becoming friends.

At that time I was questioning my sexuality, but I wasn't quite over the edge saying, "This is really what I want to be." It was just like, this is natural, this is okay, this is normal. And that's how the rest of the company looked at it, too.

What percentage would you say was lesbian?

KM: Oh, my gosh! It must have been at least a quarter of the company. It started out with eighty women per company, and we lived in one huge room, forty bunk beds, you know, top and bottom, in the barracks.

Did the other recruits say anything, or did they take a kind of "live and let live" attitude?

KM: I don't remember anything negative being said at all. And I don't even remember our company commander saying anything negative about homosexuality, at least during boot camp.

When you arrived at your first duty station, the gay men and lesbians just integrated you into their fold. Was that their gaydar going off, or did they just think you were cool by not blowing the whistle?

KM: They knew that I was probably a lesbian, and they were accepting me into the group. I didn't know that at the time. In fact, I was still so oblivious to the negative view of homosexuality that I had a heterosexual roommate in the barracks at the time and just mentioned that these lesbians were letting me in their group. "I see them hugging and kissing and making out as we're partying together," I said. "It's no big deal. I'm having a blast. Would you like to join us?" Like an idiot! I shouldn't have opened my mouth because she ran to the CO, who called me in and asked me about it

That's when I first knew that it was really a bad thing. He said, "I understand X, Y, and Z are making out, that you've seen it all." And I kind of played dumb. It was at that time that I said to myself, *Oh, my God. This is wrong, what they're doing to these people. I was an idiot to open my mouth.*

How did you get through that? Did you say, "I didn't say that"?

KM: Yes! I said, "I don't know what Mary is talking about." I don't even remember her last name. She was a petty officer third class and thought that she was just hotter than shit. I just said, "I'm new on the base. I'm just having a really good time. I don't know where any of that came from. That must be her own issues." And from that point on, she never talked to me, and we were no longer roommates.

So you got the clue. "Oh, I'd better not talk about this."

KM: Yes. And it was hard. I mean, it was a shock because I had been pretty open about who I was. I had left my abusive family, and I was finally living in a world that was—I thought—accepting, and I could talk about my life. Being in an abusive family, you can't. You have to keep your mouth shut. And I thought, *Oh, my God! Now I'm back in these same circumstances again.*

When you had your first experience with women, did you just fall into that and say, "Oh, that's what I am?" Or were you tortured?

KM: I was comfortable with it until I started realizing, more and more, that the Navy didn't accept it.

And the men were continuously asking me out, and I didn't want to say yes, so they started calling me a lesbian behind my back and writing about me on the bathroom walls. And the officers I was working with were asking about me. It was at that point that I said, "Oh, my God, I can't be who I want to be. It must be sick. It must be bad."

No one said to my face that I was a lesbian. Everything was very covert. They said it behind my back. And I would double-date with the girl that I was dating. She would go out with a guy, and I would go out with a guy, kind of as a cover.

But I would also go out with some of the officers, which, as you know, is prohibited, too. But I'd go out with them to keep up the front. But then finally I got tired of that because they were pigs! They were very inappropriate. Two of them tried to attack me, and I reported it. Basically, I was the one that was in trouble. I was told that it was me who had enticed them, and that I shouldn't be dating officers. It was just a mess, an absolute mess.

And there were a lot of my friends who were heterosexual that would say "no" and would be called lesbians and dykes, too. The guys' egos were so messed up that if a girl turned them down, the girl's automatically a dyke.

You said that once you began dating women you found it difficult to hide your newfound sexuality.

KM: I was uncomfortable with using vague pronouns, like *them* or *us* or *we.* And so I started having an observing ego watching myself as I was talking, choosing my words very carefully. And it just was uncomfortable. And it made me angry that I had to do that.

Takes some of the spontaneity out of life.

KM: Yes!

You were involved in an NIS investigation down in Florida that involved plants who insinuated themselves into the lesbian community there and then named names.

KM: That was in Orlando. When I was an E4, I applied for company commander school—drill sergeant is what you in the Army know them as. I made E5, got transferred to Norfolk for instructor training, and then I went down to Orlando, Florida, to be a company commander.

Immediately everyone's gaydar went off, and I was assimilated into the gay and lesbian group. There were males and females, but mainly females. And gosh, I had been there maybe a year when "the plant" joined the group.

She was transferred in and became a company commander. No one really knew a lot about her. I mean, she didn't talk about going to company commander school or anything like that, but she was just assimilated into the group. And everyone—even though there were some questions—just accepted her. She was a part of our group for anywhere between six months to a year before NIS really started investigating anything.

Didn't a red light go off for anybody?

KM: There was some question because she didn't seem to have the same background as the rest of us had, and she didn't seem to be quite as good a company commander or as knowledgeable. She didn't seem to have the skills. She seemed a little bit off.

And I don't remember anyone ever saying they could confirm that she'd gone through instructor training, which was mandatory. I mean there was just something that wasn't right.

But I don't ever remember anyone mentioning the possibility that there could be a plant or a witch hunt. I mean, it wasn't something overt. It was just a gut feeling for a good portion of the group.

How many people were in that group?

KM: Oh, it was huge. It was probably every damned lesbian that was on RCP Orlando. The group ranged from ten to twenty people, and as the girlfriends or the boyfriends changed, the group would wax and wane. But twenty was the core.

And then a second informer joined you.

KM: Yes. She actually started flirting with people in our group, or what seemed to be flirting with people in our group, so one of our group members started flirting back. That group member was one of the people who actually got kicked out because she had slept with the informer.

And that was really the only way you could prove someone was gay.

KM: Yep. But the informer started it. And she stayed in, but the other girl was kicked out. The primary plant never slept with anyone. She was supposedly married with kids, though I don't think anyone ever met her husband or her kids. That might have been another one of those yellow flags—that she was married with kids and supposedly hetero.

Then she just disappeared. All of a sudden she was just transferred. Gone. It was right after that that the investigation started. I might have been the first one called in. I was training drill teams, and I had just finishing training one of my teams. We worked from 4 or 5 A.M. until 7 or 8 A.M., and if there was a ceremony, until 11 or 12, unless we had duty. So I finished training my drill team, and it was around lunchtime. And my supervisor, a male lieutenant—who happened to be dating an enlisted woman, so he was doing stuff under cover—called me in and said there was a meeting and he had to escort me and wait for me. I asked him, "What are we doing? What's going on?" But he wouldn't tell me anything.

So he drove me over to NIS in his car and escorted me in and sat me down in front of this guy in a big pink frilly shirt, who was a flaming homosexual, and it started.

He was the investigator?

KM: Uh-huh.

In the pink frilly shirt?

KM: Uh-huh.

Had he just come from an undercover mission or was that his normal dress?

KM: I think that was his normal dress.

And when you sat down before the man in the pink frilly shirt, what happened?

KM: They started right out by saying they were investigating homosexuality on base and that my girlfriend and I had been seen sitting behind the barracks in my car, making out, which was absurd. Then they just kept questioning.

They asked me about things that only someone in our group would know. I had bought my girlfriend a ring, and she had bought me a ring, and they asked about the rings, saying that they knew when they were bought and the reason they were bought.

They asked me about my roommate, who was also a lesbian. They asked about other people who were a part of our group, but they didn't ask anything directly sexual, like, "Have you had sex with so-and-so?" They just said they knew that I was partners with a woman.

How do you respond to something like that?

KM: I said, "Absolutely not! I don't know where you're getting your information. This is ridiculous. What are you talking about?"

Afterwards, I found out they had brought my girlfriend in at the same time, and they were telling her the same thing they were telling me. They were telling me that she had admitted we were girlfriends, and they were telling her the same thing, but we both denied it.

It felt like it lasted forever, but I think, in actuality, it only lasted about an hour. Then they had the officer escort me back, and he had to stay there with me all day. But he didn't say anything to me.

Was that the end of it?

KM: No. NIS didn't call me in again, but then they started calling in the rest of the group over and over again. And my off-base phone had this funny *beep beep beep* sound that kept going on. We were told that it was being bugged. There was a car that always sat outside of our house, and the person in that car, at one point, I saw open our mailbox and look in it.

And it lasted for? God, I don't know. Two months? Three months? This was my last year, 1985. And I had wanted to re-enlist because I had been in six years at that time, but during this I decided, uh-uh, I'm just getting out.

It was ridiculous, too, because all of us were the top performers. We were the people who were getting the number 1 recruit companies. We were the ones who were getting company commander of the month, company commander of the quarter, company commander of the year. I had just pinned on E6. I mean, we were just really good sailors.

One of the women ended up marrying. It was a sham, but she married one of the guys who was being investigated just so they would be let alone.

The last I had heard about her, she had gone LDO—limited duty officer—and was an O3 and doing wonderfully. You have to be a top performer in the Navy to get picked up for LDO.

So we were all able to overcome it, as far as I know. But a lot of people were angry and upset. A couple of people ended up getting out, besides myself. But the ones who stayed in, the ones who hadn't slept with any of the plants, continued doing pretty well.

As a group, did you do anything that a comparable heterosexual group wasn't doing? What you are describing to me is off-duty. Off-duty, you do what kids in the service do—party. You get together, you go out, and some of you hook up, and some of you don't. But during duty hours, everything is about the job.

KM: In fact, no one in our group, as far as I know, was doing anything illegal. None of us were doing drugs or even alcohol. None of us were selling drugs or alcohol. Some of the heteros were. None of us were pedophiles.

I mean, we caught a hetero guy who was an E5, a company commander, being a Peeping Tom. They also found out he was having an affair, and he got busted one rank. That's it. And we were being looked at to be kicked out. We weren't doing anything wrong. It was absolutely ridiculous.

Defense Secretary Donald Rumsfeld was complaining recently about the military having too few people to meet our obligations. But this weeding-out of very good people continues.

KM: It sure does, and it's really disgusting.

The chief argument against our being open in the service is that our doing so would jeopardize unit cohesion. If you put us into a group, we'll immediately want to have sex with or attack all the heterosexuals.

KM: That's their own fear or their own wish, their own narcissism. Because I can tell you personally, I have never wanted to recruit a heterosexual woman to be my lover. I don't know about you, but that's not my thrill in life. And what makes me even angrier—and it's from my own experience—is that you have so many military men out there who are being inappropriate with the women and nothing's happening to them. The men are worse predators than anybody! The two officers who almost raped me had nothing happen to them. Nothing.

It's just homophobia. It's fear. And part of it is perpetuated by the senior individuals who are deciding that homosexuality is wrong. I mean, it's no longer a disorder. The psychiatric association, the psychological association, everyone knows it's not a disorder. Yet the military continues to perpetuate that it is a disorder just because of those people who are afraid.

It's very similar to the same sort of fears that people had about working with African-Americans in the 1940s.

KM: You are exactly right, and there's still some of that prejudice going on. It's really sad. At least when I was in, the majority of the mess cooks were Filipinos or African-Americans. The majority of the ship's stewards, African-American. I think it's still going on.

How do we change this?

KM: If those in the military would open their eyes, they would see that many of their fellow sailors and soldiers are GLBT and doing a darn good job. It's just gonna take time. I don't think that we're gonna be able to push anything any harder than we're already doing. We're making huge strides for gay and lesbian rights.

There's just a lot of fear and a lot of internal homophobia from individuals who profess to be heterosexual. It's their own fear that they might have homosexual feelings themselves. Research shows that a lot of individuals who are committing hate crimes against gays and lesbians themselves have some feelings of homosexuality, which they're projecting.

Otherwise, why would you care?

KM: Exactly. Why would it make a difference? There just always has to be some hot button in the world, and I think this is the hot button right now. It's the last societally approved overt discrimination.

It's still okay to hate fags and dykes?

KM: Yup. Sure is. And I feel really, really bad for the trans-sexuals and the gay males even more so than you and I, because lesbians seem to be more accepted than the transsexuals and the gay males.

Is that true? We seem to be kicked out of the service in greater numbers, proportionally.

KM: Well, part of that, too, is that some women in the military *say* they're lesbian just to get out.

Do you think that's true?

KM: I *know* it's true. When I trained companies, some of the girls were saying they were lesbians just because they wanted out. They went into boot camp, and they just couldn't do it. It's just like some of my recruits tried to get pregnant so they could get out.

That's very drastic.

KM: The recruits that we lost, or at least that I lost in my companies, weren't always lost because they couldn't do it or they weren't physically fit. At least one or two in every single company professed gayness, or were gay and couldn't hide it anymore. And it's an easy way to get out, to say you're gay. It's very easy.

That makes it tough on the troops who are gay and want to stay.

KM: It's frustrating for them. But when you went in, I'm sure you had heard that a lot of females were going in so that they could find a husband, right?

Some girls were there to find a husband or a boyfriend. You knew which ones they were because when you fell out in the morning at o-dark-30, they were the ones with full makeup on.

KM: [*Laughs*] And you wondered how they found the time!

And all to march to the PT pit and get filthy! In fact, in basic training I didn't recognize more than one or two other lesbians.

KM: I'm glad I didn't have that experience. I mean, my boot camp company was absolutely fantastic. It was fantastic, and so welcoming, and so lesbian. So full of lesbians!

Well, that would make for a very strack outfit, wouldn't it?

KM: Well, we were number 1!

Note

1. In 1977, singer Anita Bryant, then spokesperson for the Florida Citrus Commission, led a move to overturn a gay rights ordinance in Dade County, Florida, drawing national media attention. Her group, "Save Our Children," played on prejudice, claiming that gay men and lesbians shared a "hair-raising pattern of recruitment, seduction, and molestation" of minors and others. Convinced, Dade County voters repealed the ordinance by a 2–1 margin. Bryant then took her show on the road: With her aid, similar gay rights ordinances were repealed in St. Paul, Minnesota; Wichita, Kansas; and Eugene, Oregon. The gay community and its allies fought back, launching a successful boycott of Florida orange juice and forcing the Florida Citrus Commission to jettison Bryant as their shill.

About Face

This Korean War–era vet joined the Navy in 1952. Straight couples were fornicating even in trash cans, and base signs warned NO TWO IN A DUMPSTER. Her gaze fell elsewhere.

One of my friends went into the Navy, and she was writing back these glowing letters of what a great time she was having. And there was a movie that came out around then, too, where Betty Hutton played twin WAVES, and the uniform turned me on.[1] Between those two things, I made my decision to go in.

Looking back, there is another incident that made me kind of interested: My dad and my stepmother broke up for a short time, and he was going out with WAVES. And on one of my visits, he took me and two WAVES—one for me and one for him—to an amusement park in Cleveland, which was very big and wonderful. And I had a great time with those girls!

My first memory of boot camp is seeing an upper bunk. [*Laughs*] I had not been in an upper bunk before. I wondered if I could get on. I have to set my hair every night because I have straight, straight hair. And I would do pin curls in the dark, sitting on that upper bunk.

I had a crush on one girl in particular, and she liked someone else. I saw some girls pairing off, but I didn't go there. That could be very dangerous on a military base.

—Barbara Owens
CT3, U.S. Navy

Note
1. *Here Come the Waves*, Paramount Pictures, 1944. Hutton played twins Susie and Rosemary Allison.

We'll Have to Issue Soap-on-a-Rope

Lara Ballard

Entering the Army wasn't Lara Ballard's idea—it was her father's. An ROTC scholarship, he suggested, would pay for a four-year ride at Georgetown University, where Ballard hoped to study international relations and prepare for a career with the U.S. Foreign Service. She won a full scholarship, and in 1991 she graduated cum laude and was commissioned a spanking new second lieutenant.

"I really had no interest in joining the military," says Ballard, 34, now an attorney in Washington, D.C. "But my uncle had gone to VMI and was an Army officer, and my dad was briefly enlisted in the Coast Guard. He didn't have any sons; I was his oldest daughter, and I think maybe he had a little projection going on."

Though unenthusiastic about the Army at first, she caught the can-do spirit at ROTC Advanced Camp and chose to enter the Air Defense Artillery branch.

"I started meeting people who were just so dedicated," she says. "I was motivated to do a good job because I felt that I was taking care of my soldiers. And I got very gung ho."

She completed her Officer Basic Course at Fort Bliss, Texas, and joined the 1st Battalion, 7th Air Defense Artillery at Rhine Ordnance Barracks in Kaiserslautern, Germany. In 1992, her battery was deployed to Kuwait as part of Operation Southern Watch.

The Army, says Ballard, made her more of a professional and gave her an aptitude for leadership. But when her four-year tour was up, the captain was "ready for the door."

"You really meet some fantastic people," she says. "I really loved my soldiers. I thought they were interesting and funny and diverse and unpretentious.

"But it takes a lot of effort to hide your identity. I don't think I spent a day not thinking about it. I would wonder, Is this the day they're going to find out? It didn't matter that I was widely considered the best XO around. Hiding is a full-time job."

* * *

I distinctly remember the only time I was officially asked about sexual orientation. I went to ROTC Advanced Camp, and for that you had to do a physical and be weighed and everything. I can picture it clearly, sitting at these long tables, and there were these nurses asking you if you had a history of heart disease or diabetes. But one of the women said, "Are you homosexual?" I just said, "No," before I had time to think it over. I always remember coming back to that and thinking, *Oh, was that honest?* I was still soul-searching at that point. I gave what I thought, or hoped, was the honest answer, but that was around the time I was coming to terms with my sexuality.

That's one of the questions—number 37f in 1978—on the whole sheaf of forms given to enlisted persons: "Have you ever engaged in homosexual activity (sexual relations with another person of the same sex)?" I was out when I joined the service at 18, and most of the girls I knew were out. We just checked "no" and went on.

LB: Right. But part of why officers sometimes struggle more with "don't ask, don't tell"—and have an inner struggle—is that they're just pounding into our heads this idea about integrity, you know, this code of honor. I mean, I'm not saying they don't do that to enlisteds as well. But for officers, it's so much a part of the culture—you're supposed to be a person of honor, a gentleman. I think we tend to be a little more idealistic perhaps than NCOs.

And anyone who's ever been asked that question in an official capacity can often remember, like I do, the nurse and the table and the room. You just linger over it, thinking, *Was that the right thing to do?*

There are people who just really internalize this thing about the gay ban. And I'm that kind of person where it really affects your self-esteem and you feel dishonest and you can't get over it. There are people who just think it's a game, you know? This is some stupid rule that I have to play to get where I'm going. That second category of person is probably the healthier person. They just don't let it get to them as much.

Officers have a larger investment, in a way. As in corporations, there are workers and there are managers.

LB: Oh, I think that's very true. I certainly knew a lot of career-oriented enlisted, but, you know, it's not a prerequisite. But officers are very wound up in their careers and their image. And by the time I was being asked this question, I had a $60,000 scholarship at stake. I would have had to repay every dime of that money had I answered "yes."

Also an officer is typically older when he or she enters the service. The difference between 18 and 22 can be vast.

LB: Absolutely. All the things that lower enlisteds explore when they join at 18 are the things that freshmen in college are exploring. And by the time you're 21 or 22, you can have a substantial amount of experience behind you.

But that 18- to 21-year-old time period is when a lot of people come out of the closet. College, just going away from home for the first time during that time period, is when most people come to terms with who they are. But if you happen to be doing that while you're on an ROTC scholarship, you're sort of stuck.

And then you landed at Fort Bliss.

LB: Yeah. [*Laughs*] The first person I came out to in the Army was a guy that I met there. He was a West Point grad. I happened to be in a class that was seventy percent West Pointers, and they were an interesting crowd. They seemed to be living out their college freshman year that they never had at West Point—a lot of heavy drinking and running around and stuff.

But this guy was cool, and he was really interesting. He developed quite a crush on me, and we were just inseparable best buddies. Eventually I came out to him because I wanted to be fair and let him know that there's nothing developing here. And at the same time, I was getting a crush on our female instructor. I don't think he believed me for a few months, but it eventually started to set in with him that I had a crush on this woman.

And you felt safe in telling him?

LB: I really did. You know, I only came out to a handful of people in my four years. But I think I chose them well. They were, surprisingly, straight men. If I had a good vibe about somebody, I just told them.

What happened between that junior or senior year at college, where you were grappling with your sexuality, to being at Fort Bliss recognizing you're having a crush on an instructor? Something changed.

LB: I think it was a gradual realization. I don't know if there was any one thunderclap moment. I was so hung up about being gay that even after I realized, *Okay, I must be a lesbian*, it was not driven as much by attraction to women as lack of attraction to guys.

By the time I was a senior in college, I was pretty sure that it was unavoidable and not a choice. I tried to talk myself out of it for several years. I grew up with a religious background (I was probably more devoutly religious than my parents). I took that Bible stuff seriously, so there was a lot of soul searching. By senior year of college, I was fooling around with women, but I can't say it was really a satisfying experience. But I undeniably had a crush on this instructor.

And did you talk to her or did you keep your boundary, keep your distance?

LB: Oh, I was just a total teacher's pet. [*Laughs*] I didn't tell her about the crush. Actually, she ended up hooking up with a guy in my class and ended up getting out of the military because that little scandal about sleeping with one of her students caused her quite a bit of heartache. It's sort of ironic. I didn't like the guy either. I never really understood the attraction. The whole time it was funny because I used to hang out with my buddy Dave, and Dave was friends with this guy, so the four of us would hang out and double date.

Here I was secretly harboring this crush on her, and she just really liked having me around. And I excelled in the class. I think I graduated second in my Officer Basic Course class. It was largely out of an effort to do anything that would get her attention.

Whatever works.

LB: Right. But she gave us an interesting speech one day because she had done her first four-year stint at a unit in Germany and had come back. She gathered all the female OBC students together and just started giving us a lecture on what you deal with as a female officer. And I remember her saying that you really need to make an effort to get to know the wives. And she's like, "I know you feel like you have nothing in common with them, that they just want to trade recipes or something, but they don't understand you any more than you understand them. And they don't understand why a woman would join the military. They don't know if you're queer or what."

And she actually said that, and I inwardly cringed. And she said, "All they know is that you're working late with their husbands all the time. So just show your face at their little events now and then, and make sure that they have some sort of trust in you." She was a really good officer, and that's part of what attracted me to her. But I always remember that speech.

Indeed. During the era of the WAC, there was often a speech warning against "abnormal friendships."

LB: I never got that. I think they kind of assumed there were no lesbians in their military, and so there was nothing to worry about. Really, I think they warned people more about heterosexual misbehavior, which there was a lot of.

When I arrived at my unit in Germany, we had this battalion commander who was famous for giving the "perception equals reality" speech. And he gave that speech only to female officers. I wouldn't have had a problem if he had given it across the board, but it was a special speech that he gave to us. The gist of it was that an appearance alone of an improper relationship is enough to impact your career, it's enough to get the soldiers talking, to where people think you're not a fair and objective officer, you're screwing around. But clearly, it was heterosexual misbehavior that was contemplated.

It's a very interesting thing, this idea that there aren't lesbians in the military, yet this is what investigators search for—lesbians in the military.

LB: Yeah. It's a very odd thing. Honestly, I think that, in many ways, straight women have more of a struggle in the military than gay women. I had a lot of straight female friends, female officers, and they almost all got themselves into trouble at some point. A lot of them were struggling with this idea that they weren't feminine. You know, that they were wearing these ugly uniforms and no makeup and boots all day long, and they wanted to feel pretty. So I think a lot of them slept with a lot of guys to affirm to themselves that they were still attractive. Whereas, most of the lesbians I know were butch enough that this wouldn't bother them, you know, running around without makeup and in big boots. [*Laughs*]

In fact, it was desired.

LB: I was more than happy to slip under the radar screen of heterosexual attractiveness. [*Laughs*] The women I served with were all heterosexual, and a lot of them were quite sexually aggressive. A couple of them screwed around with enlisted guys. One of them got divorced, and I think she was screwing around on her husband in Saudi Arabia. There's just all sorts of misbehavior that goes on.

That's what blows my mind about the gay ban. I think I saw a quote from a general once saying, "You just can't introduce sex to the units." It's like, *Whoa, buddy! You don't think sex has been introduced to the units?* I can assure you it has.

When I was in Kuwait, I had a soldier find out that his wife was sleeping with his best friend back in Germany, and three guys were holding him down, and he was demanding to be sent home. You know, deployment is rough on everybody. Sexuality and family issues and partnerships are just inextricably part of military life. It's something that all commanders have to deal with.

Why do the powers that be assume that these things exist only in the context of gays and lesbians in the military?

LB: People just haven't accepted that our relationships are just like everyone else's. They seem to think that we're more about sex. Whereas, I probably had less interest in sex or having sexually explicit conversations than a lot of my heterosexual counterparts.

Just like white people don't realize they have a skin color, heterosexuals don't realize they have a sexuality. And their sexuality is on display all the time.

I found the Army to be a particularly sexually charged atmosphere. I mean, people are young and they're fit and they're away from home, and all they've got is each other and they just get wound up. They work hard and play hard and they drink hard, and stuff just happens because hormones are raging. You know, in the working environment, people tell very raunchy jokes and use a lot of foul language. Sex just seems to be on people's brains all the time.

I find it so ironic that somehow introducing gay people into that is going to disrupt things.

When I was in the service, the people who were fornicating were invariably straight. It was the men sneaking over to the women's barracks, the women sneaking over to the men's barracks. But there was no activity that I could ever see among women in the women's barracks. And as you well know, in training situations, you're so tired, you're really not even thinking of sex.

LB: Oh, yeah. I can't even imagine anyone thinking of sex while they're in basic training or airborne school or something like that, or even in the field or on deployment. I'm talking about garrison that they were screwing around. I mean, when you haven't showered in three days, your colleagues are not the most attractive thing on your mind. You just want to sleep. You want to shower and you want to sleep.

They get so wound up about this. You'd think that the gay ban is all about men's fear of showering with a gay man. And I'm just thinking, I can't even remember that many group showers. I just don't remember the issue coming up that much, that somebody thinks somebody's looking at somebody. In reality, after basic training, you have separate shower stalls, and you go your separate ways. I just don't remember the privacy-shower thing coming up that much.

You mentioned that you were on deployment during the introduction of "don't ask, don't tell."

LB: I arrived at my unit, the 1-7th ADA Battalion in Kaiserslautern, Germany, in March of '92, and in July of '92, a couple of days before my birthday, I got a call at 2 o'clock in the morning on a Sunday. Our whole Patriot unit was on a plane within twelve hours and landed in Kuwait and got set up. We didn't even know what it was all about. We were just going. We started getting information en route. And we stayed there for 179 days, and they kept telling us different stories about why and when we were going to get out.

This was during the final months of Clinton's presidential campaign, and I was surrounded by people who just thought he was the devil. They were really wound up because he had promised that the first order of business was gonna be to lift the ban. People were just up in arms about this. And I had always heard homophobic comments, the word "fag" used and stuff like that. But after it came up in this context of the presidential campaign, it really took on an obsessional quality.

And I had this battery commander. He was kind of an older fellow, Vietnam Vet, infantry combat. And he started to say, "You know, we're gonna have to issue soap-on-a-rope to all the GIs because it won't be safe to bend over in the shower anymore."

And every time the subject of President Clinton came up, he would just say "soap-on-a-rope" and think this was hysterically funny. I might have thought it was moderately funny in a different context, but in that context, what leaders need to understand is that when they joke like that they're giving people license to do what they please. The leadership, in doing something like that, sends a signal that it's okay to beat up fags, it's okay to make even more derogatory comments than they would make.

So on the gay issue, it was a really dangerous atmosphere. I don't know if anyone on this deployment was gay. I mean, this was a ninety-person Patriot battery, and we pretty much kept to ourselves. And whatever atmosphere that commander set, that was pretty much your whole world.

I was the only female in any position of authority. There were a couple of female E5's, but I was the only female officer. The officers pretty much had to keep to themselves. On a deployment, you can't get too chummy with the enlisted: It just leads to trouble. I did get hit on while I was there, even keeping a respectful distance. Somebody just out and out propositioned me.

A woman or a man?

LB: A man. He was my mess sergeant. I didn't tell anyone this story for many years afterward because I just felt so badly about how things turned out. But I'll tell you now.

We were driving out to the site one day. This guy was an E5. And I knew in the back of my mind he was married, but it just didn't click. Obviously, I could see there was a lot of hanky-panky going on in the unit, so I was already sort of conditioned to thinking this was the sort of thing that goes on during deployments.

And we were driving along. And just out of left field—I can't even remember what he said—he very directly propositioned me. It wasn't lewd or anything, but he was like, "You know, I was wondering if we could get together sometime?" And I said, "Well, I think that would be a very bad idea because I'm in your chain of command, and we're on a deployment, and you're married, and I'm not interested."

And he said, "Well, there's a lot of places we could go to hide." And I said, "Look, I don't think you're getting this: I'm flattered. I'm not interested. Please don't bring it up again."

And I was already worried because I thought, *What happens if you get hit on and turn it down?* I did outrank him, but I thought, *Is this the norm for people to just start getting it on? And if I don't get it on with him, are they gonna start saying that I'm a lesbian?*

So I didn't quite know how to handle it. And I was really hoping that we would put the issue to rest, and I would never tell anyone and just put it out of my mind. I also felt like it didn't *offend* me. I didn't feel sexually harassed. And he didn't bring it up again. So I just put the incident out of my mind.

And a couple of weeks later, one of his female subordinates came forward with an allegation of sexual harassment, that he was making lewd comments to her all the time and wouldn't stay off her case. And at that point, I went to the first sergeant—because this woman had gone to the first sergeant—and I said, "You know, this guy? I could see him being capable of that because it was really ballsy of him to say what he said to me."

My commander was just livid with me. He took me into

his room and counseled me for an hour. I don't even know what he was talking about, most of it. He was angry that I had gone to the first sergeant before I had gone to him, and now I understand.

And he was angry that I didn't report it to him because this was a UCMJ offense.[1] He just kept going on and on about how I'm letting the sergeant think that way about me, and now all those men are thinking that way about me. Like the whole thing was my fault!

Then I was taken over to Camp Doha one day because my battery commander really wanted to discipline this guy for hitting on me, and he wanted someone with serious UCMJ authority. He wanted to go to this colonel who was technically in charge of us. And I was introduced to a senior first lieutenant who told me this long story about how some major had hit on her, and how we have to prevent this from happening. I really couldn't decipher what her lecture was, but clearly nobody wanted to hear my side of anything. I mean, it was treated with such kid gloves.

The guy ended up not being punished for sexually harassing this subordinate because two other women in our unit rushed to his defense and said she was a liar and the whole thing just turned into a big *Jerry Springer* episode. I never knew what to make of it.

To this day, I feel bad. Had I come forward first and done something about it—I mean, it just didn't occur to me that if he was being that ballsy with me, he might be harassing lower enlisted subordinates. I feel like I let her down.

Well, you were also young.

LB: Yeah, I was young, but I was a second lieutenant. I was in charge of her. I was her platoon leader. I was supposed to take care of her.

It's so hard to figure out what is the code. How am I supposed to respond to this? And then, on top of that, just to be terrified to bring up anything that puts your sexuality on display because it might get people talking—"Well, she didn't do it with him. I wonder who she *would* do it with?" It just adds an extra level of anxiety to something that's already pretty frightening.

I've talked to women who've said, I turned so-and-so down, and then he started rumors that I was a lesbian. That didn't happen with you?

LB: I think there always were rumors that I was a lesbian; they just never rose to the level that anyone felt compelled to do anything. Who knows? Maybe I was investigated. I really have no idea. No investigation ever came to my attention. But I know there were times that people talked about me. I had a few friends that I was out to, and they would let me know if people were talking about me or speculating whether I was gay.

I lived in fear of having to pay back a $60,000 scholarship and getting a dishonorable discharge and being out of a job and having to come out to my parents. It just terrified me.

You had said that with "don't ask, don't tell" suddenly all people could talk about was gay men and lesbians in the military. During that time, did you deport yourself any differently to make yourself less suspect?

LB: I did grow my hair out. I had very long hair when I was in the military—now it's very short—because I think people just associated short hair with dykes. I don't know if that was as much a response to "don't ask, don't tell" because I was pretty afraid of being out even before. But afterwards, it was like, you couldn't even make a gay-friendly comment.

I remember one night I was in the command post, the CP, working these twenty-four-hour shifts in Kuwait, and these two infantry soldiers came in off of guard duty. They loved to hang out in the CP because it was air-conditioned. So, it was just me and this commo[2] specialist, this Spec-4, and these two infantry guys came in and they just started going on and on about gays and Clinton—"that faggot draft-dodger and his lesbian wife"—and just on and on.

I felt I couldn't tell them that their jokes were inappropriate without bringing suspicion on myself, so I just played it like, "This isn't your duty station. If you're done, sign out and go over to the other barracks." So they kind of looked at me askance—I think even that got them thinking, *She's soft on gays*—and they left.

Things got very quiet, and I was reading this book. And the specialist said, "Thanks, ma'am." And I said, "Don't thank me. They were annoying me." And he said, "Yeah. Those guys." And I thought, *I really don't want to talk about what just happened.* And there was a long pause and he said, "Well, the thing is, my cousin is gay." And I put the book down. I go, "Really?" And then this look of fear came over his face. He said, "Well, you can't tell anybody because they'll think I'm that way, too."

This gives you a glimpse of what kind of atmosphere it was that an obviously straight married man with a gay cousin was afraid for people to know that he had a gay cousin, that he thought something might happen to him, that they would hassle him or beat him up or something.

And, of course, we've seen that that could happen.

LB: Oh, yeah. Absolutely.

In a combat branch isn't there an enormous animosity toward women in general and anything that could be perceived as feminine or femme?

LB: Well, I'm not sure I'd say an *enormous* animosity. I mean, a lot of women succeed quite well in air defense. But I think the problem is the military too often motivates troops by appealing to their masculinity. Supervisors tend to push their people hard by saying what you're doing is really manly. Guys who didn't do enough push-ups would be called a faggot. Anyone who screwed up something would be called a faggot. So, there's a real bias against anything they think is feminine, and I guess they think that gay men are feminine. Most of the gay male veterans I know are quite macho. There's nothing *queeny* about these guys.

It's funny because within that paradigm, lesbians would probably be less threatening to them than straight women. They almost comfort themselves by thinking that any woman who could succeed in this branch is obviously a dyke. But there's just always this simmering resentment.

I don't think the officers are as much a problem. The officers do a pretty good job of treating men and women equally, other than these weird incidents of sexual harassment and stuff. But among the troops, they make these snide comments like, "Air defense isn't a real combat branch anymore." The upshot is that because there are women, it must not be a combat branch anymore. To have anything in the unit that they think is feminine somehow detracts from their image of themselves as being manly.

There's not really an animus against lesbians per se. It's just that the men seem to be really caught up in their issue of gay men and bending over in the shower. That's their fixation. It's almost like they forget the lesbians exist.

I think that some of the straight women in my unit are probably not crazy about lesbians because they don't like being stereotyped as lesbians. That's fair. I just wish their animosity was directed more at sexism rather than lesbians. Female athletes are often in the same boat. We shouldn't presume that people are lesbians just because they're in the military or they play rugby or they play professional basketball.

No one should have their sexuality questioned simply because they're in a traditionally male profession.

It's a curious thing, though, that being considered lesbian is still such a put-down.

LB: In the military it would cost you your job. But people still cling to this traditional notion of a lesbian as somebody who's not attractive enough to get a guy. A lot of my heterosexual female colleagues were constantly trying to convince themselves that they were still attractive to men, that there's nothing wrong with them, that they can go out and be a gung ho officer, march around in boots, fire a weapon with the best of them; but you know, at night, they're just like any other gal. They need what a gal needs, and they're just crazy about boys. They seem like they're on the defensive, like they have to convince themselves that they're "normal."

It's that supercompensation. You see it in female bodybuilders, too, who need to wear their hair very big and put lipstick on.

LB: Exactly. So in the midst of all that, there's animosity of straight women toward lesbians because the presence of a lesbian in their ranks exacerbates the stereotypes. It's like, "Oh, great, this is exactly what everyone says about us, and now this one is going around advertising it."

We were talking earlier about raging heterosexual hormones. The presence of lesbians should lessen the competition for male attention. Instead of bashing us, heterosexually inclined females could say, "Oh, well. More for me!"

LB: That's right. I got along great with most of my female colleagues, and I think they sensed that I was not competition for them, whether they knew why or not. They just sort of sensed I'm not on the make. I'm not after your guy. I'm not gonna try to be prettier than you. I'm not the competition. They occasionally took a passing interest in why I didn't pick up on the guys. You know, we'd go out to these German discotheques and stuff. But they basically left me alone. I was just their pal.

We've said that in combat branches, which are all about masculinity, the feminine is despised. But most lesbians in the military aren't femme lesbians: They're more on the butch end of the continuum. Why, if we're the perfect soldier, if we fit that stereotype, are we cashiered from the services in such great numbers?

LB I think it's a way of taking out women. It's a way of keeping women in line. If you act too feminine, the troops won't respect you. They won't think of you as just like any other officer or soldier. But if you get too masculine—or too good at your job—then they start calling you a dyke. They don't even care if you're really a lesbian. It's just a way of keeping people in line.

I think this is all very subconscious. I don't think anyone plots to do this. I just think that we make it very difficult for women to succeed in positions of authority, and that's not just the military. That's also true in law firms. Any power CEO or something. If a woman is too aggressive, then she's a bitch. And if she's not, then she's pushover. It sets you up not to succeed.

There was a chaplain in our unit who once said to me, "You know what I really like about you? You're a really good officer and yet you're really feminine." He was paying me a compliment. What does that tell you? Why are these two mutually exclusive attributes? Somehow you've managed to be a good officer and feminine at the same time. It's not an animus toward lesbians. It's an animus toward women. And the fact that you can accuse someone of being a lesbian and ruin her career—it's just too tempting not to use.

There was a time when I was competing with another lieutenant to become the executive officer of the battery. And I really wanted it, mostly because I wanted to work with the battery commander. Another guy, a West Point grad, wanted it, too, and he was competing with me. And the battery commander actually preferred me, but the battalion commander wanted this guy, Rick, to get it.

So the battalion commander and my battery commander battled for a long time. And in the midst of all this, I ended up having a conversation with this guy Rick's wife. I was thinking about coming out to her, and she told me that Rick had made her give up all her friendships with gay people because he was just so homophobic. He just thought that was so wrong, that they shouldn't associate with gay people. And then she kinda said, "Well, what were you going to tell me?" And I was like, "Nothing. Nothing important."

I remember being quite fearful. I thought, *All Rick has to do is start a rumor that I'm a lesbian or renew the rumors that were already circulating, and I could be out of there. If he wants this slot badly enough, he can take me out.*

That didn't happen.

LB: No, it didn't happen. I was probably a bit paranoid. But it was within the realm of possibility of things that could happen. It's all too easy to get rid of the competition that way.

Are gay soldiers at all safer under "don't ask, don't tell"? Statistics seem to show that there are a greater number of discharges.

LB: Well, in some ways it's better. In some ways it's worse. In the past, commanders had a lot more discretion. If your commander used his discretion wisely, people would stay in. I know people whose commanders in the '80s were quite supportive, who didn't care. Certainly in the Vietnam era, people didn't care. I mean, if you got caught in the act of sodomy, maybe they would care. Even going back to the Korean War, World War II, there were people who did not care. So if you had either a progressive-minded commander or a pragmatist who said, "I need this person," you were fine. If not, you could get yourself in big trouble. You could end with a dishonorable discharge. Even if you didn't, just being charged with homosexuality was a much bigger stigma than it is now.

Now the chances are much less of suffering severe consequences. You'll probably get an honorable discharge. You may or may not have to pay back your scholarship money. Prosecutions for sodomy have become almost nonexistent. But because the discretion is gone, everyone who comes out loses their job. And I think that's why the discharge figures, in part, are going up.

And they're going up for other reasons. People are more attuned to gay issues, and that makes it somewhat harder to be closeted. Thirty years ago, somebody might have thought that I was an eccentric old spinster, just a bachelorette or something. Now they look at me, and I'm not married, and I'm 34, and they think, *Short hair? Yeah, she's probably a lesbian.* People think about it more and ask about it more.

You said that it took an enormous amount of psychic energy to stay closeted and that if you hadn't been so focused on staying sub rosa, undercover, you might have used those energies elsewhere.

LB: I was just completely focused on my career. I did well. But in terms of stress and being able to handle stress, well, I think I would have been a more centered person. I would have had a better time. I would have been closer to people in my unit. It just breaks my heart that some of these people would have been my best friends for life, and I just feel like they knew nothing about me.

That's one of the attractions of the military, that sense of family, of unity. But to derive that benefit you have to be known.

LB: Exactly. And I just don't think straight people understand the effort and the level of deception that goes into convincing them that you're straight. It just means you can never be honest about what you did over the weekend. You can't be honest about why you don't like this guy that they're fixing you up with. I just felt deceptive every moment of every day. I've caught up with some of my former military colleagues and I've made a point of coming out to them, and they've all been supportive.

In the 1940s, it was decided that the services would be integrated— white and black together. When the chiefs of staff bridled and said, "We're not going to have this," Harry Truman essentially said, "You'll do what I say, or there's the door." Why doesn't that happen today, and what would it take?

LB: You'd have to have a commander-in-chief with a fair amount of integrity and an understanding of the military. I think Clinton's big failing is that he didn't understand the military. I think he also underestimated Congress. You know, there's a lot of reasons "don't ask, don't tell" happened. But you've got to have somebody who has the courage to do the right thing.

In terms of the American public, I think you're facing more inertia than opposition to gays in the military. Most polls show that seventy-five percent of people believe the ban should be lifted, but they're not angry enough about it to write to Congress. Even some of my liberal, very gay-friendly friends don't understand how bad "don't ask, don't tell" is, so nobody is incensed enough to write to their congressional representative, which is what needs to happen.

But if you look at the racial integration order, the vast

majority of American society didn't support blacks being integrated into the military at that time. What that experience shows us is that you don't have to wait for everyone in the military to be gay-tolerant for gays and straights to work openly and well in a unit together.

There are still racists in the military. There was a kid in our unit, a lower enlisted soldier. He had come and gone by the time I got to the unit, but I always heard about him. He was infamous because he was a Nazi. He was a neo-Nazi, white supremacist, had a swastika in his room, handed our literature, talked about it in his spare time.

And I had an African-American platoon sergeant who had had this kid in his platoon, and I asked him one day, "How did that make you feel?" He said, "Didn't bother me. He always said, 'Yes, sergeant. No, sergeant.' Absolutely polite. He showed up on time, boots always shined. He was a good kid. Why would I have a problem with him?" I think people would eventually have the same attitude toward gays. It's just not that big of a deal.

People in the military are quite used to being thrown in with a diverse group of people and, at any given point in time, there's somebody in your unit who just annoys the living daylights out of you. And you just have to deal with them. So, you know, military folks are more able than most Americans to deal with the situations.

The gay ban, when it's finally lifted, it's going to be a hiccup. I know that the top brass is opposed. When you're in charge of creating order out of chaos, you're pretty much opposed to anything that's gonna make your life even temporarily more chaotic. It's just sort of a knee-jerk reaction: "We've got things just the way we like them, please don't change it." But when someone says, "Do it anyway," you just do it and you get over it.

Detractors might say, "The military isn't the place to engage in social engineering."

LB: The military is unavoidably a social experiment. It's always throwing people together who'd otherwise never interact with each other. Different classes, races, genders. It's an ongoing social experiment, and there's always some bubbling cauldron of drama going on. I had Satan worshippers in my unit and Wicca practitioners and born-again Christians and neo-Nazis, and they all just got along.

You mentioned that it took you a long time to recover from your tour of duty.

LB: I didn't realize how much it was damaging me, to be in a homophobic environment like that and to deny such an essential part of my identity. The military's not a day job. It's your whole world while you're in it. To deny something about yourself—it's not like hiding it from your colleagues at work. It's like hiding it from your family.

Nothing particularly bad happened to me. I feel like I don't have the right to complain, compared to somebody who was investigated, who was kicked out.

A lot of vets are very wounded. I'm very involved in American Veterans for Equal Rights, and I'm always trying to get more gay vets involved. It's pretty hard. I co-chaired the Servicemembers Legal Defense Network dinner one year and stood up in front of 600 people and said, "I'm a lesbian former Army officer," and got a round of applause just for that. And it was very cathartic for me. But a lot of people really can't do that yet.

Retirees in particular, I think they convince themselves that they could lose their retirement pension if they came out as gay. I really think it's a three percent possibility and ninety-seven percent in their heads. They've just convinced themselves because they've lived like that for so long that something bad will happen if they come out. Then it's so cathartic when they finally do.

It really does wound you to live in that environment. A lot of people come out with the same experience, and it's not because they're hypersensitive or they just can't play the game. They have bad reactions to it because it's a bad policy.

Notes

1. Uniform Code of Military Justice, the regulations governing servicemembers' conduct.

2. Army slang for "communications."

About Face

This Army NCO married a man to deflect the daily barbs and divert what she feared could be a full-on queer bashing.

I was at units that could not have functioned without their queer soldiers. If they'd have put all of us out, there would have been no personnel left!

I remember a fag cook we had in a hospital unit. He used to get up earlier than the other cooks (Wow! That's early!) and make extra batches of cookies. This was done because, in his words, "I know y'all pigs."

He was the reigning drag empress in our town. He represented the bar at the state and regional drag queen-a-rama. He wore hose with his Class B's. We loved him, and he loved us, straight or gay.

A new private was assigned to our unit. This boy was making the rounds informing any who would listen that he believed a certain cook to be a faggot. We assured him that not only did this "news" have no bearing on our mission, but we had the situation under control and that if he enjoyed eating regularly he would shut his trap or become very hungry.

—A.G. Flynn

Dinah Shore Made Me Do It

Shalanda Baker

Austin-born Shalanda Baker was 17 when she was appointed to the United States Air Force Academy in 1994. A star student and competitive athlete, she was attracted to its "combined rigorous physical and mental challenges."

Baker didn't know she was gay, she says, and "don't ask, don't tell" hadn't been as much as a blip on her radar. When her awakening occurred, in her junior year, it happened on the rugby field.

"My sister's best friend is a gay male," said the second-year law student, now 27. "And after I came out, she was like, 'Well, we all knew!' But I think I was pretty naive going in."

Baker graduated in 1998 with a BS in political science and spent her first post-Academy year on recruiting duty in Dallas. From there she was assigned to the Los Angeles Air Force Base, where she worked as an executive officer in acquisitions.

Three years into her five-year commitment she realized she couldn't remain closeted: "The don't ask, don't tell" policy made her very existence—barring any conduct—against the rules, and the emotional price of hiding had become too high.

She came out, and the Air Force showed her the door.

Following an administrative hearing, Uncle Sugar presented the bill: $48,000 remaining on an original educational tab of $150,000. Baker has appealed.

"This is my inspiration to go to law school and become a lawyer," she says. "The law has so much power to oppress or free, and it affected my life so greatly. I wasn't as confident in my Air Force attorney as I probably could have been. I think he couldn't get his head around the nuance of the policy. He was a straight guy from Colorado who probably thought that I should have just kept my mouth closed anyway."

* * *

When you arrived at the Academy, you said you had no idea that you were a lesbian.

SB: I may have had an inkling, but it was so far removed it was not in my conscious mind at all. I dated guys my first two years pretty solidly, and then my junior year was when I figured it all out.

What happened that pivotal junior year?

SB: You know, I'm not really sure. I think it was rugby. [*Laughs*] I was exposed to a lot of different people, and I realized that was an option for me in a way that I hadn't thought of before. I was like, *Huh, maybe I kinda like girls.*

We often played teams from the Colorado area and also the Colorado Springs area, and we traveled a lot to other cities and played tournaments. You know the rugby community has a lot of lesbians. That's just sort of a safe place for a lot of women, and that's how I ended up meeting my first girlfriend, in fact. She had played on an opposing team, and she was out of the rugby scene but still kind of around, and she kind of wooed me. And I was like, *No, this can't happen!* [*Laughs*] But it was too late. [*Laughs*]

This is classic: The lesbian got you on the soccer field, the rugby field, the softball diamond.

SB: [*Laughs*] She got me.

So this happens to you, and you have signed this paper and checked the "no" box, and there you are in the Academy, and what are you feeling?

SB: I was definitely feeling pretty paranoid. You know, in a way I still had that sort of 19-year-old risky sort of outer being, and I was like, "Oh, whatever," you know. I'm not doing anything wrong, really. But in my heart of hearts, I was definitely petrified. This was when there was a lot of undercurrent of "don't ask, don't tell," and that would be a joke. We didn't really know what it meant, so we just threw it around. Like if someone would do something "gay," we'd be like "Oh, don't ask, don't tell." *I* wouldn't. I realized that it was a possibility that I'd be seen.

What might be something that would show up on somebody's radar to which he or she would respond, "Oh, don't ask, don't tell"?

SB: Well, for example, it became apparent that the same woman had shown up to several of my games. If someone had seen me in town with this woman, there would be sort of a chatter or a buzz about that, and that would sort of trigger the "don't ask, don't tell" [chant], sort of tongue-in-cheek, like "ha ha ha."

But as far as cadets were concerned, we weren't necessarily

into turning people in for homosexual behavior. It was more of an administrative issue. And people may have known or may have had suspicions, but in general my classmates wouldn't have made any statements. But I was afraid of the administration, for sure.

Is that disinclination to turn each other in, or make an issue of it, representative of that generation, or were you just with a cool bunch of folks?

SB: I absolutely think it was a general feeling amongst my peers, and not just my circle. My circle contained a lot of people that knew for sure. My rugby team did find out at the end of my junior year, and they actually made a vow of silence. And it was kind of bizarre. Sweet, but bad that they had to do that. [*Laughs*] But I think, as a general rule, the folks in my year and younger don't find it an issue.

How did the rugby team find out about your relationship?

SB: My rugby team went to England my junior year, for spring break. And we actually ended up playing a team in the countryside. But we'd all been drinking a lot by the end of the day, and apparently I'd been dancing with this one woman all night, and people were like, "What's going on with that? Why is she dancing with a woman? That's so weird." And she walked me on the bus on our way out and gave me a goodbye kiss. And this was like in front of my entire team. [*Laughs*]

The next day they had a little meeting without me—and I was the captain, actually, which is kind of funny. I found this out through a close friend. But she said they all decided, "We know she's gay, so what are we going to do?" And they said, "We're going to make it a non-issue." And that's what happened.

191

Were there rumors about you, outside your team?

SB: Not that I know of. I was actually in a high-profile position on campus as well. I was a member of staff, so a lot of people knew of me and knew me. I think because I had this history of dating men it wasn't an issue. It just never flew in my face as a big deal at all.

I actually had a mentor in Colorado Springs who was a former Army sergeant. And she kind of took me under her wing and just provided a safe space outside of school. She introduced me to a lot of people in her community who were also in the military, and that sort of opened my eyes a little bit.

One of my really close friends graduated a year ahead of me at the Academy, and we now talk about people that have subsequently come out, and it's just an interesting thing to realize that we were and are everywhere.

Once you realized, "Oh, I'm a lesbian," did you become more circumspect, more watchful of what you said and did, or did that not have any affect on your deportment?

SB: Oh, my gosh! You know, it's interesting. Despite the close, close quarters of the Academy and the sort of feeling that everyone's always in your business, I felt fairly safe there. And I think it was because we all sort of grew up together with this common goal, this general purpose. The Academy has a lot of faults—a *lot* of faults—but for the most part I felt safe.

But when I graduated and was released into the larger world—I think in general people go through a kind of culture shock—but to be trying to find community within the gay and lesbian community, and also figuring out how I was going to be an officer at 21, I think I just had a lot of stress. I was like, *How much do I engage in this military piece without giving away everything that I am?* And a large part of that was my lesbian identity. I was so careful.

People would always ask me, "Hey, L.T., why aren't you married?" "Do you want to come over for this?" "Do you want to come over for that?" And I had a long-term girl-friend at the time who I was just petrified they would find out about.

I definitely lied. I said, "Well, I'm not interested." Or, "I'm busy." "What did you do this weekend, L.T.?" You know, I would make up things because I just never wanted to be questioned.

It was so ironic. I mean, upon becoming an officer and pinning on my rank, I took an oath and said I'll protect the country. And to realize that I was having to lie so that I could be protected, and that all people are not equal—at least in the eyes of the military—I was definitely angry, and I felt a lot of shame. The internalized homophobia took so long to get rid of. I ultimately became angry and very resentful toward the Air Force.

Would people around you say things that were homophobic in nature?

SB: Yes, definitely. One of the incidents I recall pretty vividly happened when I was recruiting. We had a head recruiter in the office who was in charge of all the other recruiters, and I remember him saying, "That's dumber than two girls kissing," or something. And I was just like, *Whoa.* You know, like he could joke in that way without anyone questioning him. And I felt personally attacked by that.

And after I went through my board and I was discharged and everything, one of my supervisors who was a colonel came up to me as I was sort of clearing out my desk, and he put his hand on my shoulder and he said, "Shalanda, I wish you had told me sooner about this because I would have introduced you to a nice young man." And I was just like, *You have no idea.* You know? *You have no clue.* So that was definitely the general mood.

I mean, people could say whatever they wanted and not get questioned.

What's the cost of the closet, in terms of spontaneity and that kind of thing?

SB: Oh, my gosh. The cost is so huge. I think you're always wondering if there's six degrees of separation between you and someone you know in the community who may know someone in your office. So you're always sort of holding back about what you do in the civilian sector. And then on the other side, you never want anyone over to your house. You very rarely take on close friends in the Air Force. And so it sort of undercuts that community aspect, and you end up feeling so isolated.

That's really one of the selling points of the services: "Come join our big, happy family". But you can't really be a part of it.

SB: And you can't really be a part of the other community either because what if you're at gay pride and your picture gets taken and you end up on the front page of the newspaper? You're always thinking about where you are, who you're associating yourself with, and all of it. And at 21 [*laughs*], after four years of the Academy, that was not something that I looked forward to.

It's a very interesting thing: You're 21, but you have the burden of an officer, and the military kind of ages one. You feel much more grave and grim than the ordinary 21-year-old.

SB: Absolutely. In the Air Force, in the noncombat roles at least, I think it's a little less stressful, but I was still under a lot more stress than my peers in the civilian sector. And to have [being gay] over my head was certainly an added stress.

And many of your peers working at various corporations had employment protections and couldn't be fired for being gay, as you could.

SB: I think you get so sucked into the structure, the culture, that you forget there's another world, and there are different ways to be in that world. Until I started doing my own research, and until I actually started dating someone in San Francisco, I had no idea. I just thought that was the way it was going to be: It sucks to be gay. And that's just the way it is! [*Laughs*]

In San Francisco, I realized there was definitely a community that existed, and that it was normal to be a lesbian, and people accepted that, and you weren't a societal leper, which is sort of how the military paints the homosexual issue. In my mind, that is sort of what it had become. So going to San Francisco really opened my eyes to the larger community, and it wasn't an issue. Gays and lesbians were highly functioning individuals within the economic sector, and there was no conflict as to their jobs or anything like that. It was definitely a huge contrast from my day to day. [*Laughs*]

And I'm not talking about overly generous open displays of affection, but subtle things like a kiss on the cheek or a goodbye when I wasn't left looking over my shoulder. That made me realize, *Wow, this is a different way of life.* Whereas in Los Angeles, I wasn't seeing anyone, but I definitely was paranoid—just about being me—which is a really sad situation.

Would it take you a while to decompress when you went into this "new" environment?

SB: Yes. It took me a while to decompress, and I think I experienced more trauma going back. Often I would fly in on a Monday, at 6:30 A.M., and there was a shuttle that would take me from the airport straight to work. And I would just transform: The uniform was on, and I was back at my desk being the executive officer again. I had just left my girlfriend maybe two hours prior to that, so it was definitely an intense, transitional, dual life, for sure. A lot of people talk about living two lives, and I definitely felt that was the case.

And nine months later you came out.

SB: Yes. In June I wrote a letter to my supervisor, expressing my sexual orientation, which is a statement of homosexuality. My supervisor was a civilian, a longtime government employee. He was the equivalent of a one-star general, and we had a pretty close relationship because I was his person in charge of operational things.

And I went into his office and I had the letter in my hand, in an envelope. And I said, "Sir, this is a statement of homosexuality." And he threw up his arms, and he said, "Don't give it to me! Don't give it to me!" And he said, "Close my door, close my door." He was just like, "I don't want this."

It was a bittersweet sort of conversation because on one hand he was saying, "You're doing a great job. There's no need for this. Do you understand what the potential repercussion will be?" And, on the other hand, I had, of course, considered everything. I'd been in since I was 17. I'd worked hard through the Academy and earned my degree. That wasn't an easy chore by any stretch. I had served and done a good job. I knew what was at play. But my integrity was definitely more important than the potential things that I would lose.

Eventually I withdrew the letter. He wanted to give me more time to think about "my decision." And at that point a huge weight lifted because I knew that I was out.

Then I took about a week. It was a hard, hard week, you know. Long nights and early mornings. And finally one morning he hadn't come in yet. It was about 5:30 or 6 A.M., and I left the letter on his desk. I remember pretty clearly him walking by my desk after he had read it and looking me right in the eye and continuing to walk, almost as if at that point I was on my own, that was the decision I had made.

Was that decision the result of a slow wearing over time, or did something happen to prompt that?

SB: It was a slow and gradual wearing-down process. And actually I feel as if there is a gap in my story. And I want to go back because I wouldn't be honest if I didn't give you the whole picture.

When I graduated from the Academy, I was with a woman who I stayed with through my recruiting year and then through my first year in L.A. And when I was in L.A., she actually became abusive. It became a really dramatic situation. We were living together there, and I was trying to break up with her, and she was really having none of it. It was just a crazy time for me: I was going to night school to get my MBA, working a lot, and having to deal with her.

At one point I had a black eye from some sort of altercation we had, and I was actually about to call the police because she was frantic, and it was just a crazy evening. And she just looked at me and said, "What are you going to do, L.T., tell the cops your girlfriend beat you up?"

At that point I knew I had very little leverage in that relationship because of my military status, and that was when I started thinking about the danger of my situation.

I would go to work with these injuries, black eyes, and people would ask what happened, and I would just attribute them to rugby. I actually do think a supervisor had a suspicion that something was going on. She sent me to a doctor on a couple of occasions. And she was just like, you know, "Are you okay?" She ended up telling me a story about her daughter who was in an abusive relationship, and I think it was her way of being like, "If something's going on, you should say something." Ironically, I couldn't say anything to her about it because it could jeopardize my career. Eventually we broke up. I came out almost a year later.

You tendered your letter in June, and you went before an adminis-
trative board of five officers—all colonels, all white, all men, except for
one—in November. Describe that experience.

SB: I really didn't have a lot to do with the board's proceedings. No one cross-examined me: I just gave an unsworn
statement—twenty minutes of just my story, from high school
through the Academy, through my abusive relationship,
through my statement. And the colonels on the board were riv-
eted. The woman was crying. I was crying: I was emotional
because it was a huge moment for me.

And the judge, who was also a colonel—and this I learned
afterward—went to the government, the Air Force attorney,
and said, "I know how this is going to turn out. No need to
argue it. We can end this right now. She obviously has a good
reason for making her statement. I think it's legitimate. I'm
okay with not letting them deliberate."

And the government's attorney was this young whipper-
snapper—this was his first case to argue—who said, "No, I
want to argue it." The folks had their own perception of my
debt to service, and what I owe. But he apparently was more
persuasive.

And I recall pretty vividly the attorney for the government
looking at me and then looking at the board and saying, "Yes,
clearly she's articulate. And she benefited from four years of
our educating her. And for that she deserves to pay."

And I was floored. I was shocked beyond belief. I thought
it was such a low blow, given the reality of the situation and
given the irrelevance of that.

I've thought back to that moment a lot, and I haven't ever
come to terms that it was about race until just now. Here's a
white board, all white colonels who presumably paid their dues,
whatever that meant to them, and they had probably seen
some stuff and worked hard to get where they were. And here
I was, someone who had been given an opportunity to excel

and ostensibly been handed things. [*Laughs*] Clearly, you know, I had been born with a frickin' silver spoon in my mouth. [*Laughs*] Been handed things at the Academy, and now I wanted to get away without paying my debt in the way that they had. And being an African-American, I'm sure that was even more clear, because how would I have made it, how would I be articulate had it not been for the Academy? You know? [*Laughs*] I feel like all that was in play in the one moment.

"Here's this 'girl.' Look at all we've done for her and what she did with it. And we have taken her and educated her and see...

SB: Right. I heard it to mean that I was trying to get out of my commitment, that I was trying to take the money and run, the education and run, and that I owed for what gifts the military had bestowed upon me. The fact that I was willing to continue, but for this policy, should have spoken for itself.

I had a lot of pride in the school I went to and the work that I put into that. And I knew that I was risking losing it and being estranged from that. But I never wanted to lose that pride in that common experience that I shared with so many people.

Did you lose it?

SB: You know, I did for a little while. The Academy has this ethos of just like, "Suck it up!" You know? "Do it!" And I felt I had sold my classmates out by making my statement. But I also knew that their burden wasn't as heavy as mine. If I could just go to work everyday and have a picture of who I was seeing, who was important in my life, on my desk, that would be a much different scenario than having to lie about where I've been on the weekend. And hide behind every corner. I came to understand that. But for a while there was definitely a lot of shame around it, sort of self-blame, self-deprecation that went on there.

How would having your girlfriend's photo on your desk be a bar to good order and discipline? How would that affect unit cohesion?

SB: [*Laughs*] It wouldn't at all. I think there probably are people who have their partners' pictures on their desk, who are gay, and who lie about who they are. The job I was doing was about my competence, about my ability to think and do the job well. There was no time at which my personal life should have come into the equation.

The response on the other side is, "Well, then, why did you do it?" And it's because I knew if someone saw me outside of work, with my partner or whomever, they could then pursue it. That was what created the jeopardy. It wasn't anything that happened at work. Because, you know, it was all about getting the job done, and about business, and I was definitely all for that. I couldn't care less if someone was married: That was their business. You know, whatever. We could talk about it, but that's irrelevant to whether or not they could do their job. [*Laughs*] And I would ask to be treated the same way.

Was there ever a point after you tendered that letter that you thought, Well, maybe it'll go another way. Maybe they'll retain me?

SB: I did. I knew of Margarethe Cammermeyer, that case, when they actually decided, at least for a time, that it was not a big deal. I thought maybe it'll be okay because I was doing a great job. But ultimately they decided I couldn't stay in as an out lesbian. [*Laughs*]

When I ended up coming out, there was a retired major who was then a civilian, and on my last day on base she pulled me aside and she was like, "Hey, I just want to talk to you for a little bit."

I knew she was gay. I'd seen her at a rugby game of mine,

and the "head nod" occurred. And she pulled me into her office, and she said, "Hey, kiddo. I just want to tell you that I'm so proud of you."

And it just floored me because knowing that she was a lesbian, and knowing that she had served for twenty years, I thought that she would feel some sense of betrayal that I had come out with some knowledge that I could be discharged. She might think that I sold out, that I could stick it out as a dyke when she had.

And she was totally grateful. She said, "When Clinton did this, we all looked at each other and we wanted to say, "Hey, we're here, we're gay, we're not going to hide." She said, "Of course that didn't happen, but you showed tremendous courage and did something I could never do."

A friend inside the Beltway who knows many lesbian generals and colonels says that they are perfectly happy to have secret monthly brunches and will never come out. Should they?

SB: Wow! It's such an individual decision. For me, it was really hard to accept the military's understanding of who I was. And I refuse to. I think I knew, based on my childhood foundation, which was liberal, and knowing what I did about San Francisco and the fact that there are large communities of gays and lesbians everywhere, that it's okay to be gay and out and you can do a good job without that becoming an issue. And to accept the idea that I should live in secret was not a possibility once I understood the policy.

And yet, your friend the major could weather that for twenty years.

SB: She could. And there's a funny little part of that story. She was sort of tearing up as she was telling me, but one of her supervisors knew that she was gay, and when she went to every lieutenant colonel board, it came up. And it came up in a way that wasn't obvious, but it was like someone was impeding her career progress. So she retired as a major. She had many opportunities to be promoted, and she was a great officer. But she wasn't [promoted]. It was really a sad, sad thing.

And that told me that no matter what sort of good will my civilian supervisor had toward me, ultimately someone could undermine my career anyway. So his trying to protect me while I was under his care for a year or two was really not going to help me in the long run, if I wanted to be a career officer.

I'm thinking of that old Air Force recruiting slogan, "Aim high!" Unless you're gay.

SB: Right! [*Laughs*] I know it's not funny, but the ironies just continue to rear their heads.

Well, it's not funny, but it is absurd. What else are you going to do, jump off of a building?

SB: Some do. I was at the point of pretty much, you know, going crazy at 23. It was pretty ridiculous. I'll tell you the straw that broke the camel's back for me, the thing that actually made me come out. I mean, I went through the abusive relationship. I stayed in and continued to do a good job and had this long-distance relationship going. And my mom came out, actually for a week, and I took off with her. We went to San Francisco and hung out.

When I came back home, I had a voice-mail from a friend who had e-mailed me while I was away. My friends didn't really use my work e-mail. I mean, people had it, but they knew they weren't really supposed to be using it. And she had e-mailed me something about Dinah Shore, the golf tournament party in Palm Springs. [*Laughs*]

And I don't know what she e-mailed me about, but because I was the executive officer, there was always someone checking my e-mail for important things, and so someone had seen the e-mail and wrote her back, "Lt. Baker isn't in the office this week; she'll get back to you as soon as she's back in."

And my friend, of course, freaks out, understanding the potential repercussions, and left me this long voice-mail: "I'm so sorry. I hope I didn't get you in trouble... I wrote you about Dinah Shore... Oh!" You know, just freaking out, freaking out. And of course that freaked me out.

And my mom was there, and I was just like, "Mom, I cannot do this." This is an e-mail about logistics for a lesbian golf tournament, and I'm thinking I might be discharged, or I'm thinking someone might find out I'm a lesbian. And that was actually the last straw because I realized how ridiculous it was for me to be constantly on edge.

Did your mom say, "You're African-American, you're a lesbian. They're going to eat you alive"?

SB: Not in so many words, but basically. I mean, when I came out to her initially she was like, "You're really making it hard on yourself, aren't you?" [*Laughs*] I don't think I got it all then, but I definitely have it now.

About Face

This Marine training-device technician repaired everything from motion picture projectors to flight simulators. It was harder to fix attitudes.

The base I was stationed at in California had quite a few lesbians. One wing of our barracks was quietly referred to as the "dyke wing" because almost everyone there was gay. Most people knew, but the general attitude was one of "Live and let live." As long as people were discrete and did their jobs, no one seemed to care much one way or the other.

It sounds derogatory, but it wasn't. It was, "Oh, yeah. That's the dyke wing." A fact. And they would just merrily go on their way.

Women, in general, weren't well received by a good portion of the men. Their concept was that we didn't belong in their Marine Corps. The younger Marines, the boots like ourselves, weren't really bad, but the older sergeants would egg them on. They tried hard not to take us very seriously, though we worked really hard to make sure they got the point. To them we were "WMs"—women Marines—not the real thing—or "BAMs"— broad-assed Marines. Not too many guys used that term, if they valued their family jewels. But we were just heckled and taunted constantly.

—Belle A. Pellegrino, PFC
USMC, 1968–1969

Sergeant Mom

Ziva Mataric

Rumors that Ziva Mataric was gay flew from her first months in the Air Force, though she herself was the last to discover it—two thirds into a twelve-year tour. From the gate, her fellows demanded she show her straight credentials.

"Basically I was told that I had to sleep with someone on the team to prove that I wasn't a lesbian," says the Chicago native, who joined the Air Force in 1986, becoming one of the first female members of its elite security forces, troops charged with guarding air bases and their assets.

"My answer to them was, 'Just because a woman sleeps with a man doesn't mean she is or is not a lesbian.'"

Mataric joined the military for the college money she could earn, and for a leg up and out of her inner-city upbringing. A "structure" person, she loved much of it: the travel, the diversity of its troops, the opportunity to immerse herself in other cultures.

She did not love the sexual harassment and discrimination, which she says were nearly nonstop. The former abated when she married, but her second-class status as a woman in a male-dominated environment continued until her mandatory separation—honorable with a Code C for homosexual admission—in 1997.

During her last three years of service, Mataric taught at the

Security Forces Academy for new recruits and also instructed Ground Combat Skills courses for junior NCOs and officers. Her male colleagues dubbed her the "Milk 'n' Cookies Instructor," she says, because her teaching style did not mirror their own grind-beneath-the-boot methods.

"A lot of people who haven't been in the military think it's a great place where they take care of their own," said Mataric, who left the Air Force an E6. "It could not be further from the truth. They eat their own."

* * *

I did not know [that I was gay when I enlisted]. I did not have desires for women. My mom speculates that harsh military life, being in an all-male career field, dealing with sexual harassment from the day I got in until the day I got out, made me sick of men and a lesbian. She wants to write a book called *The Military Turned My Daughter Gay*. And I'm like, I don't think so. I always go back and remind her of the time I was 6 years old and I got caught messing around with my girlfriend.

I can exactly tell you the day that I had a sense of myself as gay: I saw another military woman sitting on a truck. I was 26 or 25. And I looked at her in a way that was inappropriate for a woman to look at another woman.

What was different about that glance?

ZM: It hit below the belt. There were sexual feelings. I worked with this woman, and they developed. I was married, so I never acted on it, never showed anything. It was just a crush that I had on a woman that I wasn't supposed to have. My defense mechanism said that as soon as she leaves, all of these bad, sinful feelings will go away. This desire will go away, and I'll just go on with my normal heterosexual life. Sure enough, six months later she left, and then it was another woman, and another, and it just evolved from that.

You said that sexual harassment for you in the service began almost immediately.

ZM: It happened when I got to my first base and then just pretty much continued on until I got married. Once I got married, things kind of settled down. Then it wasn't sexual harassment. It was sexual discrimination, which was very prevalent all through my career.

How are those two things distinct?

ZM: Well, the sexual harassment was obvious. Like I said, on several occasions I was approached, before I was married. "Everyone's saying you're a lesbian. You gotta sleep with me, or you gotta sleep with someone on the team." And I would be walking to work—now, mind you, I'm an airman—and I would have NCOs walking behind me saying, "I would cheat on my wife, but Ziva won't let me." Or "Look at the butt on her." At one time I got physically grabbed by a male. We were out doing a check. I walked back to the vehicle to stow my weapon, and I turned around and he was right there. He grabbed me and attempted to kiss me, and I pushed him off. Those were distinct.

As far as the sexual discrimination goes, when I got promoted to staff sergeant, I was at an air base overseas. Women are not prominent in our career field still, and I made rank very quickly. I was in a room with the commander handing everybody his or her stripes for promotions, and he was going around shaking all the males' hands, saying, "Congratulations, great job, great job."

And when he got to me, he just handed me my stripes. He never shook my hand. He put his hand on my shoulder and said, "We've never had a female team leader at this base. You're going to have a tough time here." And my answer to him was, "I'm a staff sergeant, and if someone has a problem with my being a female, then *they're* gonna have a tough time, not me." I'm very strong-willed, and I don't have a problem standing up for myself. On numerous occasions I came toe to toe with people, which, in its own right, was detrimental to my career.

The commander really was saying, "You're going to have a hard time with me."

ZM: Yeah. I did not have any support at all in my career. Thankfully, in the beginning promotions are based more on your abilities to take a test and pass it, so I was making rank really fast. My initial belief was, if I can make rank really fast and I can get up there, I can change this. I can make it better for everybody. They would finally accept me and realize that I could do the job just as good as they can. What I found in reality was that the quicker I made rank, the harder it got.

The Air Force, among the services, is considered to be the "smart service." The more progressive people allegedly are there. But that doesn't sound like a fact.

ZM: Well, I believe it is a fact, just not in a male-dominated career field. I was working with a lot of Army Rangers. They had the little Army Ranger tabs on their shoulders. I had been in the military for ten years and never had a stitch of paperwork in my career, and then I was assigned to teach at the air base ground defense school, a school I had graduated from years before. And all of a sudden...

The course itself had for a number of years been taught by the Army at Fort Dix, and we had just taken it back from the Army and were starting to teach it at the Air Force level. But the instructor cadre was comprised of a lot of Army Rangers or

Air Force members who had gone to Army Ranger school—
Army Ranger wanna-bes, as I call them. So here I am on the
team of six or eight guys. I'm the only woman among these
Army Rangers. And in their opinion, women couldn't go into
combat, so we didn't have a right to be there.

We had a commander at the base who had served in
Vietnam, and he said right out in the middle of a commander's
call that he was going to break women. Those were his exact
words. He was going to break the women. Everybody heard it.
There was no denying exactly what he said. We had eight
female instructors at that base, and within a year and a half, all
eight were gone.

We actually filed an Inspector General's complaint.
There was an IG investigation file. The report we got back
from IG said, "Yes, it's sexual discrimination." But nothing
was ever done.

What kind of things did you witness?

ZM: Really stupid things. One of the women there had her
nails manicured, and nothing in the regulations states that a
woman cannot have her nails manicured. The only thing the
regulations state is that the nail polish has to be a conservative,
natural color. Well, the commander didn't like it, so he ordered
her to wear gloves. First he ordered her to take the nail polish
off and stop having manicured nails. She confronted him. So he
said, "Well, then you have to wear gloves. Everywhere you go,
you have to wear gloves." So she had to wear gloves everywhere
she went. It was just stupid rules, how they break you.

I was trying to take leave. I was getting into a "use or lose"
situation, and I got denied. I asked a couple of months later,
got denied. So I waited for a time when I knew we didn't have
students on board. I knew there was not going to be manning
issue. I gave them a month's notice, and I said to my boss, "I
need to take a week off during this time when we don't have

students." He refused to sign my papers until I told him why I was taking leave. He said, "Well, if it's not important enough to tell me why, then it's not important enough for you to take it." I finally got tired of fighting, so I told him why I was taking vacation. It was just for me to go back to Chicago and deal with some family issues. And he came back and signed my leave form and said, "Okay, I agree you need to take leave, but I think you can do this in three days, so I'm only giving you three days." But any time a male on the team would ask for leave, he could just take it. You know, you want forty-five days off? Go ahead. Take it. It was just those separate standards for males and females every time you turned around.

The sad thing is, women had opportunities to leave the unit. We had other units trying to get us. We were overmanned, so there were mandatory cross-trains. I submitted for a mandatory cross-train. Just anything to get out from under this guy. And everything that went across his desk that involved a woman got denied. Everything. So it wasn't that he wanted an all-male unit. He wanted to break us. He wanted to ruin careers.

If we're still fighting this fight as women, for the right to participate equally and to have our efforts honored and appreciated equally, what hope do gay men and lesbians have of serving openly and being accepted and integrated?

ZM: That's what I realized when I was in: I can fight until I'm blue in the face. These people have their mentality set from when they were children. The only hope anybody has— women, minorities, gays, and lesbians—is this younger generation coming up into the ranks and coming up into politics.

I do have a firm belief that gays and lesbians are going to be openly accepted in the military. I know I'm gonna see that. You know, they said they would never let black men and women integrate with white men and women. And then look what happened. Then they said they would never let women in combat roles. Well, look where women are now. We're right there on the front lines. They'll tell us they'll never let gays and lesbians serve openly, but they will eventually.

What is the big fear about gay men and lesbians serving openly?

ZM: Honestly, I think men say that they don't want another man looking at them, but sometimes I have to wonder if men fear it because maybe they have curiosity about it themselves and don't want it looking at them in the face.

I've talked to heterosexual men who have openly said, "Yes, we've been curious about it. We've never acted on it, but we're curious." Much of male sexuality is purely physical, and it probably wouldn't be anything for a couple of men—even if they are "heterosexual"—just to experiment with another form of sexual expression. If they realized all these gay guys are there, right there in their faces, could they withhold their own desires, their own curiosity?

An airman told me a story the other day: The men in her unit would say, "We're afraid of these gay men. We won't be able to drop the soap in the shower." And she turned to them and said, "Don't flatter yourselves. You guys aren't even good-looking." And they were offended, like, "Well, why wouldn't a gay guy want to look at me?"

ZM: It's crazy. The bottom line is they have to realize gays have served in the military since the military's formation. And gays have served honorably. The only thing we're lacking is "openly."

I think some straight people have so sexualized us that they just imagine we'll be fornicating openly morning, noon, and night. But the people who seem to be all about sex are the straight men in the service.

ZM: Yes. I can't tell you how many times I was chased.

With mistletoe and everything else. Chased around tables.

Maybe they're afraid of what they've subjected women to.

ZM: Good. Maybe they should be a little bit afraid to drop the soap. I know there was times I was afraid in my dorm room. I didn't know who was going to be out there at my door. Give them a little dose of their own medicine.

When you were sexually harassed, did you report these instances? And reporting them, did anyone take any action?

ZM: I reported the one where the person physically grabbed me and tried to kiss me. I reported that one specifically because he had been carrying on. It started by bringing a *Playboy* magazine and showing me the centerfold—as if I wanted to see it. Then it went further with the comments about my appearance. I should have nipped it in the bud then, but I was a young airman. I didn't know better. Then he chased me around one time with mistletoe and tried to kiss me. And at that one point, while on duty, he physically grabbed me. I was trying to get posted so I wouldn't have to work with him. My boss wouldn't do it until I finally came down and told him what had happened. I got my position changed, but nothing happened to the gentleman who did it.

I hate to think what would happen if a woman did that to another woman. She wouldn't have time to pack her socks.

ZM: No, probably not. But sexual harassment of women was accepted. I've overheard guys saying, "Well, that's what they get for coming into a man's career field." That was the mentality. "If the women want to come in, they're gonna play our game, by our rules."

The very day you came out, you lost your instructor badge.

ZM: I came out to my husband in May. Rumors about my socializing or associating with lesbians started in June or July. My husband actually came and told me one day. He said, "People are talking that you're hanging out with known lesbians." Everybody knew he and I were getting divorced, and it was in September that I told my commander that I was a lesbian.

I talked to my husband first, and I told him I was worried about him. And he said, "Naw. Go ahead and do it." I had talked to the chaplain before doing it, and that is when I learned about the "don't ask, don't tell" policy. I was, of course, worried about getting a dishonorable discharge. And I talked to legal on base, and they told me, "No, you'll get the discharge you'd get if you had been normally separated."

So with their guidance, I told my commander. And the day I told him that I am a lesbian, I was taken off my instructor team. I was no longer allowed to teach. I had to surrender my instructor badge and also my weapons card to carry a weapon. And I was reassigned to desk duty. Because of my disclosure of my homosexuality, they said, they could not allow me to be around female students.

Suddenly you became a kind of threat, or a predator even?

ZM: Yeah. I might have sacked all those little 19-year-old girls. Forget the fact that I had been working with them for four years and never once had an incident, nor would I. I guess you can't take it personally. It's okay for a heterosexual to prey upon a young female airman, and it's all washed under the rug. Just because I'm alone in a tent with a hundred naked women doesn't mean I want to attack them. It doesn't even mean I'm attracted to them. I'm just there doing my job.

I taught for four years and totally loved teaching. The

military mentality is, you gotta beat these guys down in the dirt, dust 'em off, and that's how you make great leaders. I didn't share the same philosophy because I think our American kids are beaten down enough. So my philosophy was, I'll treat them with respect. If I treat them with respect, they're going to respect me. The male instructors didn't like my style of teaching. I got called "Sergeant Mom" and the "Milk 'n' Cookies Instructor."

But I got my point across by asking my boss to observe two classrooms. Come and sit in my classroom, I told him, and then go and sit in this other guy's classroom. My students were asking questions. They were awake. They were enjoying learning. Everybody was interacting. Everybody was talking. Everybody was respectful of everybody else. You go to the other guy's classroom, kids are just sitting there, faces down. They're intimidated. They're scared. They're not asking questions. They know if they get it wrong they're gonna get their butts chewed out. Half of them are sleeping, totally tuning out the instructor. I said, "Who is the better teacher? Me or him?"

Still, you felt obliged to come out, thereby ending your career.

ZM: I'm not a quitter, if you will. I don't quit. And my whole mentality was, I'm gonna tough this out. I'm gonna tough it out. Even when I was dealing with my own sexuality, I dealt with it. I stayed in the military. I stayed married. I hid my own sexuality and dealt with that because I was not gonna quit on the military. I was gonna do my twenty years honorably.

But I got to a point at twelve years that I realized that to stay in the military and pretend to be something I'm not, to continue to subject myself to these sexual harassments and discriminations, I was actually quitting on myself. So at that moment, I was actually proud. I was actually like, you know what? That's fine. Take my weapons key. Take my badge. Because I'm standing up for myself, and those keys and badges don't define who I am. I was proud at that moment because I was standing up honorably for who and what I was.

How did your fellows react?

ZM: Nobody said a word to me. I kind of joke about this because the leadership of that unit treated me better *after* I came out to them than when I was actually an instructor. I have to wonder if it wasn't because of the fear of the defense league [Servicemembers Legal Defense Network] in Washington. I think I was the first lesbian to come out, the first one they had to deal with, and they didn't know how to deal.

As soon as I told my commander, he left the room and was on the phone talking to legal. I'm sure legal told him, "You better not harass her. You better say nothing to her. You better treat her right because the defense league in Washington is hot on these types of cases."

I have friends in the military I still talk to, all of them being in the senior ranks, E8s, E9s. They're lesbian, and the feeling I get from them is that people don't ask, and they don't tell. Nobody bothers them. One woman's a Naval officer serving in England. Her partner—they've been partners for fourteen, fifteen years—of course wants to be with her. So she herself has to pay to go to England. She has her little worker's visa or visitor's visa, and every ninety days she has to come back to the States to renew it. That's what she endures so she can be with her partner.

With a heterosexual couple, the nonmilitary spouse would just be allowed to come over.

ZM: Exactly. And I talk with people about this all the time. People in the military, people outside of the military. A lot of them are like, "Oh, it's no big deal. People at work don't need to know my sexual orientation." And I keep trying to reiterate to them, it's not just about that. You know, I don't run around waving my banners either. It's not just about people knowing I'm gay and letting me come to work and say, "My wife did this today." It's about *all* our rights.

I talk to my friends. I asked one, "What happens if you get transferred out of Luke Air Force Base and sent to Germany? What happens to your partner? You guys have been together for four years: Do you think you can endure a long-term relationship across the pond for another four or five years if you got an assignment for that long?" Sometimes I get the answer: "She'll just come with me." Well, look at the financial burden you're going to have because you're gonna have to pay for her to go over there. Look at the financial burden of shipping that much furniture over there.

And let's go beyond that. You go to the hospital in the military because you're sick and something happens, your partner can't even go in there. Your partner can't do anything for you. Let's talk about filing income taxes. I'm a CPA right now. You can't even begin to think of the tax burdens that same-sex couples endure versus heterosexual couples. They talk about this Marriage Penalty Act all the time, and they're doubling the deductions for married people. But gay couples don't have those rights, so we get fined every which way we turn. You get a twenty-year married couple, the husband dies or the wife dies and the other one gets to collect the other one's Social Security benefits. You get a twenty-year gay couple: One of the partners dies, the other's not gonna get to collect benefits. All I'm saying is that.

Critics would say, "That's not the same."

ZM: What's not the same? Two people living together? Two people paying bills together? Two people running a household together? What is not the same? There is no difference. Two people paying Social Security together? I'm looking at two people. I'm not looking at a gender. Two people.

Two people bearing the same responsibilities, having the same feelings, entering into the same commitment.

ZM: Exactly. For however many years down the road. Social Security benefits? Whoops. You weren't married. Sorry. But what about my twenty-year partner? Nope. Not married. Not getting them. It's sad. And it's sad that even within our own community people don't see it. One of the things I always like to quote is the old "liberty and justice for all." Well, if liberty and justice for all, then for all what? Not for all Americans. It's for all white men, I guess. For all white men and the women who'll be married to them.

But you know, I keep my faith. Someone asked me once, if they were to allow lesbians to serve openly in the military, would I ever go back in? I absolutely would. I may not go active duty because in my career now I'm doing better than I could ever do in the military. But I would absolutely join the Reserves and work for eight years more to get my retirement. I honestly enjoyed the military. It was exactly what I needed at a certain point in my life, and I had fun doing it. And I could still do it. But I have to do it on my terms. I can't be told who I'm going to live with, who I can't live with, who I can see, who I can't see. It's none of the military's business, if you ask me.

About Face

When this WAC joined the Army in 1976, she had "no clue" she was gay.

Right out of AIT, 71-Lima, at Fort Jackson, South Carolina, I was sent to Germany. There were a lot of lesbians in my unit. They never made any secret of it. I mean, they didn't walk around saying, "I'm so-and-so, the lesbian." But in the women's barracks, everybody knew everybody's business. We lived in what was called the WAC Shack, and everybody knew who was sleeping with whom. It didn't matter if you were gay or straight. And nobody ever cared.

Maybe because we were all so young it just didn't matter. As long as people do their jobs, it doesn't matter who you sleep with. The three years that I was there, there was never a witch hunt. As long as you did your job, they just didn't care.

—Wendi Goodman,
Staff Sgt. U.S. Army, Ret.

Smile and Look Pretty

Major Jane Wilson

Jane Wilson served in the Air Force from 1974 to 1993, retiring as a major just six months shy of twenty years as part of a military downsizing following both the country's nominal success in Desert Storm and the end of the Cold War.

She'd had enough of hiding and feared that the new "don't ask, don't tell" policy—and its attendant publicity—had put the spotlight on gay men and lesbians. People had begun sniffing around for the queers in their command, and when the policy was in full swing, she thought, it would be harder to blend in.

"I remember talking to guys in the military at the time, and they were already saying, "Wow. You know, I think so-and-so's gay. And so-and-so too," says Wilson, who now works on the civilian side of the military-industrial complex. "All these things that nobody had ever talked about were suddenly on everyone's mind."

Wilson joined the Air Force during its beauty-pageant era—the late '60s and early '70s—when recruiters were looking specifically for pretty women to fill their quotas.

Butches and plain women need not apply. A couple of extra math classes in college, and she was in.

The eldest of four girls whose father died when she was 6, Wilson, a

Texan by birth and temperament, had developed pluck and self-suffi-ciency. She was doing what no woman in her family had done, and, she perceived, she was working without a net.

"I just decided to make it in the world at that point," she says. "I was just doing what I had to do and going where I had to go."

* * *

Before "don't ask, don't tell," people didn't think about gays like they do now. Reporters really covered it. I mean, they put a description of who we were in the paper. They said, "She's the woman that's really working hard. She never talks about her personal life, and the only time you ever run into her, she's with women. You probably didn't know, but this woman you've been working alongside for a year or two is gay." Until then, the only people it occurred to were people who didn't have a life and they'd nose into yours.

But the day-to-day people you worked with never knew. Even when I would have a roommate, nobody ever blinked. They just thought it was the standard roommate situation that you have. I mean, years ago they would have never even thought to ask, "Are you in love with this woman?" President Clinton didn't count on the fact that "don't ask, don't tell" just made people want to ask more.

In your view, "don't ask, don't tell" was just like putting a big mar-quee over our heads?

JW: Absolutely. Now people definitely think about it. "don't ask, don't tell" is what caused all the problems. It brought the subject to the forefront. If I had been around dur-ing it, I would have gotten kicked out. I know that.

Why?

JW: Because I was in a field where there were men who didn't like me. There was a lot of competition. I was an officer. You know, it was up or out. And people were always trying to find ways to cut off your legs. If a couple guys I know would have found out that I was gay, they would definitely have. These guys just didn't like me, didn't want me to be around, didn't want me to make it, just went out of their way to make my life really hard. And I had that almost all the way in the military. They decided to make sure that Janie Wilson wasn't gonna get any further than she was.

I could never confront these people like I wanted to because I knew that if I just backed off and let them look bad and I didn't react, then people would start looking at them like they were crazy, which is what happened almost every single time.

But it took a big emotional toll on me. I mean, I had one guy call me once and he said, "I've heard rumors that you're a lesbian." And I said, "Well, I've been called a lesbian. I've been called a home-breaker. I've been called just about everything in the book. So you can throw that at me if you want." And I just hung up. It was probably the only time I was ever confronted by anybody.

I mean, I had a woman who showed up in my office with a knife one day because I had to call her husband at home sometimes at 2 in the morning to come into work. And she just knew I was having an affair with him.

You were his colleague or his boss?

JW: I was his boss. You see, the problem is—and you might have seen some of that in the '70s—men weren't really ready to admit that they were working for women. So a lot of times they wouldn't tell their wives that they worked for me. They would tell them that I either worked for them or we were colleagues. And I would get to these parties and things, and I'd introduce myself and start talking to their wives, and somewhere in the conversation they'd say, "Oh, you're his *boss?*" [*Laughs*]

The problem is that now that women are more accepted, the guys are wanting to hit on them. And the minute they think they're gay, they want them out. I've seen that happen a few times when they've been denied sexual favors, and as a result, have put a spotlight on certain women.

I'm sure it's still not easy for women. I think in the military we tolerate more than we realize. A lot of people say, "Oh, yeah. The military are the first ones to push people out for being anti-woman, anti-black, anti-gay." But that's not true. The military probably is more tolerant of their people abusing others than the outside world.

You remember the Aberdeen thing?[1] How long it took before they finally got known? This was going on for ages. Or look at the Fort Campbell situation.[2] The general that ran Fort Campbell is still being promoted.

Did you always want to be in the service?

JW: I knew from the beginning that I wanted be an officer. I mean, I just loved all those movies about West Point and the academies, and I definitely found myself wanting to be a pilot and the whole nine yards. At that point, that avenue wasn't even open. They didn't even have women in ROTC, until maybe the second or third year I was in college.

So I joined a group called Angel Flight,[3] which was like a sister sorority for the men in ROTC, but not like a Greek sorority. Basically, the idea was to look beautiful, and hopefully—as a result—guys would see us in our little mock Air Force uniforms. I don't know if they even exist anymore. But they existed for a long time, and it was a big honor to be in them. Some of the most attractive women on campus were chosen to be in it.

So was it all about the uniform for you?

JW: Yeah. It was all about the uniform, and it was all about the Air Force stuff. I certainly didn't do it because I wanted to meet the men.

Did you get military training? Did you march and drill?

JW: No, we didn't do any of that. But we got to go on a lot of little trips. I remember going to military bases and seeing the airplanes. That was pretty big. We were allowed to go to classes, if we wanted to. It was about as close to the military as I could get at the time. That was about 1970.

It just wasn't well thought of for a woman to go into the service. But I met a few female military officers, and I found out they were just as normal as I was, and they got in for different reasons, and I began to think, *Well, why not? What's wrong with being a woman in the military?*

My mother fought me the whole way. I can remember almost every time I talked to her on the phone she'd say, "You can leave. You can get out. You don't need to be in the military." She was even embarrassed to tell her friends that I joined. Women were still supposed to get married, and I think that followed me well into the military another twelve years.

But for a lesbian, the military is the perfect answer. I mean, it was! I remember in the back of my mind going through all the reasons I should go in, and all the reasons I shouldn't go it. One of the things I thought was, *Well, one of the good things is I'm gonna be around a lot of women that are single.*

I was out of college, and working wasn't like college, where you have all those women in the dorm that you're hanging around. And I missed that! And somehow I thought I would get that in the Air Force, because I knew we would have to live in barracks together. I can remember thinking, *Oh, we're all gonna be great friends and we're gonna hang out like we did in the dorm and party!* And it wasn't like that at all. Pretty much we were there to work, and the women were kind of competitive about the guys. In fact, I was the only woman in my flight. We would sleep together in our same rooms, and we would see each other at night, but during the day we were always with the guys.

You had to be a looker to get into the Air Force in those days, didn't you?

JW: Yes. One of the first questions the recruiter asked me was if I was attractive. He said, "What do you look like?" Back then, those were the kinds of questions you would get. Now it seems unbelievable.

How do you answer that? "I'm 36-24-36"?

JW: Once I told him I was in Angel Flight, that's all he needed to hear. He knew it was pretty safe because most of the women in Angel Flight were attractive. That's how they got in in the first place.

I'm not a beautiful woman by any means, but when I was in college I was probably more attractive. And he just went, "Well, would you say your hair is really short? Is it long? Do you wear feminine clothes?"

He told me that they were trying to change the look of women in the military so that more women would come in. That wasn't really true because they started reducing the number of women allowed in. Maybe it was for the men that they wanted women who were more attractive. I don't know! [*Laughs*] And he said, "We usually just take a picture of the face, but because they're making sure that women are attractive, we're taking full-figure pictures." And that's what they did. They were going through a lot of trouble to choose women that were more attractive.

Does that mean they didn't want women to look like...lesbians?

JW: Exactly!

Or what they thought were lesbians?

JW: They didn't want women they knew were dykey. Look, even for our promotion pictures we were told as women to smile and look pretty. We knew that the promotion boards were all men, so we did. I even shopped for a photographer who would take the best picture.

You said you knew you liked women at that point but had not acted on it.

JW: I knew I'd liked women since I was in kindergarten. I can still remember sitting at a table and having a mad little infatuation with a girl who sat near me. There was a string of that all the way through elementary school and junior high and high school, where I would find one woman that I just would be really attracted to and wanted to hang around.

I'd had boyfriends, but they'd just kind of come and go, and I never took them very seriously. After a while, I began to realize the only time I seemed to get excited was when I was around a woman. But I didn't think I'd ever act on it because I never met a woman that was gay. When I was in college there was one woman in this sorority who supposedly was found to be gay. Everybody was talking about it. I'd seen her once or twice, but it wasn't enough for me to go and talk to her—and I wouldn't have at that point.

I'm sure I was like a lot of women at that time—they probably identified with someone like that, but it wasn't enough for them to make the next move.

You couldn't talk to anybody else about it. You were in a very straight world. You certainly couldn't talk to your mom or anyone else. It was just you and your mind. There wasn't an Internet. You couldn't go to the library and find gay literature! There was no way to know where you were supposed to go. Unless you were extremely dykey, and I wasn't in that world.

You said you experienced sexual harassment and discrimination in the Air Force right from the gate.

JW: I always thought I was equal to and had all the rights that any guy would have. I mean, I noticed I didn't get to play baseball and I didn't get to do all the different kinds of things. But I never thought that I would be treated differently. I didn't even think that in college. But I got into the military and guys hit on me from day one. The very first time I went to work, my chief sergeant announced he was going to have to quit because he was not going to work for a woman. This was in 1974–'75. He said, "I can't do it. I'm gonna ask for another job."

Was that allowed to happen?

JW: Well, he thought he could. I don't know exactly what happened. I guess he was basically told he had to come back for a while. Eventually he did. And he was the one whose wife I met, and she said, "He works for you?"

I brought it up to my bosses, and of course they didn't really care. They weren't going to stand behind me and help me or do anything. They were going to let people walk all over me. If something was done to a guy, they'd be there to defend him. But they weren't going to stand up for a woman.

And yet you succeeded?

JW: I just worked hard and people couldn't help but notice that. I went through about two or three years of having a really tough time, and then they brought in a new commander, and I actually could go to him.

He started observing my work. And, actually, to be honest with you, I was not going to make captain. My very first report, the guy said I was afraid of the dark and couldn't do my job. Put it in my report. I tried to fight it, and I'd gone to the Inspector General, and they told me that there was nothing I could do and that, obviously, I wouldn't get selected for captain because of that report in my record.

So I thought it was pretty much an over thing. And this guy came in and he started paying attention to me and watching what I was doing. And one day he called me into his office. And I thought, *What is he calling me into his office for?* And he said, "I just read your record, and I saw the report that's going to stop you from making captain. And I want to know what it's about and where it came from."

And I just told him, "This is what I know, and this is where I think it came from." I said, "The guy who wrote it is still on base. Go ahead and talk to him."

Anyway, he called me back two days later and said, "I've decided that you have been harassed. I've seen your work. I've talked to other people that have worked with you, and there's no basis for this report. And I am going to personally get this thing out of your file."

I don't know what he did, but he called every friend he had. He got some people from the Judge Advocate General Corps. And they went to bat for me and got it pulled, and I made captain. I couldn't have done it myself.

It's a very odd thing to say somebody is afraid of the dark.

JW: It was easy for them to figure out once I had somebody on my side because the only person that would know somebody's afraid of something is a trained psychotherapist or a psychologist. How can a layman make that call? And I wasn't afraid of the dark. I mean, a couple of guys threw me to the ground trying to rape me one night in the dark, and I decided that instead of riding around on a bike, I should have a car.

There was an attempted rape?

JW: One of my sergeants—that I obviously didn't know was attracted to me—just threw me down and jumped on top of me one night. I said, "What are you doing? You better get off of me. This is going to ruin your career!" And he did. I never reported him, but I went to my commander and said, "Look, I'm having some incidents, and I don't feel safe walking around. I would feel a little bit better if I had a car."

I was working on the flight lines making sure that the planes were getting refueled and that the work was being done to get the planes ready for the next day. It was nighttime, and they didn't have very many lights. We didn't even have a closed base. People could drive right in off the freeway.

And in the course of your work this sergeant attacked you?

JW: Yeah. Guys would call and they'd whistle at me. It was crazy. It was not like today. You know, I was 24 years old!

It's a very interesting thing when people say gay men and lesbians disturb good order and discipline. From all the accounts that I've heard, it's sexual harassment that disturbs good order and discipline.

JW: Oh, yes. That's the biggest problem in the military. The gay thing, to me, has nothing to do with anything. The gay thing is more men having a hard time with men.

They need to be educated that we're just as choosy as they are about partners. I don't see a man wanting another guy who isn't interested in him. He would just move on. The problem is that men haven't had to really deal with it [sexual harassment]. Women have had to deal with it all the time. I think that's why women aren't as afraid of women being gay in the military. It's the men that have the problem.

So you're saying that women don't really care.

JW: More or less. I think there's a couple of things that go into it. Women that get into the military know that they're outside the typical norms, and they kind of expect that there are going to be women who like women. They kind of understand that from the beginning. I've been around women who knew, but it wasn't talked about. Women are just more accepting than men are.

Do you think that the women you worked with knew about you?

JW: I had people that I eventually came out to. It wasn't like it was obvious, and most of the time I was usually dating somebody. I was always going out with a guy at least once in a while. And as a curve ball, I never talked about hanging around women. I don't know. Other people have said it was obvious. People who were gay said they could tell.

Gaydar.

JW: Yeah. And I think it's much tougher for the enlisted women than it was for the officers. They were thrown together and put in barracks. They weren't allowed to live off base. They weren't allowed to have a life outside of the military. And as a result, they ended up becoming close to their roommates, and some of them would end up in relationships. And that's when they would get caught. Whereas, I was allowed to live off base, and when I finally did become gay, I was able to have my relationship outside of the military and do whatever I wanted to because there wasn't really anybody there to see me.

How did that come about? Earlier you had doubted that you would ever act on your feelings.

JW: Well, I was just kind of going along, and I remember I was the OIC of one of the maintenance shops. And there was this one little shop that had all these people in it, and one of them was a woman. And every time I'd go by and check on them, I'd keep getting into a conversation with this one woman. I don't remember how it even got started. But we ended up over at her house. She had a roommate. It didn't even dawn on me that they were together. I didn't even think about it. Like I said, nobody ever thought about it in those days. And they asked me if I was interested in playing softball, and I said, "Well, I'm not really good at it, but I'll come along anyway."

So I started playing softball, and somewhere along the way things started coming out that the women on the team were gay. And finally, I started talking to one woman, and next thing I knew we were in the back of a car and kissing, and that was kind of it. It was actually just a one-night thing. And the next day she was like, "You know, I'm really not interested in you." And I said, "Well, that's okay. I'm not really interested in you either."

That worked out well.

JW: It worked out really well. But actually there was a woman I had a crush on that was on the team. So we started hanging out and doing things together. A few months went by, and finally I just couldn't take it any longer: I tried to touch her, and she jumped up and said, "You know, I'm not a lesbian. I don't know where you got this idea."

I decided at that point that I wasn't going to be gay anymore. I basically went off and said, *I don't know what I was thinking. I don't know why I thought this was okay.* Two months later, she started calling me again, and we dated for a year after that.

She was just scared.

JW: Yeah, and she didn't really know what she wanted. That was 1976, the bicentennial year.

It was interesting to me that you said you perceived that a lot of gay men and lesbians get caught in the military because they've lied about financial issues.

JW: Definitely. I know of two, personally, and I've heard stories of other people. In the military, anytime you lie about anything to do with finances, they will kick you out. I mean, you can turn in a travel voucher that is wrong, they'll look at you. People are kicked out for any kind of financial fraud.

I'm in a situation right now where I've got a top-secret clearance, and the thing that they looked at more than anything was my financial standing. Was I bad credit risk? Was I doing anything over the Internet? Those things are a big thing.

Well, anyway, I do remember there was a woman who was married to a guy, and they were both gay. Of course, they were claiming themselves as husband and wife. And they weren't kicked out because they were gay. They were kicked out for saying they were husband and wife yet they were not living together. And because they were taking advantage of getting more money because they were married. And that's why they were kicked out. Actually, I think only one of them was kicked out.

And this story will probably flip you out. There was a girl. She worked at the Pentagon. She was about to retire. She was, again, one of those people that's worked hard, done great things. Being at the Pentagon is just an amazing thing. So she hands a list over to the general's secretary for people to invite to come to her retirement ceremony, and this woman, this stupid woman, has on there her roommate, who happened to be an NCO. But obviously she has the same address because this is her lover.

Well, this secretary took this a little further and found out that both of them had lived in the same house for some years, and they both were drawing cost of living adjustments (COA). And there was a regulation that if you have two military, only one of you can pull the COA if you're living in the same house.

And that's regardless of marital status or whatever?

JW: Even if it's a case of being married, only one of the members can get it. I remember signing statements every year that I wasn't sharing a room with anybody who was getting COA. In the Washington area, it's a substantial amount that you get, and they figure that one person is enough to pay for that additional rent.

Well, anyway, they kicked her out even though she was about to retire. She got no retirement or anything.

And of course they probably figured out she was gay, too. But the reason they kicked her out was financial. Maybe "don't ask, don't tell" played a part, but on the sidelines.

But your point is that it was the financial impropriety that drew that fire?

JW: And if they kept clean about that, they probably would have sailed right through. I mean, she was living with an enlisted person and had been for years, which I thought was pretty stupid because the officer-enlisted stuff is outside the bounds, too. So they were really treading on some very, very loose things. But again, nobody did anything until it was brought up as a financial situation.

So you were absolutely fussy about your financial issues?

JW: Oh, God. And actually, it saved my butt, if you want to know. Because I was gay, I knew that was an issue that people could use as an excuse. You just try to keep your back covered all the time. You figure it's gonna come from your back. It's not going to come from in front of you.

And why wouldn't they take the frontal approach? Why would it necessarily come from the back?

JW: Because in the front, I could probably defend myself. But if they caught me and said, "Well, we checked these three travel vouchers, and these are lies, and you're out," there would have been nothing I could have done to defend myself. It's the way I felt they would do things.

What other measure did you take to avoid detection?

JW: I've been stationed in big cities for a while. After Sacramento, I went to the Dallas–Fort Worth area. I was able to pretty much be out and go to bars a little bit because I figured the numbers thing. I was hanging out more with civilians than with military, and there weren't any big military bases in Dallas, so I was safe there.

And I went to Boston, and I was stationed there and, God, again, I was just very lucky. It was just a very civilian gay area, and I could pretty much do what I wanted to do. I even went to Provincetown.

Then I got stationed in Dayton, Ohio, and I bought a house. There was an area where all the military people lived, so I definitely didn't move there. I moved to an area where more civilians lived. I paid more, but I figured anything to get me away just in case I do start dating a woman. I didn't want them to start seeing only women coming out of my house.

So anyway, I did date a woman in Cincinnati, and I began to realize that Dayton was just too small. I'd go to the store and I'd run into somebody from work. I'd go to church, and I'd run into somebody from work. I had to get out of there. I was just too close to retirement. I was definitely gay. I was definitely dating women. I needed to be in a bigger place, so I moved to Cincinnati and drove sixty miles each way.

And the people at work were like, "Why are you moving to Cincinnati?" And I was like, "I like big cities. I don't like this small-town stuff." Anyway, I put my house on the market and I had a hard time selling it. Finally, two offers came in, and one was a really, really good offer. It was from a military guy that worked in the same place I did, but we didn't know each other. He worked on the floor above me, but he worked with people I knew, and I worked with people he knew. And I tried to get my Realtor to reject his bid and go to the other bid. But he couldn't understand why. And I said, "I just don't want it."

I couldn't be honest with him about what was going on, but there was no way the guy could move into my house and not figure out that I was gay once he started talking to the neighbors. My neighbors knew me fairly well. They'd seen women coming in and out of the house at all times of the day. And I had been dating a woman who used to have little lesbian signs on her car, so my neighbors knew.

I think I lost anywhere between $30,000 and $40,000 because I decided not to sell him my house. Then we went into a big recession, and I finally ended up selling the house a year and a half later. I just felt like I couldn't take the chance.

Those are the kinds of things that we all did.

When I would leave Cincinnati, to drive the sixty or so miles to the base, I'd wear a cape over my uniform. You know, the kind you wear when you go to the beauty salon? I bought one and put that over my uniform everyday so that nobody in my neighborhood would know I was in the military.

You would walk to your car wrapped in the beauty cape?

JW: Yeah, I would go to my car in that. Then I'd go to the base and take it off. Usually I'd take it off before I got to the base. I remember I actually got to the base one time, and some guy said, "Why are you wearing that?" And I said, "Oh, I drink coffee in the morning, and I don't want it to get all over my uniform." [*Laughs*]

You said everybody did these kinds of things. Would you all trade your best method, like recipes? "Oh, Jane. You should try this! It works for me."

JW: Well, I say everybody was doing it, but at the time I didn't have anybody to talk to. I think I met a couple of women that were in the military and gay in California, and we did talk a little about what they were doing to try and stay covered up. But again, to me they were doing stupid things. Officer-enlisted living together. As a result, we stopped being friends because I knew I was putting myself in danger.

And I can remember every day wondering if today I'm gonna get called in. You know? Will I come in and my stuff will be gone? How will they take me down?

It was definitely a drag, and I was constantly trying to do everything to keep myself circumspect. The only people who knew were my lovers and immediate close friends. The fewer people who know, the better chance I have that it's not gonna happen. And it served me well. I made it and never got investigated, and I'm lucky.

But part of it was I was in a professional field, too. I didn't work with standing military all the time, and I think had I remained in aircraft maintenance, where I began, I wouldn't have made it all the way through.

I moved out of aircraft maintenance into contracting, and I was working with civilian personnel. Those people didn't really give a hoot. And that's another dichotomy in the military. In today's world, there are more and more contractors and more and more civilians that are doing the jobs the military used to do, and those people couldn't care whether they're working with gay people or not. They don't care. Why should they? It's just the military people that care.

The funniest part that's going on in this whole Iraq thing is that during Desert Storm, ninety-five percent of the people overseas were military people. Active duty, reserve or whatever. Today in Iraq, I would say it's sixty-forty: sixty percent military and forty percent contractors. It could even be fifty-fifty. My best friend right now is a civilian head of reconstruction for Iraq. She's in the Log Cabin Republicans.

If the military is already working cheek and jowl with gay people who are contractors—never mind the members of allied forces who have already lifted their own bans—what is the problem with gay people serving?

JW: I don't know if I really understand it, but I did have an experience that was thought-provoking. I was at a squadron officer school in 1980 because before you go up to major you're supposed to go through this kind of senior service school, to get you ready for the next part of your career.

And these generals came up and they were actually still talking about black and white integration. The average person who enlisted at that point was 18 or 19 years old, they said. He is in the Army. He has a GED. He comes from a very poor family, and he has very little cultural or moral views at all. And if we put blacks in the same barracks as them, they said, they're gonna just tear 'em up. And at one point in the discussion, one general even said, "We can't even think about having gays in there. I mean, they'd kill 'em. They've been brought up to hate these people. So we can't put them in there."

And it made me realize that's what they're looking at. They're looking at the average Army person that comes in, that they have to talk into going to war and giving up their life. They're not even able to drink 'cause they're not old enough. How are you going to get people to do that? They have to be desperate because they're not doing well wherever they are. And these are the kinds of people that killed the guy at Fort Campbell. They have a very closed view of the world. And the general said, "We need those people," and so, as a result, we're going to try and eliminate any friction that could take place.

They're going to keep those people and just eliminate gay people.

JW: They're going to eliminate anything that's gonna keep them from doing their job.

What's the solution to thinking like that, and have things changed at all since 1980? That's a quarter of a century ago.

JW: I think that's the only reason the military still says what they say: They still think the same way.

Many enlisted gay women I've talked to largely went into the service to escape hard economic situations. The factory in their town closed, or they didn't have the money to go to college. That situation hasn't really changed very much.

JW: That's always gonna be the case in the military, and that's one of the best things the military offers lots of people: the ability to step up. If a young woman came to me and said, "Would you advise me to go in?" in most circumstances I would say "yes." "No," if she were gay.

Why should a young gay man or a gay woman not have that same opportunity to step up and get a lift out of impoverished circumstances?

JW: They do. They pay their taxes like everybody else. And there's nothing going on in the military that's gonna keep them from doing it. It's prejudice. It's just prejudice, plain and simple.

Notes

1. In 1996–1997, investigations were triggered by numerous allegations of sexual assault against female trainees by their drill sergeants at the Army's Aberdeen Proving Ground in Maryland. The army-wide investigations took eight months to complete and resulted in more than 35,000 interviews at fifty-nine bases around the world. Among other things, investigators found that sexual harassment exists throughout the army and that respect is not well taught in basic training.

2. In 1999, Army Private First Class Barry Winchell was beaten to death in his barracks at Fort Campbell, Kentucky, by fellow soldiers who perceived him to be gay. An investigation revealed that Winchell had endured daily anti-gay harassment at the post, where cadre were later cleared of any responsibility. Two soldiers were convicted for their role in the murder. The post commander, Lt. Gen. Robert T. Clark was later promoted. In 2000 Pentagon officials added "don't harass" to the "don't ask, don't tell, don't pursue" policy. The general that ran Fort Campbell is still being promoted.

3. Angel Flight was founded at the University of Omaha in 1952, as a separate (and unequal) women's Air Force ROTC–flavored program.

About Face

This U.S. Army Persian Gulf veteran served well, but at tour's end came home tired of deep cover.

In Saudi Arabia, in the hospital unit I served with, we all pretty much knew about each other. We were never harassed, but there were whispers. I was an E5 and had been promised E6 if I went over. I didn't want to be found out, and I was really scared. At that time I had 10½ years in the military, and I thought I was going for twenty. I had read about people who had been outed, and I was afraid. I didn't want to go to Leavenworth.

Everyone kind of knew about the lesbian tent. But it was a wartime situation, and there was a kind of suspension of values. Men were fucking women all over the place. Everyone was sleeping with everyone else, and it didn't seem to be a big deal.

My partner was in the same deployment. It was difficult being together and not being *together*. When we arrived in Bahrain, we slept next to each other in a tent that held 400 people. Scuds were coming in, and we were put into full MOPP [biochemical] suits. I was scared to death, and I couldn't be comforted by my lover. It was okay for husbands and wives, girlfriends and boyfriends to comfort each other. That was hard.

One woman came out, and they told her, "So what? Carry on, soldier." If they need you, they don't care what your persuasion is. When there's no real demand, then they start focusing on things.

—Jane

Okay, I Won't Wear Shorts

Donna S.

Donna S. entered Army ROTC in 1981, her freshman year of college, and completed cadet basic training at Fort Knox, Kentucky. She liked the challenge, she says, the physicality of it, and made many friends.

The Boston native—who came out when she was 30—never met anyone gay, nor knew anything about it beforehand. If she had, she says, she would have been the last person she suspected.

"I was 18 when I went to basic training. I didn't know anything about gay people," she says. "I wasn't interested in men, but I just thought that would come when I met the right one."

A member of the Quartermaster Corps, she was stationed at Fort Lee, Virginia, then served with a National Guard MP unit.

Throughout her ten years' service, she was all about the job: "Let's get it done."

A captain, Donna was deployed to Saudi Arabia with a National Guard unit from Maine in 1991 and served as the transportation officer in charge of all trucks that came into the theater and all roads.

Duty in the Persian Gulf during Desert Storm was an opportunity to put her skills to the test, she says. But the most serious threat came from within her own ranks, in the form of sexual harassment and gay baiting.

Such harassment of women in the military and bad heterosexual male behavior are the leading bars to "good order and discipline," she suggests.

"I was not interested in any women or men as a partner. I don't believe in mixing social life with work life," says Donna, now 40 and employed in the health-care industry. "That was the policy that was taught to us in training, yet many people I encountered seemed to be pre-occupied with our lives outside of work.

"As long as 'don't ask, don't tell' exists, the military does not have to acknowledge gay people, and does not have to take care of this group. I did my part. I went in harm's way. The military needs to take care of all of its soldiers."

* * *

I met one girl in basic training. I don't remember her name; she just told us to call her "Spike." She was cool, and we all liked her. She was fun to hang out with, and she was really good at spit-shining boots. Unfortunately, she didn't hide her sexual orientation from us.

Anyway, one girl, her bunkmate, claimed that Spike hit on her. None of us knew what really happened. It was all very quick. Spike was gone. And then the cadre asked us who she hung out with. Did she hit on anyone else?

We were all really angry with the girl who turned her in. Basic training was all about making it through, and Spike was very athletic and definitely pulled more than her weight. She was a big loss to our platoon.

I didn't come out until I was 30, after I got out of the military. There was this guy, a higher-ranking officer, who harassed me when I was in Saudi Arabia, and that was the first time someone else saw it in me and pointed it out. He would harass me, allude to the fact that I was gay. He would try to get me in trouble. But

I didn't know what he was talking about. I was kind of scared. I was afraid for my career, and I was also afraid I would not have the respect of my troops and would not be able to accomplish our mission. I thought I could go to jail or something. But the thing that bothered me was that I hadn't really done anything, and when it happened to me—this is in '91—I would still adamantly say that I was not gay. I just didn't believe that I was. It's weird how light dawns on Marblehead. [*Laughs*] You know? But all of a sudden, it all came to me. It all fell into place.

Sexual harassment seems to be the biggest bar to "good order and discipline" in the ranks.

DS: Yeah. Every unit I could think of that I was in—except for basic training—every place I went to, there was some guy who would give me a problem. They'd either want to go out with me—and I always felt that this was work: I don't mix the two. So it wasn't even an issue with me. But he would want to go out with me, do something to make it harder for me if I didn't want to go out with him. And that's how I looked at this other guy [in Saudi Arabia], but he was the first one to say that I was gay.

He said it just like that?

DS: No, he never said, "Are you gay?" or anything. There was another guy in the unit who wanted to go out with me. I had no interest in this: He was married. He had children. He was fifteen years older than me. But this other guy, this captain, he just figured, if she doesn't want to go out with Bill—the one who asked me out was named Bill—if she doesn't want to go out with Bill, she must be gay. So he started out by saying, "Well, you're 27 years old. Why aren't you married? Why don't you have a boyfriend?" And I would say, "Well, I just don't. Let's talk about work now." [*Laughs*] You know? And it would get worse and worse.

And then one time he was reading a newspaper, *The Stars and Stripes* or something, and he said, "Oh, Lieutenant, you should be interested in this." And I said, "What's that?" "Well, this person, this woman, in the Army, she's gay and she wants to get out, and she doesn't want to go through a personnel board." And I said, "Why would I be interested in that?" And then later I thought about it, and I said, [*breathes a surprised breath*] *He thinks I'm gay!* That's the first time.

And then one time in front of our battalion commander he said, "Well, lieutenant, who *have* you slept with? Or have you *ever* slept with a guy? Tell us."

And I was like, "I don't even want to talk about that. It's none of your business." And the battalion commander, he was standing behind the captain, his eyes got so big. And I thought at that point, *I need to go talk to the battalion commander.*

I had already talked to my supervisor about the problem, and I didn't get anywhere. But I didn't feel comfortable going to the battalion commander because I didn't know him. We were a small unit, all combined into one big unit. So I had only known the battalion commander for a couple months. You know, he was a colonel. I didn't know how it would be taken, whether he would say, "Well, *are* you gay?" You know what I mean? So I was afraid. But I decided that the next time I saw him, I was going to ask him if I could talk to him.

That night, after all that happened, my supervisor called me into his room and said, "You're not going to believe this. I can't believe what's happening. I just can't believe it." And I said, "What's going on?" And he said, "You're going to Germany tomorrow morning." And I was in Germany for two months. So that's how the battalion commander solved the problem.

Get you out, then redeploy that other fellow somewhere else.

DS: Yes. But when I came back, the captain actually was on our shift for a while, and he wasn't really working out. I don't remember if he was still harassing me at that point. But then the war started, and it got very busy.

The captain was also a Vietnam vet, and I guess he was having some flashbacks. He got really crazy, and I was really worried that he would flip out or something. So I went to my supervisor and tried to tell him I was very worried. And the supervisor thought that I hated the captain because of all the trouble he had given me, and that I was trying to get back at him. So nothing happened. And this captain—every night it was really scary. You don't want to have a crazy person in your office at night. He would just go crazy.

The other people on my team were four guys who were very young. One was 18, and the other three were like 25. They hadn't been in the Army long. And we needed people we could depend on. And they weren't feeling good or comfortable. And I didn't want them to worry. I wanted them to be able to do their jobs.

My supervisor said, "Well, try to get along with him. Try to work it out." And I thought, *Oh, great.* But then it happened again. And one of the guys in my unit went to the supervisor. And the captain was shipped out.

Your supervisor believed the young man—but not you.

DS: Yeah. [*Laughs*] And it all worked out. It wasn't exactly the way I had hoped. But once this captain was gone, I hardly ever saw him, and the other three people on my team, we all bonded really well. They were probably the best friends I'll ever have in my life. How many times they stood up for me and backed me up.

That's what you expect in a unit.

DS: I dunno. These guys were incredible. It's amazing when you're terrified—it's amazing how people react. The ones you think will back you up and talk a great game, they generally don't.

And the ones who are normal and have normal feelings, who aren't afraid to say when they're afraid, they'll step up for you. Fortunately, I had three guys like that. We worked really well together. They treated me as a professional, and I treated them the same. We spent ten months deployed together in the Gulf. They were my family.

What was that like?

DS: For the most part it was boring. When we first got there, they didn't know what to do with us. We were sent out to the desert, actually, to the wrong unit. So we sat out in the desert for three weeks. Then we found our unit. And our unit was called the 93rd Infantry Battalion. And it was composed of smaller units of guard, reserve, and active duty units from all over the country, so we didn't know anybody except the people on our team. We didn't have a place to live, and we lived on the end of the pier. It was kind of cool: We lived in these big sheds, and we had helicopters in the sheds. And we'd say "Our bedroom is a helicopter." [*Laughs*] That's where they'd repair the helicopters or store them when they'd come off the ships. And our beds were there, too.

You all slept together in the shed?

DS: Yeah. It was huge, about the size of a football field. We had no choice. You worked around it. We had a lot of time on our hands, so we found these pallets on the end of the pier, and we built a dressing room, and we put our tents around it so everybody had privacy when you got dressed. And we built other things, like a movie theater. Someone had brought a big-screen TV and a VCR, so we closed it all off and made it all dark. Then we built picnic benches and other things. We went there Labor Day weekend. Then by, I think it was the end of October, they moved us into a compound.

You didn't know you were gay, and let's say you didn't turn out to be gay. If you were merely a heterosexual Army officer, this fixation with sexuality, who's gay and who's not, would create stress for you as well, if you constantly have to prove it.

DS: Well, that's the thing. If they just let people be whatever, then that wouldn't happen because it's not an issue. Then I could have gone to someone, and I wouldn't have had the fear that they would ask me if I were gay, question me, that I would get into trouble—not that I had done anything that I could get into trouble for. But I had heard about the witch hunts and all that.

You heard about those?

DS: Oh, yeah. Spike, in basic training. She got kicked out. She was kind of stupid, in a way. Even I knew that being gay was not allowed. And she was just right out there with us. "Yeah, I'm gay. What're they going to do about it?" And I was like, "Okay, whatever." But there was one person who didn't think that, unfortunately, and made it an issue, and that was enough.

You never know who—even where I work, you can't just put it out there, because you don't know how they'll react, and they can react any way they want because there's no system in place that says that's not allowed.

You feel that's true even in your civilian life?

DS: Well, I'm now a contractor, so I'm dependent on the government and the military for my job. And they could just come in tomorrow and say, "Well, we don't like Donna, so you need to get rid of her." And in Virginia you can fire someone for their sexual orientation. There is no law protecting you. So it's just not a risk that I'm willing to take.

It's not necessary for my job to have people know I'm gay. Now, some people have come and asked me, and I tell them. But I'm not going to wear a sign.

Actually, one guy I was working with was giving me a hard time, and I told him. He was another contractor. One day he said, "Let me take you to lunch." And I said, "Sure."

So we went to the Olive Garden. And he started in. And he said—and I've had this happen to me a couple of times before—"You never talk about any boyfriends. Who do you hang out with?" And I said, "Oh, I have a lot of friends." "Well, what do you do on weekends?" "Go out with my friends." "Well, where do you go? I don't know much about D.C. I want to know what to do and where to go." "Well, I go to Capitol Hill, Adams Morgan, Dupont Circle." "Well, what's in Dupont Circle?" And I said, "Bars and things." And he said, "Well, you never talk about any boys or guys. Do you always just hang out with girls?"

And I said, "Oh! Are you trying to ask me if I'm gay?" And he went, [*startled*] "Huh? No. No." And he didn't know what to say. And I said, "Well, if you are, I'll tell you that I am. But it's really none of your business. It doesn't have anything to do with work, so what's the deal?" I said, "I'm proud of it, and I'm not going to hide it. But what's your question?"

How did the rest of the lunch go?

DS: We talked about work or something totally different. Then the next day he was a little odd.

Maybe he was embarrassed by his behavior.

DS: Well, he should be. He said, "I don't want to know anything about it." "And I said, "Well, then don't ask me. That's the way I am, and I'm proud of it, and I don't like to be judged."

What is the fascination, do you suppose, with people's sexuality? Why does it matter to the company commander or to the CEO, your fellow workers?

DS: I don't know, but the people it comes from seem to be older. This guy at work is about 55. And he's also from India. I have another friend that I work with—he's gay as well—and he said, "Don't worry about it. It's a cultural thing."

With the captain, he was a Vietnam veteran, and he'd be about the same age now, in his 50s. And I just wonder if, as the new generation takes over the Army, it's changing. 'Cause I find that the younger people don't seem to care.

I have friends on active duty now who are gay, and they say, "Oh, it's no big deal. My commander knows, and he doesn't care." It's good to hear that. But I would like a legal statement from the military that it's okay.

You got out of the Army in 1991 after ten years' service. Why didn't you make it a career?

DS: I'd had it. I felt like I was constantly having to justify my social life—even when I didn't know I was gay. We always had to go to a lot of parties and affairs. And I usually brought a date. You don't ever want to stand out, you know? I felt like every single unit I was in, here I was just trying to do my job, and somebody'd want to go out with me. And they would cross that line. I don't find it like that in the real working world, and I don't understand why it has to be that way in the Army.

Every unit! I could tell you stories. Here I'd work with somebody really closely and think I had a good working relationship, and then they would want to go out with me. And then they'd be upset if I didn't want to go out with them. I mean, I'm not a flirtatious person.

You're a nice Catholic girl from Boston.

DS: Yes. [*Laughs*] Like there's this one girl at work. And she gets asked out a lot. But I know why she gets asked out a lot.

Why?

DS: She flips her hair around and giggles and does all that kind of stuff. [*Laughs*] I don't do that. I don't even wear a skirt! [*Laughs*] I felt like some men just thought that's what we were there for. How sexy can you look in a green Army uniform? You just don't. So it's not like somebody could say, "Well, you were wearing that short skirt."

Or a push-up bra with your BDUs.

DS: Yeah. I just don't know. I just acted like myself.

And the men were married and not married?

DS: A lot of them were married.

Enlisted and officer?

DS: Both. Maybe they did this to a lot of women. When I first went into the military, I really looked young. Maybe that was it. I looked 16. I don't know.

Were you ever worried that somebody would bring you up on charges for being gay—even though you didn't know you were? If you're not putting out, all it takes is a "reasonable person" who suspects a "propensity."

DS: Just that time in Saudi Arabia. That's why I was afraid to go to anyone: I thought, *They're going to say, "Are you gay?"* I really could say that I wasn't. I hadn't done anything. But I had been training in the military for ten years, and it was the first time in my life that I'd gotten to use my training, and I didn't want to ruin that. This was my opportunity. I wanted to prove myself, and I didn't want to make waves.

Some authorities believe that if gay men and lesbians are allowed to serve openly, men will show up in drag and women will be having orgies in the barracks.

DS: Well, they might, but that's not allowed. Right? We have regs to deal with those issues. Men and women can't have orgies in the barracks, right? So if there is one, then they discipline them. But that doesn't have anything to do with doing my job

You're suggesting that the Uniform Code of Military Justice has certain rules about behavior and deportment in and out of uniform, and if you violate one of these rules—you fraternize, show PDA in uniform, or something outrageous—then regardless of your sexual orientation, you will be punished.

DS: Yes. We've been through this once or twice before when women were integrated into the military and when blacks were integrated into the military. I wonder what was said about them at the time: "Oh, black people can't be with white people"?

Yes. "We can't dare let those people in our ranks"—the same thing that was said about women in the '70s and gay people today. That there's just something fundamental about us—gay people, black people, women—that causes a stir, and they can't have that.

DS: Well, the people that cause the stir aren't gay, aren't black, and aren't women. It's funny. I kind of got a sense of what it must have been like, because women were integrated in the '70s, and I went to my first basic training in '82, and a lot of the NCOs who were in charge of us weren't happy that we were there, and they let us know. One guy just flat out told us, "I don't think women belong in the Army. I'm not married. I don't like women. And all you're doing is taking the place of a man." You know, he was this crusty old NCO.

And when we went to basic training we had what I called the "rape talk." They would gather the women officers who were in charge of us and the male NCOs would tell us, "You're in Fort Knox, Kentucky. There's not a lot of women here, and those men come out of the field, and they haven't seen a woman in weeks, so they can't handle themselves. So you should not travel in groups smaller than five people, and do not wear shorts. Don't wear tight clothing. Because if you get raped, we're sending you home."

Who's a threat to good order and discipline? That's very interesting, putting the responsibility on you.

DS: Well, yeah. And I don't know if that's just what happened at Fort Knox, or did that happen throughout the military? You know, I just wanted to make it through. I knew I was going to be there for six weeks, and I thought, *Okay, I won't wear shorts.* [*Laughs*]

We hear a lot about the threat: Gay men are going to get us in the showers. But the real threat in the American military seems to be aggressive heterosexual men.

DS: That aggressive behavior is encouraged. I'm sure it is in the combat units. And just by virtue of their telling us, "Well, these men haven't seen a woman in weeks. They've been working hard, and they just want to go out and get drunk and they're going to do crazy things. And that's okay because they've been in the field for weeks!"

They're just being wild and crazy guys.

DS: Yeah. But in a way they want them to be like that because they're going to be fighting and killing people. It's a fine line. You kind of have to have that, but you have to have discipline as well.

What is the solution? More education?

DS: Education, definitely. Remember that Tailhook[1] thing? And after all that happened, they came up with all these programs. And now if something happens to a woman in the military, it seems to get a lot more visibility. It seems like a woman can now go, from what I read, to her supervisor and say, "This guy's harassing me," and he will be dealt with because it's come from above. No officer on his watch wants that black mark, that he allowed that. So, I think [with gay and lesbian troops] it's the same thing. Learn from that. The same classes!

It's a cultural thing, though. I talked to this guy, he just got out of the military because he realized he was gay. He's only 22. So he went to his supervisor and said, "I'm gay." He said they were really good. He was in Korea and really isolated. And he said that so many people, so many officers and NCOs, came to him and said, "If anybody gives you a hard time, you come to me, and I'm gonna deal with it."

When I heard that, I said, "That is so cool." At least people out there are willing to deal with it. They don't have good guidelines, but they're willing to deal with it. And the fact that they're willing to back him up like that, you know? I thought that was very cool. So I think the people in the military are changing, and the older people who aren't as flexible, they're gradually getting out. And the younger ones coming in, I think, are a little more liberal.

It's just a matter of attrition and time?

DS: That and the law needs to be changed. Because not everyone's going to accept it. You'll always find one asshole. Because he's 21 or 25 doesn't mean he's going to accept it. That's why you still have to be careful who you talk to, and that's why I'm careful about who I talk to. You don't know.

I have talked to women who were raped on the job, had rape attempted, women who were pestered day and night...

DS: That's how it was for me most of the time. And because of my experience in basic training, it was my worst fear. I always thought, *Oh, if I get raped, I'm going to lose my career or get kicked out.* I think it's changed now, but I shouldn't have to think like that. I should have somebody that I know who'll protect me from that, so that I can do my job.

The one thing in Saudi Arabia: They took care of everything, the military did. How to write a will. How to get a power of attorney. They helped me get a power of attorney for my parents, so that they could pay all my bills. They had someone stay in my apartment. They had someone take care of my cat. I mean, they took care of everything.

But they didn't take care of the one thing I really needed. They didn't take care of it. There was this person harassing me. They said, "We'll take care of everything so that you can focus on your job." Clearly, I was not able to focus on my job because this person was harassing me. They needed to take care of that.

It scares me that there might be someone right now serving in Iraq. And it'd be worse for them than it was for me because the threat is so much more severe. So they're dealing with that, and they're also dealing with the guy next to them who is harassing them because they're gay. God! And there's nothing they can do.

Or just a single woman and not gay.

DS: Exactly. They can get away with that as well. You should be allowed to focus on your job. There should be a system in place so that when someone isn't allowed to focus on her job, someone is harassing her, she can get help. And until there's a legal declaration that you can be gay and serve in the military, it's not going to happen.

Note

1. At the 35th Annual Tailhook Symposium (Sept. 5–7, 1991) at the Las Vegas Hilton Hotel, 83 women and 7 men were assaulted during the three-day aviators' convention, according to a report issued a year later by the Inspector General of the Department of Defense. The scandal was made public by Navy Lt. Paula Coughlin, an admiral's aide who was attacked at the event. DoD investigators—critical of the Navy's initial handling of the incidents—interviewed 2,900 people who attended Tailhook '91, and obtained photographs, documents, and other evidence of crimes and misconduct by Naval aviators. Few perpetrators were ever named or charged; fewer were punished.

About Face

This fleet support officer was investigated for homosexuality twice in 4½ years. The Navy's aim: to deep-six her career.

My first time, I was investigated under the guise of a security clearance that I did not request or need. When the civilian investigator asked me if "anyone thought that it was odd that my roommate was a woman," I was incredulous. I was 24 and living in an expensive locality, Hawaii. I simply replied, "My daddy wouldn't approve if I was living with a man to whom I wasn't married." But inside, all I could think was, *Don't fuck up. Don't fuck up. Don't fuck up. Don't let them know you're nervous. Don't let 'em know.* I was terrified.

I was this young officer with student loan debt and couldn't afford to lose my job. And I'd come home with my stomach in knots. But I got the clearance.

I don't know what prompted that investigation. It could have been a midlevel enlisted person in my command who didn't like me and just decided to say I was a dyke.

The second time there was a larger thing going on. I was already out and in the reserves, but unaffiliated. I was in my first semester of law school, and they wanted me to come down and make a statement at the NIS office at Treasure Island. This guy said, "You're being investigated for homosexuality." But I said, "No, I'm not coming out to Treasure Island." He said, "Well, we're just gonna have to make a note of this." And I'm just like, "Make a note of it in your kangaroo court!"

A friend who was an admin officer told me later that a report did come out, that my name was all over it. So-and-so said he saw me kissing a woman at a bar. Some straight male sailor at my base. There was a lot of made-up stuff in the report. But nothing ever happened because I was already out and gone.

—Jamie P. Roberson, LT.
U.S. Navy, 1985–1989

Pick It Up, Put It Down

Vicki Wagner

It may have been naive for Vicki Wagner to believe that bisexuality would be an adequate shield, protecting her from discharge from the Air Force in 1990, two months shy of two years' service. After all, queer is queer, a fact she failed to grasp.

Maybe if she had married a man quickly—as others have done—as a counterbalance to having kissed a girl and been seen doing so. Maybe one more letter of testimony from a male airman she'd slept with could have saved her from that world of hurt. Maybe more discretion. It's all academic now.

More than a decade later, Wagner, 33, still seems incredulous that she was cashiered for something so minor. After a grueling nine-month investigation, the Air Force Office of Special Investigations could not prove that the gung ho 19-year-old command post coordinator with a top-secret clearance was gay. They didn't have to. Her own actions suggested "propensity," an elusive, ever-changing standard that can be as obvious as same-sex affection or as vague as an affinity for athletics.

Her discharge had nothing to do with job performance or her abilities as an airman. Her perceived sexuality was her central disqualifier, burden on the accused.

It happens all the time.

"Now do I define myself as a lesbian? Yeah, I do," says the former Catholic schoolgirl and self-described "party girl" who, like many women, was slow to label her sexuality. "But when I first got out of the Air Force, I had to go down to the county recorder's office and record my discharge paperwork, and right there for anybody to see was VICKI WAGNER, HOMOSEXUAL. I didn't tell people the real reason I got kicked out. I couldn't bear it. I'd say that I got a medical discharge."

Wagner now works out her demons onstage as a comedian— "Vicki Wagner and Her Amazing Homosexual Act." And she's come a long way.

"Someone asked me the other day, 'What would you say to a gay or bi person who was joining the military?' I'll tell you right now: Don't do it," says Wagner. "It's horrible that we can't have the same opportunities, but given how they treat us, what happened to me, I would never want anybody to have to suffer through that ever, ever, ever."

You joined the military when you were 18. Why did you do that?

* * *

VW: It's funny because my brother tried talking me out of joining the military. He was already in the Navy. He tried telling me every single thing. "Don't join. It's horrible!" But I really couldn't grasp that concept. I mean, you have the recruiters coming to your high school, and they make it seem like this great vacation.

And the uniforms look so great.

VW: Oh, yeah. They look so good. I do think the Marines have the best outfits, though. Everyone thinks that. They look the best.

We didn't grow up with a lot of money. My parents got divorced when I was 12. So it really wasn't like, "Okay, we're gonna finance your college." It was more like, "Get out of high school and get a job." My dad never really supported our family, so my mom worked. She had three jobs, and he never really paid child support. We could have used that money when we were growing up for food, for clothes, for anything! So you think, *What happens after high school?*

So my brother and his best friend both joined the Navy together. I was still in high school. And he'd come home on leave, and I'm like, "I'm gonna join the Air Force!" He's like, "No! You cannot join the Air Force. The military is a horrible institution. It's not what it's cracked up to be. They treat you like shit, and they kick you around, and they call you names."

Well, you know, he was on a big carrier. He didn't get a specialized job, so he was one of the grunts, one of the people who had to swab the deck or chip the paint off the whole boat and sand the thing down. He'd tell me these stories about how he was in this tiny, cramped hole that was just big enough for his body to fit in, sanding, welding the surface or whatever. So, of course, he's gonna think it's a horrible experience.

But I was convinced. My Air Force recruiter was this guy who was really nice, really likable. "Oh, we're all over the world, and you can pick your place." Here's me thinking, *Oh, I'm gonna go to Spain or Italy, Holland.* I actually went to the library and started researching countries to see where I was gonna go. Yeah, right! Next! So, I was completely snowed.

But the Marines have snappier uniforms. They came to your school. Why didn't you join the Marines?

VW: Because I did my studying on the military, and the Air Force is the top of the top.

You got to be the smartest to get into the Air Force, and I'm a smart person. Not to say that the other military branches aren't any good. They all are, but you know I wanted to be where the opportunities were the best. And I kept thinking about my brother, like there's no way I'm gonna be some grunt. I wanted to learn.

Michael ended up getting killed in a car accident on his way back to his station.

Your brother?

VW: Right. That really solidified it for me because that brought home the fact that life is really short. I wasn't gonna make the military a lifetime thing. I was planning on going, checking out the world, growing up, and getting some money for college, which is basically what they sell you on.

I actually wasn't even gay, you know what I mean? All throughout high school I dated guys. I was always a popular girl, had a lot of friends. I didn't get selected for Homecoming Queen, but I got nominated, which is a big deal. And I actually had a couple of experiences with women, but I always had a boyfriend.

When I was a junior in high school, this one girl who I knew—I knew there was something. You know what I mean? I didn't know what it was, though, because when you're that age, how do you know? Even though I was from a suburb of Chicago and lived in this huge metropolitan area, there really wasn't any gay stuff going on. So I never even thought about me being gay.

Did you know any gay people?

VW: No, I didn't know any damn gay people!

So you didn't know what to call yourself?

VW: I had no clue. And I had this boyfriend at the time. He was a little older than me. He always wanted me to have a three-way with him, with another girl. And I was like, "No, I'm not gonna do that. It's not my thing." But the more he put it in my mind, the more I thought about it.

And when I was a junior in high school, my brother had thrown this party, and I was high, smoking. And this beautiful girl—the most beautiful girl ever—came into the bathroom with me. At the time I was really thin, and the style was little silk shorts and half shirts. And they were pink, of course. And she had these long nails, and she just rubbed them across my stomach and told me that she thought I had a great body and just kissed me.

And I was like, *Whoa! What was that?* And I didn't know what to think. I just let her kiss me. And that experience to me was not like kissing any guy. You know what I mean? But I still didn't know, *Hey, you could pursue this option because you might be a lesbian.* You've just won the lesbian gene! Or whatever. I had that incident, and I'll tell you what: It blew my mind. But I didn't know.

So I get to the Air Force recruiter's office, and he asks one of the questions right on the form. "Are you gay?" And I'm like, "No." I mean, I answered it that fast. "No, I'm not gay." I mean, I had a boyfriend. My boyfriend's name was Vince. He was an Italian guy. We had been dating for like six or seven months at the time I signed up for the Air Force.

But my old boyfriend from before, who would always try to get me hooked up with a girl, we kept in contact. And he still said, "I think you'd like to try it with a girl." To make a long story short, his best friend's sister was gay. So he set us up on this like blind date. Right? This was in November 1988. Okay? So I meet this girl, and well, before you know it, we're together. I was 18 at the time, and she was 24.

That's when I found out—Wow! This whole lesbian world exists that I had no clue. And I mean *no* clue of. So anyway, I met Julie and she was really a hot-looking girl. She takes me out to the bar. And it's packed with women. And I'm like, *Oh, my God! All these women are gay?* I couldn't believe it.

So anyway, I started having like, not a relationship, but I guess a relationship, when I was still dating Vince. And Julie was like, "You're not dating a guy and me at the same time." So, I thought, *Well, I can date a guy anytime.* I mean, I had so many boyfriends. So I was like, *I'll break up with my boyfriend because I might not have this opportunity again.* You know what I mean? *I'm going into the Air Force anyway, so I might as well have some fun while I can.* So I started dating her. And still I didn't think that I was a lesbian. I did not think that I was a homosexual.

You were just someone who was dating a girl?

VW: Right. And my mom finds out. And I told her, "I must be bisexual. I'm not gay because I still like guys." I told her, "I don't know. I like both. I like everybody." So she deliberately picks out a bisexual psychologist for me to go to.

Even though I had answered "No" to that question that the Air Force had asked, "Are you a homosexual?" I figured, *Hey! If I'm a bisexual, then it doesn't make me a homosexual. If I still like guys, I'm still half straight. So why couldn't I be in the military?* Never even thought about it any other way.

The bisexual psychologist said that it's completely normal for there to be bisexual people. Now that I'm older, I don't believe it. You know, you're one way or the other or you haven't picked yet. I broke up with that girl before I went into the Air Force anyway. I wasn't dating her anymore.

That was just a fling?

VW: Yeah, a couple of months. It wasn't like I had this long, lost love affair with her. Trust me!

Anyway, I go to the Air Force boot camp. It was Lackland Air Force Base, San Antonio, Texas. I went into the military on April 12, 1989. It's one of those things you just don't forget. You forget everything else: your parents' anniversary, whatever. You're not gonna forget the date you went into the military because that's really the day your life changes. And boy, I was in for a big surprise. It certainly wasn't the Taj Mahal they had talked me into believing it would be.

What delights awaited you on your first day of boot camp?

VW: It was terrible! The whole entire first day was horrible. First of all, I couldn't fall asleep. You have to spend the night in this hotel before you have to go into the MEPS, the Military Entrance Processing Station. I couldn't fall asleep all night long because of anxiety and everything, and then our alarm goes off at 4 A.M. And you get bussed down to the MEPS and lined up with everybody. And you go through all the tests.

Then we get to Texas. It's pouring rain; I haven't ever seen rain like this. I didn't even know it could rain like this. It was like they picked up the ocean and just dropped it.

By this time it's like 2 or 3 in the morning. I've been up for almost twenty-four hours, and I was dead tired. So we drive onto the base, and it all begins. We got our one little suitcase that we're allowed to bring, and they made everybody stand outside. And I'll never forget this. All of a sudden, it was like an orchestrated movie. BAM! Five doors fly open and these TIs appear. It was like their grand entrance. "Welcome to our world! We own you now!"

They started calling us every name in the book. "You motherfucking slackers!" Every name. They wore the big

Smokey the Bear hat and their stupid uniform. They should just have an outfit that says on it I'M AN ASSHOLE [*laughs*]. "TI" stands for "too ignorant to get a better job." It's the truth. How stupid do you have to be to be this mean to people? It's cruel and unusual punishment. You have to have some sadistic vein in your body to want to be the person in this job. To want to be a military training instructor? There is something wrong with you. There just really is. [*Pauses.*] You weren't a TI, were you?

No, but I always wanted to be a drill sergeant. It looks like a lot of fun.

VW: Fun? To be mean? Oh, my God. I can't believe it. So anyway, they're like, "Pick up your luggage. Put it down. Pick it up. Put it down," for an hour because some guy who hadn't had sleep can't do it right. And I'm thinking, *Oh, my God! Just pick up the damn luggage when he says pick it up!* You know what I mean? And if everybody doesn't pick it up at the exact same time, we had to do it again. We did this for like an hour. "Pick it up! Put it down!"

So we finally get to go in, soaking wet, freezing cold, dead tired. Your arm feels like it's gonna fall off from picking up your damn luggage and putting it down. Then they're like, "Take a shower! You filthy little dirty people! Take a shower!" So they make us take this shower. And all you can think of is, *I just want to go to bed. Please, please! Let me go to bed.*

And they're like, "Now, clean up this shower!" And we don't have any towels because they told us not to bring any towels. So they're like, "Use your clothes!" So we had to use our T-shirts from our luggage to wipe down the showers. Okay? And they're like, "Pick your bed!" And you pick your bed, and then finally you get into the scratchiest, nastiest, squeakiest, most uncomfortable bed with the scratchiest covers. I can't even believe they use those for covers. I just can't. It's like a burro! You think, *Okay, it's the late 1980s. You could have come up with something better than this horrible, 100-year-old pet bedding.*

But that's all a part of making it the nastiest experience possible. It's not meant to be Club Med.

VW: Horrible. So I get into bed, and I'm totally gonna fall asleep, and then all of a sudden it starts all over again because you hear them coming in with a whole new group of people. So that was my first day, and that's why I never forgot it. You can ask me what happened the second day and the third day and the fourth day. I have no idea, but I remember that day. And I thought to myself before going to bed, *What the heck did you get yourself into, Vicki Wagner? What have you done?*

Some people say that having gay people in a training situation like that creates sexual tension, but as anyone who's gone through it...

VW: [*Interrupting*] What sexual tension? All I wanted to do was go to sleep.

Then the two people they had picked to be the squad leaders, I guess they got fired. And I can remember there was this other girl there from New York, and I was from Chicago. And for whatever reason, they nicknamed me "Chicago."

That's a stretch.

VW: Hmm. You think? So she's like, "We're from the city. All these other farm girls don't know what's going on. We're just gonna keep getting in trouble over and over. Let's take over!" This chick, I'm telling you. She says, "Let's volunteer to be the squad leaders." And I'm thinking, *I don't want any trouble. I just want to get through this damn POW camp that we're in right now so we can move on.* I didn't want to do it. But my natural self is a leader, so I just said, "Fine."

And trust me, that's probably why I was so thin, because I ended up being the squad leader. Our unit was 3707. That was our group. And everyday for like twenty to thirty minutes, we had to stand out there going, "3707, best of the best! 3707, best of the best! 3707, best of the best!" Over and over and over and over.

Well, you know what? By the time we got out of boot camp, we not only were the best in the whole entire base, but we had broken all base records for boot camp in like ten years. They trained us to be the best.

You completed your technical training as a command post controller at Keesler Air Force Base, Biloxi, Mississippi, which you've described as "Home of the KKK."

VW: At Keesler, I dated a black guy. His name was Chris. So I'm going out with Chris, and we're at this bar, and we're just having fun. And all of the sudden, the fact that we are in the South sets in because these guys with their giant pickup trucks and their gun racks in the back and big-ass Confederate flag scream, "Hey, nigger lover! You damn Yankees! You Air Force bitches! You come down to the South, and you're nigger lovers." And I'm like, *Holy shit!* And the one guy—just the thing that you would imagine, the truck hat on, the mullet, whatever.

And I'm thinking, *They're gonna start shooting us.* And that was my first taste of Mississippi. Wow. Like that song from *Deliverance* [*Hums "Dueling Banjos"*]. It's alive and well in this world. And you start seeing it everywhere. Confederate flags. People calling you names under their breath.

And when I was down there, I did meet a couple of girls in technical training school, but I was like, *Okay, I'm dating this guy.* You know? Same old pattern. I'm still not gay. Gay, straight, whatever. I started dating this girl down there. And she had never been with a girl before me. I was the first one. But there was something about her that I just knew.

I had volunteered to help out with the local Special Olympics, and afterwards we had this big party and they were having barbecued chicken and pitchers of half beer, and we're drinking, and one thing led to another, and I hooked up with her. And I actually was with her for—I don't know—two months. She was in air traffic control school.

Where did you go?

VW: I don't remember, but we rented a hotel room once. We went down to New Orleans once. Went down to the French Quarter.

You didn't go back to the base.

VW: Nah, we did it on the base a couple times. You know, we found ways. Her roommate was, like, dead. You could launch a rocket in her sleep, and she wouldn't even wake up. So I actually did hook up with her a couple of times in her room with the roommate sleeping in the next bed. And my roommate knew, but she didn't care. So sometimes she would trade and go sleep in the other room.

But the whole time I was dating her, I was also dating a guy, too. I really didn't discriminate against men or women. [*Laughs*]

And you met other gay people?

VW: Oh, yeah. There was a lot of gay girls when I was in training school, and good looking ones, too. A lot of dykes, too.

How did you know they were gay?

VW: I don't know. You just kind of know they're gay, I guess. Kind of the same way you know now. I am the worst person. I do not have gaydar. I never know who's gay and who's not gay. My mom's got better gaydar than me!

Anyway, I'm in the military just going along, and I actually really like it, too, because now I'm in Washington state. There's pine trees everywhere. It's gorgeous. I mean, it's boring to live there. It's like this little tiny town with 90,000 people, and it has one main street. Know what I mean? But I got a ton of friends really fast, and I had a boyfriend right away. I never met any gay women—I didn't—until right before I got out of the military. But it wasn't like how I was saying in technical training school, where there was gay chicks.

Was there any realization that you all had to keep this below the radar? You couldn't be too out about it?

VW: Oh, yeah. We knew that. But when I got to my regular base, I mean, now you're doing your job. And you have to learn all this stuff. There wasn't really any time to socialize that way.

So I had my job. And I liked everybody I worked with. And while I was there I dated some guys. But this one girl, Erin, I had dated before I went into the military, I kept in touch with her. Back and forth. And that was my extent of gay life.

Your mom, stepdad, and Erin came for a visit around New Year's 1989, and that led to your undoing, didn't it?

VW: They all came, and we all celebrated New Year's Eve together. We had a good time. My mom rented a fancy hotel room in Spokane, and we went and stayed at the hotel for New Year's Eve, and we just had so much fun. They knew about Erin and I. They did not judge me. They only wanted their daughter to be happy.

Then my parents flew back home, and Erin stayed. We had talked about a relationship and really liked each other. We slept together every night. I took her around the base. I had so many friends, and I introduced her to my friends—actually three of the guys knew I was bisexual and didn't care. Then we became careless, and that's when someone saw me kiss her.

I wanted to bring this point up because a girl who was in my squad when I was in basic training ended up on my base. And she was security police. Now, I don't know to this day if it was her—I'm pretty sure it was—but I was kissing Erin in my room, and she walked in.

How did she walk into your room?

VW: People used to come to my room all the time, just walk right in.

So she walked in and what did you do?

VW: I didn't do nothing. Just looked at her. What can you do? You know, pretend like it didn't happen. And you know, Erin had long blond hair. We weren't two people who looked like what you think the stereotypical gay person looks like, back at that time.

But you were two girls kissing.

VW: But back at that time people's idea of a gay chick was short hair, wearing flannel, boots. And neither of us looked anything like that stereotypical image. And I'm not sure if this person was like, *Oh, I'm gonna get my revenge on her now because she was our squad leader.* But after that, I never heard anything about it. Erin went back home to Chicago, and I actually got sent to Carswell Air Force Base near Dallas[1] for advanced training for three months. And again, I had a fabulous time there.

And I came back—I don't know if it was the day I came back, but within the week—and my boss was like, "We need to talk to you." So I'm like, "What's the matter? What do you need to talk about?"

So all of a sudden, they're like, "Well, we need you to talk to these people." And I'm like, "Okay," not knowing what's happening. So I go, and it's the AFOSI, the Air Force Office of Special Investigations. "Well, we're investigating you for homosexuality."

You know, I had been gone three months. I hadn't even thought about it. I mean, I never even put the connection together. *Oh, my God! This girl saw me kissing and then turned us in.* And of course, they're like, "You know, you cannot be in the military and have a top-secret clearance. You just can't."

So I started getting investigated. They took me down to their office and started giving all their harassment.

How does that look?

VW: Well, I go back into their little office, and it's me and these two guys in suits. They're dressed as civilians, not as military people. And they're just, "Are you gay? Do you know any gay people? Somebody said you were with this girl." And blah, blah, blah. Of course, I'm denying everything because now I'm like, *Oh, my God! No, I'm not gay.* And it was ironic because at the time I was dating a guy. I was never like, "Yeah, I'm gay!" I was never like, "Oh, this is my girlfriend." It was always like, whoever was there at the moment. I don't want to come across as slutty. But I had a fun time! Know what I mean? I was 19. Nineteen years old. And my work was hard.

You worked in a top-secret, ultraconfidential environment running war-game simulations that required split-second accuracy. That you were entrusted with so much, how did it feel being in this office, being questioned?

VW: Horrible. Here I am. I come to work everyday. I do my job. I'm good at doing my job. I'm smart. I'm totally going above and beyond.

How did being investigated affect your job and security clearance?

VW: My boss was like, "We don't know how long this investigation is going to last, but because you're getting investigated, you can't work in here." I'm like, "What do you mean?" They're like, "Don't worry. It's probably only gonna take a few weeks. It's some misunderstanding."

So they took away my top-secret clearance and my job, and I'm like, *Well, where am I going to go work?* Well, the commander of the 92nd Bomb Wing[2] was a captain, a woman I credit with saving my whole life. Her secretary was gonna have a baby, so I was assigned to go down there and be her secretary. And you know, this woman, the commander, she was the nicest lady ever.

You mentioned another girl who may have turned you in out of jealousy, because her boyfriend had a crush on you.

VW: There's motive there. And she'd actually seen me in the pool hall with this girl Erin. I'll never know to this day who it was that turned me in. It was one of those two girls, though.

The security policewoman, was she gay?

VW: No, she wasn't gay, but she probably could have been. You know what I mean? I'm looking in hindsight now. But no, she had a boyfriend.

Well, so did you.

VW: Yeah, I had a boyfriend. See, I liked guys.

How many times were you called back in?

VW: Oh, constantly. They're like, "We're gonna have to do some background investigation on you." I'm like, "Okay." "And we're gonna have to go through your stuff." I'm like, "Okay." And they went through my room.

I got a little paranoid and took all my letters and gave them to a friend of mine who was a civilian to keep at her house. Then they were like, "Well, you have to go see a lawyer." I'm like, "Why?" "Because you're getting investigated, and we're probably gonna put you in prison." And I'm like, "But why?"

So I go to see this lawyer, and it's kind of good luck, bad luck for me, because the lawyer was just about to get out of the military. Okay? He was just serving his time. He always used to say, "I hate the military, and I hate the Air Force, and I can't wait to get out." He was just a straight-up guy. He was like, "I'm gonna tell you right now. I don't think you're gay. But you know what? I don't care if you're gay. The fact is there's a ton of gay people in the military. The difference is that you have a top-secret clearance and a military job, and you have access to a lot of information. And if you're gay and in the military and have a top-secret clearance, you can become blackmailed."

But if you're allowed to serve openly, you can't be blackmailed.

VW: Exactly. So I'm like, "What are you telling me?" He goes, "What I'm telling right now you is they're gonna investigate you. Then they're gonna say whether they think you need to go before a board. It's gonna be five people. Half enlisted. Half officers. And if they decide you are in fact gay, you're gonna go to prison, five years in Leavenworth. Because in the military, you're a criminal if you're a gay person."

So here's me, still not even claiming myself as a gay person, not believing I myself was gay, just never knowing really what was going on. Like I say, I had boyfriends and girlfriends. So I believed I was half straight. Wasn't that good enough for them? That should be good enough to do my damn job. I come to work everyday. I'm at the top of everything constantly. Why are you doing this to me?

Did you ask them that?

VW: No. I didn't say anything. Then I started losing all my friends. The investigation continued on and on. One month went by. Two months went by. I was up for a promotion. Now I don't get my promotion. And nobody wanted to hang out with me because I'm known as that person on the base—stay away from her! Whether I'm gay or not. They just didn't want to be associated with me.

So I started like totally throwing up everyday. I would come home and just throw up. You know? Like, what's gonna happen? And I'd have to go talk to these OSI guys all the time. And I'm like, "Why can't you guys just make up your mind one way or the other?" But no, it just kept dragging on. 'Cause they couldn't find anything. You couldn't find any concrete evidence that I was a homosexual.

This was the horriblest time because our commander had her baby, and we got this new first sergeant who hated gay people. So he said to me, "What are you doing? Why aren't you standing up for yourself?" And he started harassing me on a daily basis because I'm still working for her in this office.

And my lawyer in the Air Force says, "If I was you, I would waive your rights to a discharge board because if they find any reason that they think you're gay—even if you're not—you're gonna go to prison."

If you waive your rights to a discharge board, what you do is you submit your package of information, your side of the story, and then whoever's information is more convincing, they say, "Okay. This is the way it is."

So I got all kinds of letters from all the people I worked

with. These majors, my colonel. All the officers, then all the enlisted. Then a bunch of civilians, then all the people I knew who said they knew I had boyfriends and blah, blah, blah, and even some of the guys I was dating at the time. "I am dating Vicki Wagner right now. She obviously can't be gay because I just had sex with her." Whatever. And that was true. I was still sleeping with guys. And I never slept with any girl on Fairchild Air Force Base. Never even met a gay girl, except for an Army veterinarian stationed there.

It started getting worse and worse. And this first sergeant, he was the meanest guy you can imagine. "You're just a piece of shit scum. You can't even stand up for yourself. And if you're a homo, I don't want no homos underneath me," and constantly like that. I would just be reduced to tears by that guy. It's kind of getting me upset right now, as a matter of fact. He goes, "You can't work in my office. I don't want you working here no more, and you don't have your captain to protect you."

And he made me go work with the prisoners, the people who were getting kicked out of the military, the people who had committed rape and who had done really bad things. He said, "You're getting convicted of a criminal activity. You're gonna go work with the criminals."

So for the last three months I was in the military, I had to go work with these criminal people. What we did all day long was clean dorms, scrub toilets, and shovel snow. And Fairchild Air Force Base was in a little valley, and we had fog every single day. The base would shoot propane up into the air, and the fog would be dispersed and come down like snow. So for eight hours a day, every day, I would get out there in the snow and shovel the sidewalks of the base till my hands bled. I shoveled so much my gloves got worn out.

The investigation took nine months. Nine months of harassment. Nine months of no friends. Nine months of doing this shitty work. Why? Because someone saw me kissing a girl?

How many times did you have to go in and talk to the OSI?

VW: At least four or five times a month.

Did they ever say, "Listen. Why don't you just tell us the truth?"

VW: They would be like, "If you're gay, tell us you're gay because we're gonna find out you're gay. And if you are gay, you're making it harder on yourself." Kind of like the same stuff you see when they interrogate people on *NYPD Blue* or something. You know what I mean? "Make it easier on yourself." And I was thinking, *I'm not fucking going to prison. I'm not going to prison.* It kept going through the back of my mind.

I called up my mom to tell her what was happening. Of course, she just totally broke down in tears because Michael, who had served in the Navy, had just died two years earlier. As a matter of fact, just so you know, my grandpa was in the Marines, and my uncle was in the Air Force. So I come from a military family. Here I am. I have a long history of my family serving this fucking country, and now it comes down to me. And my cousin was in the Air Force, too. So my mom's like, "They're gonna send you to prison for five years? Five years is a long time for nothing."

But of course the military doesn't have to prove you're gay. That standard belongs to the past. Now it's you prove you're not.

VW: Yes. And the OSI do their interrogations over and over and over again. "Who's gay? Do you know any other people that are gay?" The fact of the matter was I didn't know any other gay girls. I didn't! I didn't fraternize with gay people. All of my friends on that base were straight people. I didn't even meet any gay people, except for that one girl I told you about, the veterinarian.

You told me on the telephone that you knew a number of gay guys.

VW: Yeah, I knew a number of gay guys. The guy who lived right across the hall from me. Beautiful looking guy. Totally popular. Any girl would have wanted him. His name was Jay. The guy down the hall: He was a staff sergeant. The guy downstairs: His name was Peter. He was gay. Another guy down the hall, his name was Patrick. He was gay. All these guys were gay.

Did they know about you?

VW: Oh, they knew. I told 'em. They knew I was getting investigated and everything. They were like, "We want to make sure people don't see us together." So we actually would meet outside of the base. And I went to Seattle with these guys three times because Seattle was only like a three-hour drive away. We tore it up and went to gay bars and had a great time.

But you were still being investigated?

VW: I kept thinking that the investigation would be over, and that they wouldn't be able to prove anything because the whole time I was being investigated, I watched my p's and q's. I was on my best behavior.

But after this first sergeant made me go work with these criminals, that's when the tide turned for me, when I just wanted to kill myself. I mean, nobody really wanted to be my friend after that. It was the worse type of limbo.

Finally at the end of the nine months, they said, "Okay, we'll let you go out of the military." And it was to my good graces that this lawyer had told me to waive my rights, to not go before the board, because the board would have found me gay, and they would have sent me to prison.

So I said, "Well, what's gonna happen now?" He says, "Well, you're gonna get kicked out of the military. And it's up to your commander to decide what kind of discharge you get." He says, "I'm gonna let you know right now: I've never heard of a person getting kicked out for being gay that got an honorable discharge. As a matter of fact, five other people are getting kicked out of the base this week for being gay, and they're all getting dishonorable discharges."

So I went to my commander. I hadn't worked for her for three months. And she said, "I want you to come in here, and I want you to close the door." And I just kind of sat across from her. I remember she had this huge oak desk, and she loved Ansel Adams and had all these pictures up. And she goes, "You know, I've gotten a chance to get to know you, and I've known your record and I've known what a great worker you are." And she goes, "You're pretty young. You have your whole life ahead of you. I don't really know what your sexual orientation is. And it really doesn't matter to me because you're such an exemplary airman. The Air Force would do well to have more people like you. And it's a shame that we have to let you go."

And her exact words to me were, "I cannot *not* give you an honorable discharge. You deserve an honorable discharge." And I got one. And she actually had tears in her eyes when she told me that. Under the reason why they said I got kicked out—they could never even prove I was a homosexual—it says "Discharged for a homosexual act."

Kissing that girl.

VW: Kissing. It was an act of homosexuality. They never did prove I was homosexual. Want to know why? Because I wasn't a homosexual. I wasn't a homosexual at that time in my life. I was living the life of a bisexual person, but I wasn't a homosexual. That wasn't the life I was leading.

It wasn't me who decided I was gay. It was the military who decided I was gay. And it was stamped on my discharge paperwork. And the most ironic twist of all is that day when they kicked me out. We have a little Department of Defense sticker on our car. That day was freezing cold. The last day on my base. They said, "Pack up your stuff. You need to go. You got a week. We'll give you enough money for like a one-way bus ticket."

My mom flew out to the base, and we drove home in my car together. They gave me like eighty bucks or something like that. But the very last day, I was outside and there was an armed security guard standing over me with a razor blade. And he said, "Scrape that Department of Defense sticker off your car." And it was snowing. So I sat there in tears, scraping this off. That was it.

I got kicked out December 27, 1990. Two months shy of two years in the military. Nine months of that was spent being investigated. $75,000 of your taxpayer dollars. Plus who knows how much it cost them to train me. Millions and millions of dollars wasted because somebody saw me kissing a girl. It didn't interfere with my work. It didn't interfere with my ability to work. I never even had a girlfriend on that base. Not on that base. And they kicked me out. Because I kissed a girl.

Notes
1. Carswell AFB was selected for closing in 1991 but reopened in 1994 as the Naval Air Station Fort Worth Joint Reserve Base (NAS JRB Fort Worth).

2. The 92nd Bomb Wing was redesignated the 92nd Air Refueling Wing in July 1994. Fairchild AFB, its home, is dubbed "the tanker hub of the Northwest."

About Face

Sports were a great way to meet girls, but the Army's investigators had a simple equation, "sports = butch = lesbian." The other great danger, found this Army athlete: trespassing.

Senior enlisted have a secret cadre. They get to know one another over time. They have been to more classes together, competed for some of the same assignments, served together. In it, there is a well-defined "old girls club," a cadre of lesbians who have traveled the world together and who can communicate through the most interesting channels.

I was taking a sweat after boxing practice one day. In the dark of the sauna, I was told that a certain senior sergeant, currently stationed in Turkey, was informing me that I best stay away from her girlfriend, stationed in San Antonio, or I, stationed in El Paso, might regret my actions. The clandestine weirdness of this one-way conversation is still haunting.

—A.G. Flynn

Able v. United States of America

Brenda Vosbein

Army Lieutenant Colonel Brenda Vosbein was LTC Jane Able in the 1994 case Jane Able et al v. United States of America. *Brought by Lambda Legal Defense and Education Fund after "don't ask, don't tell" was made law, the case sought to declare the policy invalid under the First Amendment—freedom of expression, freedom of association, and right of assembly—and the Fifth Amendment—right to privacy, due process, and equal protection. It also asked for an injunction to prevent the Department of Defense from enforcing "don't ask, don't tell." It was the first case to challenge the policy.*

The U.S. District Court for the Eastern District of New York, in crisp, direct language, found that the policy was based on prejudice alone and promoted no legitimate military interest. Further, it said that the policy punishes lesbians and gay men for reasons unrelated to fitness and ability to serve, and is based on sexual identity (status) rather than on sexual conduct.

The government appealed, and in 1998 the 2nd U.S. Circuit Court of Appeals reversed the lower court, saying that the district court had not shown "deference" to Congress and the military. In its mazelike opinion, the higher court offered no real evidence but instead, in circular language, insisted the policy was good because it was.

Vosbein—the lead plaintiff in the case—loved the Army, but when she joined in 1970 she had wanted to go Air Force.

"They told me I wasn't young enough, cute enough, or slim enough for them," she says.

Their loss became the Army's gain.

She completed basic training at Fort McClellan, Alabama, then home of the WAC, taking top honors. She became an Army medic (91B) at Fort Sam Houston, Texas, before taking up hospital duties at Fort Knox, Kentucky. In 1971 she applied and was accepted to Officer Candidate School, again at Fort McClellan, graduated second in her class, and stayed to become a WAC training officer.

In 1973 she moved from active duty to join the active reserve, where she served as an AG officer, rising through the ranks to lieutenant colonel. She retired in 1996.

"I loved the military and was a gung ho troop," says Vosbein, who was known as "Jane Able" in the case not for reasons of anonymity but because attorneys designated hers the lead case, and an 'A' placed her first alphabetically.

Vosbein, like many Army women who were WAC, has a certain esprit, a pride in that association and a strong sense of belonging.

"I had a great career," she says. I really enjoyed it. Definitely, we were WAC."

* * *

In the early '70s, Air Force recruiters didn't just recruit you. After they did your recruitment packet, they'd take a full-length picture of you and then send everything to a selection board at Lackland Air Force Base. That board did final selections.

I was not 18; I was 23 maybe. And they had me lose weight, ten or fifteen pounds. They said they liked their women to come into the Air Force very slim because they tended to gain weight after they got in. The recruiters made no bones about it. They could get away with it because discriminating against women was easier to do back then.

The recruiter said this right up front, "Well, we'll try to get you in. You have a good background. You have a good education. Your scores are off the top. But you're not young enough, cute enough, or slim enough."

I didn't get selected for the Air Force. One of the things I was interested in was health care. The Army was the one that offered me what I wanted to do, with a guarantee that I could be trained as a medical corpsman.

And they didn't require you to be 36-24-36?

BV: Exactly.

When you entered the service, you were a little bit older. Did you know you were gay?

BV: No, I didn't. I knew I had never been interested in boys or dating, but I didn't really know why. So when I hit the paperwork that asked, "Have you ever been interested in a person of the same sex?" I wasn't lying because I did not really understand at the time that I was gay.

When you were serving as a training officer at Fort McClellan, home of the WAC, did you see anyone you recognized as gay or lesbian? Was your consciousness tuned to that yet?

BV: Believe it or not, everybody else except me knew I was gay. I would have drill sergeants come in and talk to me about their problems with their girlfriends. I mean, everybody was very open and taking for granted that I was one of the sorority. And it just didn't dawn on me yet.

Now, while I was at Fort McClellan, I got to be very good friends with someone who was also stationed there. I realize in retrospect that I had intense feelings, and this relationship with this woman later guided my decision to leave the Army. But there was nothing overtly sexual. I was just too dumb to be tuned into what was really going on. And we would never have admitted to ourselves, or each other, that we were gay. That's for sure.

The women who would come in and tell you their innermost secrets and dramas, did you ever say to them, "Listen, that's really nice. But did you know: I'm not gay"?

BV: Well, I told somebody that once, and she kind of laughed at me. [*Laughs*] In fact, it was the company clerk. This other woman came into the office one day. She was not assigned to the training company. She came in because she needed something and then left, and the company clerk said to me, "Your girlfriend's kind of ding-y," 'cause the girl was not a strack troop. And I said, "That's not my girlfriend." She looked at me and said, "You gotta be kidding." But I was not in touch with it to the point that I could admit. My coming-out process took a long time.

But it didn't bother me at all when other people talked about it, which was probably a clue there, too. There was, to a degree, some curiosity, so rather than saying, "Oh, I don't want to talk about this," it was, "Oh, I'm kind of interested in this." [*Laughs*]

Were there a lot of identifiable lesbians at Fort McClellan?

BV: At that time, most of the women who liked to do the training at the training battalions tended to be lesbians. The people who wanted to be prissy took other assignments and went elsewhere. The women who wanted to come back and be drill sergeants or training officers liked being there. The majority seemed to be gay. Some of this is retrospect, but some of this was obvious to me at the time, too.

Was the WAC a more welcoming place for lesbians than the larger Army?

BV: Yes. At that time, definitely. Look at the history. When I first went in, women couldn't be married and couldn't have dependents under 18. Then they changed it, and they could be married but they couldn't have dependents under 18. Now, of course, you can be married and you can have kids. But when you couldn't be married and you couldn't have dependents, who made careers out of the Women's Army Corps?

Most of the women who were there wanted to get their education or came in to do something different. Some met people while they were in the Army and got married. A lot of the enlisted women I knew when I was stationed at Fort Knox met guys and got married. And that was one of the reasons a lot of them came into the Army.

But the ones who tended to be careerist seemed to be gay. And in retrospect, the more I think about some of the people I knew who were career WACs at the time, they tended to be gay.

Was there a sense that we could talk about this among ourselves, but we really shouldn't be too overt? Or was there just kind of a blitheness about everything?

BV: No, it was like we can talk about it ourselves, but we have to be very careful. Like one of my female drill sergeants was married to a gay male soldier, and that was their cover. They could have housing on post, but then they could have men and women over to the house. So it was like, "We can talk about it ourselves, but we have to keep the cover."

Were there witch hunts during your time there?

BV: I was never part of a witch hunt. The only thing that ever happened is when I was at Fort Knox that one year, there was a woman who was kind of overtly lesbian. And there was another woman who had come in, who, I think, didn't know what she was yet. At any rate, they were caught in bed together, and it was like, *What are they gonna do?* Well, the one went out and got married right away. Just by getting married, that immediately got her off the hook. The other one, she stayed in but she took an assignment and went someplace else. So neither of them were discharged.

And at that time, what to do with a troop was more up to the commander?

BV: Yes, definitely.

Which is no longer the case.

BV: Exactly. They could choose to turn the other way. If the woman caused no problem whatsoever, then you were fine. But if you caused problems.... We even had one woman who was so clearly a dyke, and she was a real problem maker. She was getting into fights, beating people up. She intimidated everybody, including me! She'd come around and say, "I'm broke, and I want money." And it was like, "Okay, good. I'll give you ten bucks just so you don't beat me up." They were working on getting rid of her. But most of us did our jobs and had no problem.

So if a person was a troublemaker or didn't play well with others, being gay could be used as an excuse to discharge him or her?

BV: Right.

But it wasn't a foregone conclusion that someone would be discharged merely for being gay.

BV: Right. One of the things that I did at Fort McClellan when I was working as a platoon officer is that sometimes women would come into the military and then decide they made a big mistake. They didn't like it. And whether they were or not, we would have some who would come in and say, "I'm gay. I want out."

So I had to interview some of my troops who had said they were gay and needed to be discharged because they were homosexual. And I learned a lot about homosexuality from interviewing them, because I was kind of naive at the time myself. [*Laughs*] It was kind of like, "Oh, that's interesting, that's interesting." I kind of enjoyed those interviews.

Then, after the training officer interviewed them, we'd usually have to send them to the post psychiatrist. And the post psychiatrist was supposed to determine if they really were. And then if they really were, we would proceed with discharge.

Now all you have to do is say, "I'm gay," and you're out the door without any questions being asked. But you basically had to prove you were gay in order to get discharged in those days.

How could you prove it?

BV: Well, again, you'd just ask them questions. And since I didn't know a lot, I'd gotten some copies of some interviews from files and looked at the questions people asked, and then I'd ask them similar questions.

My company commander at the time was a lesbian. I knew that because she was living with the executive officer, and they both left there and went to Fort Lewis together. And I had asked a question that I had seen on another file: "Are you a butch or are you femme?" And she said, "That's getting to be passé. We don't really identify that much by butch and femme anymore." And I go, "Oh. Okay." [*Laughs*] So she kind of taught me things to ask or not to ask, but I find today, people are still identifying to some degree. And it's still a valid question. But at the time, she told me that wasn't a good one to ask.

Among these desperate women was anyone proved not *to be lesbian?*

BV: No, I don't think they could ever prove anyone was not. The questions were just to make it a little more difficult. Anyone who kept pursuing it definitely ended up getting discharged. Unless you were serious about getting out, you didn't want to put up with the hassle.

How did the light come on for you?

BV: Years later. Let me go through this evolution. Again, this woman who I knew at Fort McClellan—I left there and went to a school, and then I was assigned to Fort Huachuca. Well, then she was reassigned to Rock Island Arsenal in Illinois.

And we had $100, $200, $300 a month phone bills, talking constantly. I missed her so intensely. Then she decided she was going to get out of the Army and come to California. Her getting out largely influenced my decision to get out. So it was like, "Oh, yeah. Let's go to California and room together."

So we came to California, and she was at loose ends as to what to do with herself. I started using my veteran's benefits to get into a nursing program, which had been my original interest long before I joined the Army. And she got into therapy. The psychologist that she was seeing kind of first clued her in that we were playing house. We were doing everything like a married couple, except being married and except having sex.

So she decided she wanted to move out, go live by herself, and didn't want me to come along with her. This put me into a major crisis. I was just devastated. This had been five years that I'd had an intense emotional relationship with her, without any kind of sexual relationship. So I was falling apart.

It turned out that there was this lesbian in my reserve unit who was more than willing to step in and comfort me. [*Laughs*] And that's the first person I had had sex with. That relationship did not last. It was never a live-in relationship, but we did have an on-and-off-again relationship for about a year or so. And after that I did indeed accept and realize that I was gay and then got into the relationship that I'm currently in. We're celebrating our twenty-fifth next month.

Mazel tov! Did you never hear from your friend again?

BV: For a while after she moved out, she would call, or I would call her. And then she realized that Diana and I were together, and that I had a life that was very different from hers. She moved more and more into religion, getting involved with some very evangelical, fundamentalist Christian group.

I loved the military! And like I said, if I hadn't been head-over-heels infatuated with this woman, I would probably have been a careerist. But then after that, it was my relationship that governed what I did more than just my love of the military. I knew that there was no way you can maintain a relationship and a military career unless you'd have somebody who'd be willing to move all over the country with you all the time. And Diana was very well established professionally, and it wouldn't have worked out at all.

So much of what the military seems to be afraid of with gay men and lesbians is based on a vampiric model of homosexuality: Put us in a group of people and we'll immediately prey on some poor soul. In a training situation at Fort McClellan, where the cadre were primarily gay and the training body was presumably mixed, did you find that the drill sergeants and others were hitting on the troops, or was that a strict boundary that was kept?

BV: That was a very strict boundary. People had their private life, and people had their work life. Any kind of fraternization with the troops was a complete no-no. I was never aware of that going on. I'm not saying it never happened; I'm just saying to my knowledge. I never saw it, and I don't think it went on. And if it did, it was certainly not the norm.

In my own basic-training cycle, a woman was raped by a male drill sergeant.

BV: From what I've observed, I'm definitely convinced that there is much more harassment of men against women than lesbians against women or gay men against other men. Definitely.

Yet we don't make heterosexuals at the time of enlistment sign an agreement saying they will keep their sexuality to themselves.

BV: No, but it wouldn't be a bad idea. [*Laughs*]

You brought the Jane Able case in 1994, right after "don't ask, don't tell" was made law. Your case essentially declared that the "don't ask, don't tell" policy violated First and Fifth Amendment guarantees, and you asked for an injunction to prevent the Department of Defense from enforcing it. And the U.S. District Court for the Eastern District of New York agreed with you![1]

BV: Oh, yes. Judge Nickerson. He wrote a wonderful opinion. He was just great. It was at higher levels that we had our problems.

Judge Nickerson wrote his opinion very fast and delivered it, by my calculation, in little more than two months. In very direct language he said that the only interest being served by "don't ask, don't tell" is prejudice. He also said that the policy failed to bear even a rational relationship to a legitimate government interest. How did it come to be that you were a part of this case?

BV: Soon after "don't ask, don't tell" went into effect, Lambda Legal Defense and Education Fund began running ads in some of the gay-oriented press seeking volunteers to be part of a lawsuit challenging this policy. They said that our identity wouldn't have to be made known and that they would do everything possible to protect us, although they couldn't guarantee that.

So I called them, and I talked to them about it. I was certainly willing to take the chance. I already was a lieutenant colonel with over twenty years of service. I already had my retirement years in, and I just wanted to go for it. I think I was one of the first ones to get on board.

We had some guys come on later, but most of the folks that they talked to dropped out along the way. I was the only woman and one of the few people who stayed with it until the end.

And why did you stay with it?

BV: Because I just believed in it, and I really wanted to try to do something to lift the ban and see if we could get "don't ask, don't tell" struck from the books.

When the lower court's decision was handed down and it was so very much in your favor, what did you think and feel?

BV: I was indeed excited. I got a call at work from the lawyers when they got the decision, and I was just ecstatic. I really hoped that this meant that it was really going to go somewhere. I was, needless to say, very disappointed later on, but I really thought we were off to a good start.

At the time of the case, you were very out in your personal life as a member of gay or gay-friendly organizations, marching in pride parades, etcetera, but you were still very circumspect in the reserves. Were there other gay people in your unit?

BV: Oh, yeah. You know how you drop hints to get to know? When there's somebody that you think is, you mention someplace that you've gone or something you've done. For instance, one year we were at annual training, and this one sergeant says, "Golly, I haven't worn this jacket in a time, and I reached into my pocket, and I found these tickets to *Last Summer at Blue Fish Cove.*" And then she said, "Did you see that?" And I said, "Oh, yeah. It was great."

Then this other time there was this other sergeant, and I was quite sure she was gay. And I said something about, "Oh, I'm gonna be taking a cruise. It's with Olivia. Have you ever heard of that?" And she said, "Oh, yeah. Olivia!" You know? So we got to know people. It was this open but unsaid thing.

We had this one lieutenant—a male lieutenant—who was extremely nelly. And we had a female battalion commander, and she called this O6, a colonel, who was kind of openly gay but not. And the battalion commander said, "Can you come help this guy butch it up a little bit?" She said, "He's so obvious. I can't stand it!" You know? So we had this senior officer take this younger lieutenant under his wing to try to get him to butch it up so that he wouldn't be so obviously gay. But the battalion commander wasn't about to start saying, "Let's get rid of Sam because he's obviously gay." It was, "Let's get him to butch it up a bit so he doesn't look so gay."

And perhaps won't come show up on someone's radar.

BV: Right. There was a lot of protection. Again, that's if you did your job, if you were good. If you were a troublemaker, then that could become a very good reason to get rid of you. But if you didn't want somebody to get negative attention, then you protected them and saw to it that they didn't get under any kind of investigation.

When President Clinton first proposed lifting the ban and even suggested issuing an executive order, what did you think?

BV: I was definitely thrilled by that! But I was very disappointed with him when he got into office, with "don't ask, don't tell" and with signing the Defense of Marriage Act and some of the other things he did once he was in office. But I definitely rallied around him because I thought he would be the champion of gay people.

But when things began to sour and the policy was instituted, you were alarmed enough to take action.

BV: I thought, *I have a pension. I can take the risk for the sake of other people coming along who need to stay in, in order to get their pensions.*

The government appealed Judge Nickerson's very lovely opinion, and in 1998 a higher court reversed the earlier decision.[2] The government argued essentially that the district court had failed to accord the judgments of Congress and the military the "proper deference" in deciding eligibility requirements for military service. And they said that under that "correct" standard, "don't ask, don't tell" is constitutional. In essence, they said, "The military knows. We don't. We should just let the military do whatever."

BV: It went back to the circuit court twice. And like our lawyer said, the first time they thought it was really a valid inquiry when they wanted more information. And then after the second time, the lawyers said, "The courts are passing the buck. They're saying, 'We're not going to get involved in this. We're going to let Congress handle the military. We're not going to touch this. It's too much of a hot potato.'"

The opinion of the higher court is so circuitous that it's mind-bending. It's highly uncritical of any of the government's positions and national security claims. It all mistakenly comes back to conduct, not status. In contrast, the policy itself is very much about status. How do you see this case in retrospect?

BV: One of the best things it showed to me was this: One of the other plaintiffs was an Army captain who I knew because he was in my same command. He was a company commander. He was protected during the trial because they did get the assurance from the Army that they weren't going to discharge or take any action while this was in progress.

So the captain managed to maintain a command. He wasn't relieved. He probably had a successful tour as a commander, with his troops respecting him enough to do what had to be done. After the appeal—but before we decided not to go to the Supreme Court—he came down on orders for Bosnia. So, he's openly gay, and no one seemed to be treating him any differently. I don't know about the enlisted men, because they weren't from my area. But what I was seeing was here's an openly gay company commander, and I don't see it having any effect on either his troops, his unit's performance, or his career.

And I thought, *Why can't people look at this?* You can multiply this hundreds of times, and you'll see the same thing. You'll have people doing their jobs, being respected—or not—based on the jobs they do, not on their sexual orientation. He's a successful company commander, but we've got to keep this policy because terrible things are going to happen if people knew servicemembers are gay?

Why is there that disconnect, do you think?

BV: Prejudice. That's the only thing I can think of. There is this fear of homosexuals. After the case, after the trial, I moved on to another unit, and I was at Fort Lee during summer training and a group of us, officers, were out having dinner. And one male officer said something like, "If they allow fags to serve, I'm going to demand to shower with the women. Because if I can have guys in there ogling me, I can go in there and ogle the women."

So I think there is this concern, especially with men and especially about the showers. It's their biggest hang-up: "I don't want to share a shower with someone who might be looking at my private parts."

What is it about the showers?

BV: Heaven only knows. It's a hang-up that men have more than women. Women have a thing with public showers in general. It's not based on the sexual orientation of the people using the showers. It's a privacy thing.

I remember we had this warrant officer in my unit who was a lesbian. She was very open and out to me. I knew her partner, and her partner was also in the reserves. And when we would go to annual training, we had one shower that had four shower heads. She would hang out in the bathroom until there was nobody else in the shower, and then she would go in and take a shower. She would never take a shower with anybody else. It wasn't like she was afraid of the sexual orientation of the people in there. I could be in there or anybody else. She just had a privacy thing, which most women have but they overcome when they're in the military and deal with it.

Men, on the other hand, are usually very comfortable in showers with other men because they do it all the time on sports teams and stuff like that. They're just so afraid that someone's gonna take an interest in them sexually when they see their nude body in the shower. [*Laughs*]

That's very self-confident.

BV: I'm thinking of something that someone told me once. There was a man at our hospital who needed to get catheterized. And our policy was that whenever there was a male nurse available to do that with a man, he would get the male nurse, even if he was not actually taking care of the patient.

So I said to this man, "Let me go get so-and-so. He usually does the catheter on our male patients." And he says, "No, don't!" And I said, "Why not?" And he said, "I would hate to have an erection with a man fondling my genitals." Often when you catheterize somebody, just from the manipulation you have to do, they'll have an erection.

He did not mind it if he had an erection with a female nurse, but he would not have been able to stand it if he had an erection with a male nurse, even though a male nurse would understand just as much as a female nurse that it isn't anything sexual. It's just a physiological response.

It gives you a little bit of an insight into a male mentality, that they don't want anything at all to indicate there's any sexual interest of a man in them or them in a man.

A group-shower situation doesn't typically happen except maybe in basic training or out in some field situation.

BV: Well, it happens wherever you have troops living in the barracks. The barracks are getting better and better all the time. They have a lot of semi-private rooms in the new barracks, with two guys sharing a bathroom. But the Army, especially, still has a lot of old barracks where open showers is the norm—unless you're married and you can move off post or you have enough rank to get more privacy.

Someone interviewed Joseph Steffan, the gay midshipman who was forced to resign from the U.S. Naval Academy just a few weeks before graduation.3 The interviewer said, "I would feel uncomfortable showering with a group of women. I would find myself getting sexually aroused. How can you say that you won't?" And Steffan said, "Men grow up showering with men all their lives. You don't go into the shower with the mental intent to get aroused, whereas a man going into a shower with a group of women would probably go in with the idea that he's going to get aroused. When you grow up showering with the same sex, it doesn't bother you any more than seeing a naked woman bothers a doctor or a nurse. It something that becomes old hat after a while."

I'm not talking about a stalking-type situation or anyone who is aggressive in his or her pursuit, but what if someone is aroused and does nothing about it? So what if someone is attracted to you? Big deal.

BV: Some kind of way it reflects on them and makes them fags, some kind of way. It's this mind-set that if someone responds to me, there must be something wrong with me.

I want to read you a quote from Stormin' Norman Schwarzkopf: "In my years of military service, I have experienced the fact that the introduction of an open homosexual into a small unit immediately polarizes that unit and destroys the very bonding that is so important for the unit's survival in time of war."

BV: That's bullshit.

The little clause "in time of war" is very interesting because typically in time of war we're not discharged.

BV: Exactly. Now, are you familiar with the Perry Watkins case?4 That is a good example. As long as we had a war in Vietnam, they had no intention of getting rid of him. But then after the war was over, then they wanted to get rid of him.

It goes back to something that was said once about the integration of blacks into the military. It was much easier to integrate the foxholes than it was to integrate the officer's club. Because in time of war, you don't care *what* the guy next to you is as long as you can depend on him to cover your back and be there for you. But the social aspect was more difficult.

A female Marine told me, "No Marine wants to die. Gay or straight. And if we're in that foxhole, we're going to fight just the same as anybody else."

BV: But I think a lot of men have the idea that all gay men are pansies, and that they won't be there for them. I know cops are kind of that way with gay cops, "I can't be sure my partner's going to back me up because when push comes to shove he's a pansy and he's gonna turn tail and run on me." Lesbians, on the other hand, should be highly valued in the military because they usually bring all the qualities you want in a troop: They're aggressive. They tend to be very career-minded. In general, pretty well disciplined. I remember a sergeant major of mine was talking about one of the troops in the unit. And she said, "So-and-so's really good. I think she's gay. The best women usually are." And this is coming from a straight sergeant major.

Generals Kerr and Richards and Admiral Steinman are the highest ranking servicemembers now to break the silence and come out as gay and critical of "don't ask, don't tell." They've said that the policy undermines the military's core values of truth, honor, dignity, respect, and integrity. What impact do you suspect their coming-out will have in the long run?

BV: In the long run, the more people that you can get on board the better. But again, it's going to take a long time because now this has all been codified into law. Trying to get

Congress to actually change the law is going to take more than just a few people coming out as being opposed to it.

Retired General Evelyn "Pat" Foote was the only person who had actually served in the military to testify at our trial. Pat had been my career manager when I was a lieutenant. The person you go to and say, "Well, I'm ready to rotate from Fort McClellan. Let's see where you're going to send me and what you're going to do." She was a major at the time. And she testified against the policy. She had commanded the WAC training battalion, and she knew that all of her best drill sergeants, probably all of her best platoon officers and company commanders, were all lesbians. And she said the same thing about the policy—that it didn't make sense. And it just ended up getting good, well-qualified women discharged from the military.

Do you view the Able case as one in a series of cases, like Brown v. Board of Education was one in a string that secured rights for African-Americans?

BV: Yes. It's going to take numerous court cases that nibble away. You're not going to have one big thing that changes everything overnight. It would surprise me if it did. Each time you do something like this, you make a dent.

One of the reasons Able did not go to the Supreme Court is that the lawyers were concerned about the Supreme Court coming out with a decision against us. Then every court in the country could quote a finding of the Supreme Court to uphold discriminatory laws. Whereas this way, we were only dealing with this one circuit court's writing.

We have to get to the point where there are enough cases floating out here that are conflicting with each other in various circuit and various district courts, and the Supreme Court has to get involved. And we hope that, at that time, we'll have a Supreme Court that is inclined to take a slightly more liberal slant. I'm not sure when that's going to be.

What should gay and lesbian troops do in the interim?

BV: People can probably pretty much survive the way I did. You come out selectively, to people that you know and you can trust. If you're an officer, you don't get involved with the enlisted. When you start doing things like that, it does set you up. You have to be circumspect in who you come out to, who you have relationships with, and where you have those relationships.

And for your social life, you have to seek that primarily off post. Not that gay soldiers can't go together someplace, but being too overt under the nose of the military probably is still dangerous. You just have to live a double life. You hate to do it. But you don't have to lie.

For years, Diana, to the military, has been my roommate. When I was a captain, I served with this major, and Diana had come to the unit for something, and he had met her. Years later I was a lieutenant colonel and he was a colonel, and we were back together in another unit and sharing an office. And Diana called, and he said, "Oh, are you guys still together?" Was he overtly thinking of us together as life partners? Maybe. Or maybe he was just responding like, "Oh, you're still with the same roommate."

Diana went to activities at the unit. She went to my change of command ceremonies. She went to things when I got promoted. She went to open houses, and everybody knew she was my roommate. Anybody with an ounce of sense would have known more. She was also listed on my "who to notify" in case of emergencies and everything else that I could legally have her on. She was all over my records, but I never came out and said to anyone, "I'm gay, and this is my life partner." It was like, "Here I am. I do my job, and Diana and I live together." It worked well for me. I found it comfortable. I didn't feel like I had to walk around lying.

The only time I really made a choice is when I was filling out paperwork to see about getting a top-secret clearance. And it tells you to list all the organizations you belong to. Well, this was *after* the Able case, and I belonged to—you name it, every pro-gay organization. I was going to try to be an inspector general for my last assignment before retiring, and then I thought to myself, *At this stage in my career, putting all this stuff in my packet for my security clearance isn't worth it, and I don't want to lie, so I'm just not going to go for this clearance.* That's the only time that I felt my affiliations with a lot of gay organizations would have been detrimental.

I admire your calm realism. On the other hand, it's a shame that a very good officer couldn't strike for that position.

BV: You do have to accept limitations. There's no doubt about it. You can't do everything you'd like to do. But I could be at peace with it. Now, some people, if there was really something they wanted to do and it was early in their career, may have had a lot more heartburn.

There's something about "don't ask, don't tell" that always puts my brain in a knot, and it's this: The policy says that you can be discharged "if you have engaged in, attempted to engage in, solicited another to engage in homosexual acts, unless the member has demonstrated that he or she does not have a propensity to engage in homosexual acts." How do you demonstrate that?

BV: This is the one who can say, "This was a fling or an experimentation or I was drunk, but this was not my norm." But basically it's impossible. Let's say they took away the "don't tell" part, but they left the conduct part in. If you told, you're basically saying that you have the propensity. So as long as the conduct part is still there—even if they say you have the free speech and you can tell anybody you want you're gay—what does it mean to say you're gay other than to suggest you have the propensity to engage in conduct with a member of the same sex?

It's like going down the rabbit hole. The word "propensity" is very interesting. I happened to look that up, and it means "a natural inclination, an innate or inherent tendency existing in one from birth, not choice." So if you have a "propensity," that must mean we're talking about status, not conduct.

BV: That's true. From that definition.

So with "don't ask, don't tell," no matter what you do you're screwed?

BV: Definitely.

Notes

1. *Able v. United States*, 968 F. Supp. 850 (E.D.N.Y. 1997)

2. *Able v. United States*, 155 F.3d 628 (2d Cir. 1998)

3. Steffan was kicked out of Annapolis in 1987, one week before graduation. Ranking in the top tenth of his class, he sued. His case was dismissed in late 1991 in Federal District Court in Washington, D.C. In a 1993 *New York Times* interview, Steffan said of straight-male shower panic, "Heterosexual men have an annoying habit of overestimating their own attractiveness."

4. Watkins, an openly gay man, was drafted into the U.S. Army in 1968, during the Vietnam war. He served in Korea, Europe, and the United States, re-enlisting three times as an openly gay man before being dishonorably discharged as gay in 1984. With support of the ACLU, Watkins fought his discharge in federal court. In 1989, the Ninth Circuit Court of Appeals ruled he should be allowed back in the Army because it had allowed him to reenlist knowing he was homosexual. The Supreme Court refused to hear the case, and the lower court's ruling stood. Watkins was reinstated and retired from the Army in 1989 with the rank of sergeant first class and full benefits.

Glossary of Military Terms

AFOSI: Air Force Office of Special Investigations. Its mission: to "deliver special investigative services to protect Air Force and DoD people and resources worldwide." Its motto: "Eyes of the Eagle."

AG: Adjutant General. The section of the Army responsible for administration and preservation of personnel records.

AIT: advanced individual training (specialty training following basic training)

AWOL: absent without leave

bars: rectangular insignia that in the Army, Air Force, and Marine Corps equal lieutenant (single) or captain (double)

BCT: basic combat training (also known as basic training or "boot camp")

BDU: battle dress uniform

Beltway: The Capital Beltway (I-495), an interstate highway encircling Washington, D.C. "Inside the Beltway" refers to the elite power structure of the federal government and its workers.

bird colonel: a full colonel, from the eagle insignia of grade, to distinguish from the one-grade-lower lieutenant colonel, whose insignia is a silver leaf

butter bar: an Army second lieutenant; from the rank insignia's gold appearance. Used dismissively.

CID: U.S. Army's Criminal Investigation Command (USACIDC). (What the "D" stands for is anyone's guess.) Its motto: "Do what has to be done."

Class A's: ordinary suit service uniform sometimes worn in office-type work, always when wearing a uniform on leave

Class B's: a variation of the suit uniform, minus the coat and, optionally, the tie or tab

CO: commanding officer (also: conscientious objector)

CQ: charge of quarters

DADT: "don't ask, don't tell"

DI: drill instructor. Sergeant specially trained for training recruits. "DI" is a Marine Corps term; "Drill Sergeant" is the Army's variation.

DoD: Department of Defense

ETS: expiration of term of service (scheduled date of separation from active duty)

GI: government issue; originally used for government-supplied equipment. The term often is used by soldiers to refer to themselves.

GI party: a group scrubbing effort; can also be a hazing given to someone who is an habitual screwup

IG: Inspector General

JAG: Judge Advocate General's Corps (military attorneys)

low quarters: lace-up oxfords; the military's "sensible" shoe

MOS: Military Occupational Specialty. A job classification, usually expressed as a number or number-letter combination (e.g., 91B, medic).

MRE: meal ready to eat, the modern descendant of the C-ration

NCIS: Naval Criminal Investigation Services. "A team of federal law enforcement officials dedicated to protecting the people, families, and assets of the U.S. Navy and the Marine Corps worldwide." Its motto: "Beyond Boundaries."

NCO: noncommissioned officer (senior enlisted)

OCS: Officer Candidate School

OER: officer effectiveness report

OIC: officer in charge

OSI: Office of Special Investigations

PCA: permanent change of assignment (new assignment at same base or post)

PCS: permanent change of station (reassignment from one place to another)

PT: physical training

rack: a bed, in Navy and Marine Corps parlance

RDCs: recruit division commanders, the Navy's term for drill instructors

RE1: reenlistment code number 1, the most eligible for reenlistment.

ROTC: Reserve Officer Training Corps

short: nearing the end of one's enlistment

squared away: sharp, together, handled

strack: sharp, together, by-the-book

TI: training instructor; also MTI, military training instructor, an Air Force drill instructor

WAVES: Women Accepted for Voluntary Emergency Service

TDY: temporary duty

XO: executive officer (officer second to CO)

UCMJ: The Uniform Code of Military Justice is a federal law, enacted by Congress, governing all members of the U.S. Armed Services. Its provisions are contained in United States Code, Title 10, Chapter 47.

About the Author

Zsa Zsa Gershick served in the U.S. Army Reserve from 1978 to 1983. She is the author of *Gay Old Girls*, winner of *Foreword* magazine's Best Gay & Lesbian Book of the Year Award in 1999, finalist for the Lambda Literary Award, and nominee for the American Library Association's Best Gay & Lesbian Book Award. Her bylined work has appeared in numerous publications, including the *Advocate* and the *Texas Observer*. A series of articles profiling high-achieving servicemembers cashiered merely for being gay led to this book. An Angeleno, she holds advanced degrees in nonfiction writing and playwriting from USC, where she also has taught.